£5.00

COUNTY COUNCIL OF DURHAM

COUNTY LIBRARY

The latest date entered on the date label or card is the
date by which book must be returned, and fines will be
charged if the book is kept after this date.

DRIFTING APART? THE SUPERPOWERS AND THEIR AND THEIR EUROPEAN ALLIES

Also available from Brassey's

COKER
A Nation in Retreat? Britain's Defence Commitment

COKER
British Defence Policy in the 1990s

CHARTERS AND TUGWELL
Armies in Low Intensity Conflict

CUNNINGHAM
Hostages to Fortune: The Future of Western Interests
in the Arabian Gulf

DEFENSE ANALYSIS
An International Journal

GODSON
Comparing Foreign Intelligence

GOLDSTEIN
Clash in the North

GOLDSTEIN
Fighting Allies

HOLMES
British Security Policy and the Atlantic Alliance

RUSI
RUSI/Brassey's Defence Yearbook 1989

TAYLOR
The Terrorist

DRIFTING APART? THE SUPERPOWERS AND THEIR EUROPEAN ALLIES

Edited by

CHRISTOPHER COKER

BRASSEY'S DEFENCE PUBLISHERS

(a member of the Maxwell Pergamon Publishing Corporation plc)

LONDON · OXFORD · WASHINGTON · NEW YORK
BEIJING · FRANKFURT · SÃO PAULO · SYDNEY · TOKYO · TORONTO

U.K. (Editorial)	Brassey's Defence Publishers Ltd., 24 Gray's Inn Road, London WC1X 8HR, England.
(Orders)	Brassey's Defence Publishers Ltd., Headington Hill Hall, Oxford OX3 0BW, England
U.S.A. (Editorial)	Pergamon-Brassey's International Defense Publishers Inc., 8000 Westpark Drive, Fourth Floor, McLean, Virginia 22102, U.S.A.
(Orders)	Pergamon Press, Inc., Maxwell House, Fairview Park, Elmsford, New York 10523, U.S.A.
PEOPLE'S REPUBLIC OF CHINA	Pergamon Press, Room 4037, Qianmen Hotel, Beijing, People's Republic of China
FEDERAL REPUBLIC OF GERMANY	Pergamon Press GmbH, Hammerweg 6, D-6242 Kronberg, Federal Republic of Germany
BRAZIL	Pergamon Editora Ltda, Rua Eça de Queiros, 346, CEP 04011, Paraiso, São Paulo, Brazil
AUSTRALIA	Pergamon-Brassey's Defence Publishers Pty. Ltd., P. O. Box 544, Potts Point, N.S.W. 2011, Australia
JAPAN	Pergamon Press, 5th Floor, Matsuoka Central Building, 1-7-1 Nishishinjuku, Shinjuku-ku, Tokyo 160, Japan
CANADA	Pergamon Press Canada Ltd., Suite No. 271, 253 College Street, Toronto, Ontario, Canada M5T 1R5

First edition 1989

Library of Congress Cataloging-in-Publication Data
Drifting apart?: the superpowers and their European allies/edited by Christopher Coker.—1st ed.
p. cm.
1. North Atlantic Treaty Organization. 2. United States—Military policy. 3. Warsaw Treaty Organization. 4. Soviet Union—Military policy. 5. Europe—Military policy.
I. Coker, Christopher.
UA646.3.D75   1989   355'.031'094—dc 19   88-38998

British Library Cataloguing in Publication Data
Drifting apart? the superpowers and their European allies.
1. North Atlantic Treaty Organisation countries. Military power, compared with military power of Warsaw Pact countries. 2. Warsaw Pact countries. Military power, compared with military power of North Atlantic Treaty Organisation countries. I. Coker, Christopher, 1953-.
355'.0332'1821

ISBN 0-08-036711-9

Printed in Great Britain by A. Wheaton & Co. Ltd., Exeter

Contents

About the Authors

Alfred Cahen is Secretary-General of the Western European Union (WEU), and a Lecturer at the Free University of Brussels. He was *Chef du Cabinet* to the Minister for Foreign Affairs (1977-79) before becoming Political Director, Ministry for Foreign Affairs, Foreign Trade and Development Co-operation (1979-85). He has written extensively in such journals as *NATO Review, NATO's Sixteen Nations*, and *The European and Studia Diplomatica.*

Michael Checinski is a Professor of Economics at the US Army Russian Institute. From 1947 to 1967 he served in the Polish Armed Forces, between 1959-1967 he was a Senior Lecturer at the Military-Political Academy in Warsaw and a Senior Researcher in its Institute of War Economy. He has published widely on military-economic and Soviet-East European relations issues.

Christopher Coker (Editor) is a Lecturer in International Relations at the London School of Economics. He is the author of *A Nation in Retreat?* and *British Defence Policy in the 1990s* as well as numerous articles in a variety of journals including *Survival, Strategic Review, International Affairs* and *International Defence Review.*

Keith William Crane has worked for the Rand Corporation since 1983. He has a Ph.D. from Indiana University. His RAND published books include: *Creditworthiness of Eastern Europe, Soviet Economic Dilemma of Eastern Europe, Military Spending in Eastern Europe* and *Specialization Agreements in the CMEA.*

Jonathan Eyal studied Politics and Law at the Universities of Oxford and London and completed a Doctorate on East Europe's ethnic relations. He is currently the Soviet and East European Research Fellow at the Royal United Services Institute for Defence Studies in London and the author of two books on East European Affairs.

Walter Goldstein is Professor of International Relations at Rockefeller College, State University of New York, in Albany, and the Ira Wade Professor of International Political Economy at the SAIS Bologna Centre in Italy.

David Greenwood is Director of the Centre for Defence Studies at the University of Aberdeen. Since moving to Aberdeen in 1967, he has directed several major research projects, published a monograph on *Budgeting for Defence* and contributed to various journals. He has also edited the Aberdeen Centre's series of research papers—*Asides*, and is the author of two of the most recent numbers: *The Polaris Successor System: at What Cost?* and *Reshaping Britain's Defences*. He is a specialist adviser to the Defence Subcommittee of the House of Commons Select Committee on Expenditure and a member of the Foreign and Commonwealth Office's Advisory Panel on Arms Control and Disarmament.

David Harvey is an accountant; he is assistant political officer to the Bow Group as well as a former Secretary to the Bow Group Defence Standing Committee.

Dexter Jerome Smith is Strategic Affairs Editor of *Defence* magazine, and a member of the Bow Group Council.

Dr Harry Maier left East Germany in 1986, where he was Vice-Director of the Institute for Theory, Organization and History of Science. Between August 1986 and December 1987 he worked at the IFO Institute for Economic Research, Munich. Since January 1988 he has been Professor for Industrial Economics and Innovation Research at the Nordic University, Flensburg.

James Sherr, formerly Director of Studies of the Royal United Services Institute for Defence Studies, is Lecturer in International Relations at Lincoln College, Oxford and a Research Fellow of the Soviet Studies Research Centre, Royal Military Academy, Sandhurst. He is the author of *Soviet Power: the continuing challenge*.

Stanley R. Sloan is the specialist in US alliance relations for the Congressional Research Service, Washington, DC. During 1987-88 he served as Study Director for the North Atlantic Assembly's Special Presidential Committee on NATO in the 1990s. Previously he served as head of the Europe/Middle East/Africa Section, Congressional Research Service; as Deputy National Intelligence Officer for Western Europe (CIA); and as a member of the US Delegation to the MBFR negotiations. He is the author of *NATO's Future: Toward a New Transatlantic Bargain* as well as numerous scholarly reports and articles.

Introduction

The first conference of the Standing Committee on Atlantic Organizations (SCAO) met in 1973, so that the 1988 Cambridge meeting was the fifteenth in a series of deliberations which have spanned the Presidencies of Richard Nixon and Ronald Reagan, and the transition of the Soviet Union from Brezhnev to Gorbachev. During the years, SCAO has attempted to address the problems and challenges in the Atlantic relationship in a way that has become peculiarly its own, and which—through the publication of its proceedings—may have contributed something of value to the political debate.

The essays published in this volume—some of which were presented as papers at the conference while others were specially commissioned by the Editor—illustrate SCAO's willingness to range over well-trodden ground in the hope of casting new light on old issues. The decision to consider how economic constraints also affect the Warsaw Pact reflects SCAO's belief that NATO cannot be looked at in isolation. If one of the principal aims of SCAO has been to break down barriers of misunderstanding within the Alliance, this can often be helped by understanding some of the dilemmas faced by the Soviet bloc, which mirror our own.

This book is one of the few *comparative* approaches to NATO and the Warsaw Pact. Collected together, the papers suggest that if the authors may agree on little else, broad agreement has been reached on five general propositions:

1. Both alliances face an economic crisis, largely stemming from the escalating cost of defence procurement.
2. Although their responses to the crisis may take different forms, the European members—East and West—will almost certainly be expected by their respective Superpower allies to shoulder a greater defence burden than they have in the past.
3. This process is likely to involve changes not only in the military, but also the respective economic institutions, notably Comecon and the European Community.
4. It may also involve the revitalization of old institutions such as the Western European Union (WEU), or possibly the invention of entirely new organizations.
5. Paradoxically the procurement and deployment of new technology as a means of cutting costs may bring in its train political difficulties, which could well offset its economic merits.

In a book of this nature it would be invidious to single out any particular author. I would like to thank, however, Alfred Cahen, the Secretary-General of the WEU for agreeing to write the Preface, as well as Professor Harry Maier, who until recently was based in East Germany, for agreeing to provide the Conclusion, thereby adding a new perspective to the purely academic essays in this volume. Special thanks must also go to Inga Haag, whose enthusiasm and helpful advice kept the Editor up to mark, as well as Walter Goldstein and Otto Pick for their invaluable advice and assistance. Without Sir Frank Roberts, the Conference would have been less successful than it proved to be. His long and invaluable association with SCAO deserves special mention, as does that of NATO which once again supported SCAO with a generous publication subvention.

Both SCAO and the editor were especially pleased to be associated with Brassey's, which published the previous volume of essays. I would like to thank Jenny Shaw, in particular, for her general support.

CHRISTOPHER COKER
London School of Economics
1 May 1988

Preface

ALFRED CAHEN

There could be no better time for publishing this book dealing with a problem which is new neither to the Atlantic Alliance nor to the Warsaw Pact, but is one which has recently become particularly acute for both.

Neither is there anything new in the fact that the Soviet Union and its allies have to make an agonizing choice between increasing their military budgets and developing—or even preserving—their economies.

It was only about three years ago, however, that the Soviet leadership openly recognized this fact and began to face its consequences. While we can discuss their true substance, precise scope and possible duration, the reforms emerging in the Soviet Union do exist and are developing, and thus they deserve our attention. Without necessarily accepting at face-value developments whose substance and future remain open to question, the reforms are a challenge to the West—a challenge to take the right initiatives when faced with the new perspectives which are emerging.

Within the Atlantic Alliance, the Europeans have had to face budgetary constraints which have compelled them, in varying degrees, to seek to stabilize or even reduce government spending, particularly on defence. Such contraints are more recent for the United States which, particularly from the start of the Reagan administration, has devoted considerable effort to its own and to common Atlantic security. But at the present time budgetary realities are proving to be more pressing and the consequent cuts that the Pentagon has had to accept have been sufficiently serious to bring about major changes in defence policy, and even the resignation of the US Secretary of the Navy.

The Press which—quite rightly—is always attentive to such changes has already found an expression for this problem which has recently been described by the celebrated columnist Flora Lewis, as the 'econo-military' phenomenon.[1]

This stage of affairs arises within an international situation that is undergoing significant change or, more precisely, changes *viz*:

— a change in the Soviet Union and the Warsaw Pact;
— a change in the context of East-West relations;
— a change in the transatlantic context.

We have already referred briefly to the changes taking place in Moscow and hence in the East-East relationship. There is no doubt that what is happening in the Soviet Union is significant, particularly in that the reforms would seem to stem rather from an absolute necessity and a change of generation than from the single will of one man or group of men. But their precise meaning—whatever the indications given by the chief promoters of reform themselves and particularly Gorbachev in his work devoted to *Perestroika*—remains relatively unclear.

Moreover, there is reason to have some doubts about the possible duration of this phenomenon. It is not the first time since the death of Stalin that a reformer has emerged. It has to be said that, although this will to reform may never have seemed so strong, it should nevertheless be recalled that previously old habits and the *Nomenklatura* have ultimately proved to be the stronger and that the bold reformers have either been overthrown—like Malenkov or Khrushchev—or have gone back to the old line—like Brezhnev. In any event, the result has been a return to 'normality'.

Nevertheless, this new 'thaw' in the USSR has had an impact on the countries of the Warsaw Pact that cannot be ignored:
— positions have been hardened by a worried 'establishment';
— it has led to a movement—a cautious movement—through fear stemming from lessons of the past (Czechoslovakia, Hungary)—towards a certain self-assertion at a national, European and international level.

This last phenomenon is not entirely new. A country like Romania, which internally is extremely rigid, has attempted to develop a relatively independent international policy which, however relative, has nevertheless been perceptible. For almost thirty years Hungary, within the limits imposed by caution, has been following more-or-less original lines and this has also been reflected externally. It has become a member of the International Monetary Fund and the World Bank, organizations which Poland has also joined. Today, this movement appears to be gathering greater strength than in the past.

In this context arms control negotiations have gained momentum. The Washington Treaty has been signed providing for the abolition of both long-range and short-range Intermediate Nuclear Forces (INF)—the so-called double zero option. START negotiations, the aim of which is to secure a 50 per cent reduction in both US and USSR strategic arsenals, are progressing. The scene is being prepared for making progress both on:
— conventional force reductions—hopefully, for the West, asymmetric reductions—which could secure some balance between the Atlantic Alliance and the Warsaw Pact on various European fronts;
— the gradual elimination of chemical weapons.

In this process of movement and progress in the field of disarmament, the future of short-range nuclear weapons (a possible third zero option), dual-capability weapons and even the French and British nuclear deterrents may be on the agenda.

Beyond that, in the more general context of relations between East and West, the problem of the political dialogue with its important human rights dimension and the economic and technological exchanges between countries of the Warsaw Pact and the Atlantic Alliance, are being discussed in particular in the Conference on Security and Co-operation in Europe, a process which began in 1973 and is currently continuing in Vienna.

In the case of West-West relations, it must be said that the Atlantic Alliance—which for forty years has been and still remains the guarantee of European security in the context of common Atlantic security—saw one *status quo* survive the late 1970s and the early 1980s. Of course, there were problems such as popular opposition in Europe to the deployment, in conformity with the Allies' dual-track decision of December 1979, of cruise and Pershing 2 missiles. This decision, it will be recalled, consisted of opening negotiations between the United States and the Soviet Union which might make deployment unnecessary or, if deployment had taken place, which would secure balanced reductions or even the elimination of the US missiles and the Soviet SS-20s. If such negotiations failed, then the deployment of these missiles in Western Europe would proceed as planned.

Such problems, however, did not prevent things from remaining essentially the same. NATO's political doctrine, defined in 1967 in the famous Harmel Report, which rested on the two notions of defence and *détente* remained the same and was solemnly reconfirmed in Washington in June 1984, even if they were adapted to a period characterized more by increasing tensions than by *détente* between East and West. Its strategies were not seriously questioned and were discussed mainly in order to find ways and means of making them more efficient. The old quarrels that had been going on between both sides of the Atlantic—such as that over burden-sharing—were still there, but had lost much of their meaning. The possibility of American troops stationed in Europe being recalled by their government—once a real threat—seemed very remote, and almost non-existent.

Certainly, a *status quo* is not a very dynamic position to be in, but it is rather comfortable and one to which an alliance becomes easily accustomed. This *status quo* is now a thing of the past. Events have moved at such a rapid pace that it seems like an eternity since it disappeared. And this disappearance is a worry to the European allies.

What are the reasons for these changes? Recent developments in the Soviet Union and in East-West relations, certainly constitute an important one. But there are also the developments in transatlantic affairs. The transatlantic relationship has never been an easy one. On the United States' side, Henry Kissinger spoke in the 1950s of a 'troubled partnership'. At the end of September 1986 his former aide in the National Security Council, Larry Eagleburger, referred to an 'intolerable relationship'. This evolution in the qualification of the state of the Alliance indicates, I am afraid, that some progress may have been made but, unfortunately, in the wrong direction.

As for the European evaluation of the transatlantic situation, I shall refer to a recent book written by a British journalist, John Palmer, entitled *Europe without America? The crisis in Atlantic relations* in which the author writes: 'The economic, military and political world of the Atlantic Alliance, in which two generations of Americans and Europeans have grown to adulthood since 1945, is visibly crumbling. ... Even the most sober of observers now openly discuss the crisis in the Atlantic partnership and how long it can survive in anything like its present form.'

This debate is, of course, healthy in itself. It is good for allies to air the views they may have about the state of their Alliance. It is important to review periodically the adequacy of its politico-military doctrines and of its strategies in a world that rarely stands still. That said, I do not support the apocalyptic way in which some people—including the authors I have just quoted—approach this problem. I, for one, believe in the absolute necessity of Atlantic solidarity and in all the possibilities for adapting it to a transatlantic relationship that, in a changing world, is indeed in transition.

It is in this perspective that we must approach the problems—fundamental in the present situation—of East-West, East-East and West-West relationships and, in that framework, of the economic constraints of Alliance politics. There are a number of dimensions. The first relates to the economic-military situation of each of the Superpowers and of each of the Alliances, both as regards their internal problems and their reciprocal relationships. The second dimension, which is linked to the first, relates to:

- defence, with the vital effort this involves (irrespective of economic and budgetary constraints), burden-sharing (as well as responsibility-sharing among Allies) required as part of this effort and the optimum use of new and especially technological possibilities to ensure the most effective security at the lowest cost;
- arms control, whose progress—in the same security context—is equally important and which must form part of an overall policy of dialogue.

In this context, we might quote from the Platform on European security interests adopted on 27 October 1987 in The Hague by the fourteen Foreign and Defence Ministers of the Western European Union: 'The balanced policy of the Harmel Report remains valid. Political solidarity and adequate military strength within the Atlantic Alliance, arms control, disarmament and the search for genuine *détente* continue to be integral parts of this policy. Military security and the policy of *détente* are not contradictory but complementary'.

The third dimension, which is especially important for Western Europe, relates to the emergence of a Western European security identity—and in particular the reactivation of the WEU—within the framework of Atlantic solidarity without which there can be no credible defence of the West.

These then are the issues which this book sets out to address in detail. Perhaps I might dwell on the West European aspect which, by virtue of my position, concerns me most directly. Co-operation in the field of security is steadily growing among the states of Western Europe. The movement is taking shape at a multilateral as well as a bilateral level where at present the most spectacular manifestation is undoubtedly the relationship between France and the Federal Republic of Germany. This is not an isolated case. On the contrary, initiatives of this kind are increasing all the time.

At the multilateral level the framework for these developments has been provided by the WEU, which was reactivated in 1984-85—though not without some difficulty. Indeed, a number of handicaps had to be overcome, including:

— the sporadic nature of the European commitment among the member states. This is something fairly common to the work of constructing Europe as a whole, whether we are considering the European Community or WEU. In a word, it simply means that it is rare for all the member states to seek the same thing at the same time and with the same intensity as far as the process of European construction is concerned;

— the fact that—as well as having common motives—certain member states had their own, sometimes contradictory, motives for reactivating the WEU;

— the sensitive nature of the subjects addressed; security problems are amongst those which most directly relate to national sovereignty;

— the position of the WEU at the crossroads between the Twelve States of the European Community and the Atlantic Alliance, which means that while asserting its personality it must avoid harmful duplication;

— the fact that the organization had been inactive for ten years.

In spite of these handicaps, however, reactivation is now a reality, as stated in the communiqué issued by the Foreign and Defence Ministers of the seven member states at their Luxembourg meeting on 28 April 1987. The WEU is beginning to fulfil the role which its contracting parties hoped it would.

It has succeeded in establishing a dialogue aimed at reaching, in the field of security, a convergence of views or even common positions and thus a European security identity. In so doing, it is able to create a European awareness in this area which will extend to public opinion through the open democratic dialogue that the Council of Ministers can now have with the WEU Parliamentary Assembly. Its significance is great. We must remember that a growing section of public opinion tends to distance itself from our security problems and that the vital consensus which must provide the basis of our defence policies has been eroded. It is only, I believe, through a democratic, ie public debate at the European level that we can narrow that distance and restore a consensus.

This dialogue between the Western European Union's seven member states has already begun to bear fruit. First, there has been a continuing process of consultation, leading to a growing harmony of views. Striking evidence of this was first seen at the Ministerial Meeting on 13-14 November 1986, in the aftermath of the Reykjavik Superpower summit. The joint conclusions reached by the participants enabled them to speak in harmony to their allies, and in particular to the United States, of their parallel concerns.

This has continued in the various East-West disarmament talks and also in those between the United States and the Soviet Union. This has not always been easy. But the dialogue, now covering all essential security issues, has continued among our fourteen (Foreign and Defence) Ministers and among their immediate associates, thus allowing views to be jointly expressed.

This dialogue and its results have shown quite rapidly that such convergence of views on topical problems was—in the indispensable context, of course, of Atlantic solidarity—in line with the basic longer-term policies of the countries of Western Europe. In fact, this is nothing new. It was recognized, for example, in the 1974 Ottowa Declaration which laid down the principle of the unity of the Alliance in the face of the threat to all its members. It also emphasized the specific vulnerability of Europe, which thus had a special position in the context of Atlantic solidarity. There had never been any attempt, however, to clarify and define these fundamental joint policies, nor had their consequences been considered.

It is a task that the WEU has undertaken at the instigation of its member states. It met a need identified in November 1986 in the post-Reykjavik situation and with the appeal made in December 1986 by the then French Prime Minister Jacques Chirac, in an address to the Parliamentary Assembly of WEU in which he called for a 'Charter' defining the 'principles of western European security'. Serious and in-depth work was begun and lasted nine months. Its fruits were embodied in a report which in turn led to a 'Platform' adopted by the fourteen Ministers on 27 October 1987 in The Hague. In adopting this 'Platform', the seven member states fulfilled one of the essential roles assigned to them, namely the creation of a European identity in the security area.

In the context thus defined the seven Atlantic allies which are members of the Western European Union are clearly attempting to resolve some of the problems facing the Atlantic Alliance, in particular the economic constraints which, in consolidating the base for a European pillar of this Alliance, they can overcome together more effectively than they could separately.

Furthermore, and in the same context, what may the role of WEU be as regards arms and defence equipment co-operation? Such co-operation is admittedly not a universal cure for the problem of the increasing cost of military equipment and the inherent danger of structural disarmament. But, properly conceived, it could play an important part in this respect.

This question can be approached in two ways that are not contradictory but, in fact, complementary:

— Joint projects can be set up. This is the province of the Independent
  European Programme Group (IEPG)[2] and intergovernmental co-
  operation;
— A more open market can be organized. This possibility may stem
  from the Single European Act of December 1985, signed by the
  twelve member states of the European Communities in spite of
  Article 223 of the Rome Treaty, which excludes this kind of item
  from the European Common Market.

The aim of WEU member states is not to duplicate the work done in the
two other wider fora. But the organisation, whose members have a politico-
military likemindedness (even though France is not part of the integrated
military structure of NATO) and industrial homogeneity, can give serious
political impetus to the progress that should be made both in the Independent
European Programme Group (IEPG) and in the European Economic
Community.

This is, moreover, its role as formally recognized in the Rome Declaration
of 27 October 1984 which states: 'The Ministers ... decided to hold comprehensive discussions and to seek to harmonize their views on the specific
conditions of security in Europe, in particular ... the development of
European co-operation in the field of armaments in respect of which WEU
can provide a political impulse'.

The Rome Declaration also stated that 'they (the Ministers) may also
consider the implications for Europe of crises in other regions of the world'.
The responsibilities thus conferred on WEU for concerting the action of the
seven member states—outside their immediate defence zone—was recently
given concrete expression in the Gulf. Five of them sent ships to the region
while two others, the FRG and Luxembourg, expressed their political
solidarity with their partners. Germany, constitutionally precluded from
taking part in such operations, agreed, if necessary, to replace within the
Alliance area, any of its partners' units that had left for the Gulf. Luxembourg
made a financial contribution. The national operations were technically co-
ordinated both on the spot and at admiralty levels.

Recalling the academic discussion about whether the Alliance could act
outside its formally-recognized area—a discussion which often prevented
concrete action from being taken—one must recognize that the possibility
given to the WEU is important both for it and for the Western Alliance.

A publication entitled *National Security Choices for the Next President*,
edited by the Centre for Strategic and International Studies (CSIS) Working
Group on Presidential National Security choices gives the incumbent of the
White House the following advice: 'Your basic theme in approaching our
strategic predicament should be: think smarter, not richer'.[3] Given the
economic and budgetary circumstances facing the two Superpowers and the
two Alliances, 'smarter, not richer' is assuredly of the essence. But the key
word in the formula adopted by the CSIS Working Group is certainly 'think'.

That, of course, means thinking about the impact of the economic constraints which have indeed become an essential new factor in the Alliance's security policies.

These are the problems which this book discusses both in relation to the Atlantic Alliance and the Warsaw Pact. It is a book which I wholeheartedly welcome.

Notes

1. 'Traditionally the realm of the Departments of State and Defense was considered to be foreign affairs, while Treasury and Budget were the senior domestic posts. But economics now enters every aspect of international relations, from the big, basic issues of how much should and can be spent on defense to the attempt to use money as a carefully targeted weapon, by denials as the United States is doing with Panama or by supply as with the Afghan and Contra rebels. ... The great majority (of US citizens) want to explore "a fundamentally different relationship with the Soviets" but with caution. They do not seek or trust instant *détente*. And they are keenly aware of costs. Econo-military is coming in'. (*International Herald Tribune*, 3 April 1988).
2. An organization of which the following thirteen states of the Atlantic Alliance are members: Belgium, Denmark, France, Federal Republic of Germany, Greece, Italy, Luxembourg, Netherlands, Norway, Portugal, Spain, Turkey and the United Kingdom.
3. CSIS-Volume IX, Number 3-'Significant issues series', 'Leadership choices for the 1990s'—'National Security Choices for the Next President'—Page ix—1988.

SECTION 1
Buying into a Crisis

DEFENCE *economics has become a growth subject since the mid-1960s when it became clear that both Alliances were beginning to find they had too many commitments and too few resources, while the cost of equipment seemed to be spiralling out of control. In the West, the traditional response until recently was to go for cuts which stretched NATO's forces, followed by a major retrenchment, followed by further cuts—a debilitating process which left NATO weaker every cycle. In the 1970s its manpower fell by 20 per cent, while defence spending rose by 10 per cent in every country except the United States.*

More recent studies have shown that the Soviet Union and its allies are not immune from the phenomenon of defence inflation, and that the cost of equipment is much the same. Both Alliances are in danger of disarming themselves through inflation, a process which Thomas Callaghan has termed 'structural disarmament', a problem which is no less real for the Warsaw Pact than it is for NATO. The economic problems of defence are by no means the only challenge both blocs face in the 1990s, but they are one of the most significant, as David Greenwood argues persuasively in the essay that follows.

At the Conference, he was asked to concentrate on 'NATO's Defence; Needs and Budget Constraints'—and how to get better value for money. Many of the same problems, of course, apply to the Warsaw Pact—as the later chapters make clear.

CHAPTER 1

Defence Economics: A Problem in Search of a Solution

DAVID GREENWOOD

As NATO celebrates its fortieth anniversary its members face a challenge no less daunting than that which presented itself when the North Atlantic Treaty was signed. To be sure, they do not face now, as they faced then, an adversary of seemingly implacable hostility and apparently boundless ambition. Quite the contrary: in the Soviet Union, and increasingly elsewhere in Eastern Europe, economic reform and domestic restructuring are the present preoccupations and, if attention is to be concentrated on these, the strategic competition with the West must be regulated and ideas of forcibly extending socialism's frontiers must be suppressed (if not abandoned). Hence the Kremlin's new-found enthusiasm for arms control, for 'sufficiency' and 'stability'. Nor are the countries of Western Europe now, as they were then, economically weak and exhausted from wartime exertion. Far from it: despite oil shocks and the difficult adjustments that these and other developments made necessary, their economies are fundamentally sound and their citizens are unprecedentedly prosperous. So where is the 'daunting challenge'?

It lies in the fact that, precisely because so much has changed, less significance may be attached to what remains unchanged. The Moscow-led Eastern bloc is still the preponderant military power on the Eurasian landmass, fielding formidable forces equipped with an impressive and improving inventory of nuclear and conventional weapons. This places on Western governments a continuing responsibility to keep their own apparatus for deterrence and defence in good repair, and to bear and share the associated burdens. We can hope that it will not always be like this, by all means: but we should let experience (and prudence) guide day-to-day decision-making, until the reality and durability of some new security order is assured.

More precisely and more practically, the central challenge is to manage the maintenance and modernization of the Alliance's forces—the substance of its 'apparatus for deterrence and defence'—despite tightening resource *constraints* ; and to exploit in these circumstances such *opportunities* as may present themselves for making more effective use of resources (getting better value for money). The question of greatest interest and importance as NATO enters its fifth decade is: what are the *prospects* of successfully meeting this

3

challenge? If this formulation appears to give too little prominence to arms control, the explanation is straightforward. How much maintenance and modernization is required, and of what, will naturally depend upon the headway made in future negotiations on both strategic weapons (including space-based systems) and conventional armaments (plus related measures concerning military dispositions from the Atlantic to the Urals). But the fact that such negotiations are being conducted cannot—or should not—be a pretext for neglecting force improvements.

Constraints

Needless to say, the impact of resource constraints is not a novel factor for NATO members to consider in their security calculations. The tension between commitments and resources is a perennial problem. What is foreseeable on the threshold of the 1990s, however, is an *intensification* of both general (financial) constraints and specific ones (notably manpower).

FINANCIAL CONSTRAINTS

So far as defence financing is concerned, the writing is on the wall—or in the forecasts—even now. Put simply, defence ministries face a dual predicament. Because of the rising real cost of all military inputs—and especially high-technology weapon systems—they find themselves getting less defence for their money year-by-year (in terms of the familiar indices of military power, numbers of warships, armoured fighting vehicles and artillery pieces, aircraft and missiles). At the same time, because of the pressure of other public and private claims on resources, Alliance governments are inclined to allot less money for defence year-by-year (in real terms), or at least not enough more to sustain existing force structures and force levels, while keeping equipment up to date and up to scratch.

The phenomenon of rising real costs of military equipment is well documented. It is the result of the operation of a set of interlocking vicious cycles. In the quest for qualitative offset to the Warsaw Pact's many quantitative advantages, NATO weapons designers have been encouraged to push the state of the art at a pace and across the board. This has had the effect both of increasing the technological risk and lengthening the development time for new systems. By way of compensation, and also to take account of changes in the threat during protracted development, Service purchasers have felt it necessary to ask for frequent design modifications, typically in the form of a demand for higher performance. The consequent development cost escalation has impelled governments to buy fewer items of each successive generation of equipment, but over an extended time-scale (partly for financing reasons, partly to keep industrial plant occupied). This has meant further cost escalation—production cost escalation this time—through the loss of any benefit from economies of learning and economies of scale. Small wonder that in one Alliance country an in-house study has suggested that up to one-half of each year's equipment outlays may be attributable to expense not foreseen—and hence not taken into account—when the relevant procurement programmes were started.

Nor is this the whole tale. Unexpected cost growth, arising from the pursuit of higher performance, can actually result in lower combat effectiveness. Experience with a recent NATO anti-tank guided weapon (ATGW) illustrates the point. Although marketed as 'the $10,000 missile to kill the $1,000,000 tank', its buyers found that the high cost of the item precluded regular live-firing by their troops. The exercise scores achieved by operators were correspondingly poor: 'kill probabilities' of less than 30 per cent under field conditions, compared with the 90 per cent achieved in acceptance evaluation (by experts on a test range).

The 'less money for defence' proposition is readily verified too. Looking back over the past decade, the statistical record shows that only one or two NATO members consistently honoured the commitment to strive for annual real increases in defence spending in the region of 3 per cent, even though all subscribed to it in 1977-78 and the target has been regularly reaffirmed in Ministerial 'resource guidance' since then. Looking ahead, no nation's current budgetary projections aim that high, several countries envisage more-or-less level funding (after inflation) as they enter the 1990s, and in quite a few expenditure at constant prices will, in fact, fall.

A country-by-country review is instructive. In the United States the focus of political concern is the troubled condition of the economy. The most graphic manifestations of this are the stubborn deficits in the federal budget and in the country's international accounts, the latter associated with an unprecedented accumulation of international indebtedness—and in 1988 an unprecedentedly weak dollar—plus a substantial flow of inward investment. Part of Washington's response has been to curb the Pentagon's spending. Over the turn of the decade defence outlays are going to be held on a plateau, at a level of around $300 bn. (at 1988 values).

The United Kingdom has opted for 'level funding' too. According to present projections, Mrs Thatcher's third administration will be allocating to defence no more at the end of its term (in 1991-92) than at the beginning. The period should be one of steady growth. But the benefits of that growth will accrue to private consumption (through tax cuts), to industrial investment (building the 'enterprise economy') and to selected civil programmes (health care and urban renewal, for example).

Another NATO member that has recently framed less ambitious spending plans is Norway. The country's five-year defence plan for 1989-93 assumes real expenditure growth of only 2 per cent a year, compared with just over 3 per cent in the previous period. The Netherlands government has lowered

its target rate of increase as well, while in neighbouring Belgium the experience
of recent years is that the construction of each new fragile coalition is accompanied by a scaling-down of the national defence effort. Much the same is
true of Denmark.

As for the 'big spenders' of continental Europe, France's military plan for
1987-91 projected annual budget increases in the region of 6 per cent.
Performance, however, has not quite matched that, and the follow-on plan
is expected to incorporate more modest aspirations. In West Germany the
Bundeswehr Plan for the fifteen years 1987-2001 assumes some extra funding
year-by-year to 1991 (in line with the Federal Republic's 21st Financial Plan)
but it assumes zero growth thereafter, the 'baseline' defence budget for
1992-2001 having been set at around DM 55 bn.

One could go on, noting the resource allocation dilemmas of Spain and
Portugal, Greece and Turkey, observing that while Italy plans an important
defence reconstruction, her ability to finance it remains open to question; and
that while Canada has recently completed a major review of her defence
provision—and has adopted a bold blueprint which includes, among much
else, the acquisition of nuclear-powered fleet submarines—the chances that
this plan will be fully realized are not rated highly, even in Ottawa.

SPECIFIC CONSTRAINTS

On top of all this, some Alliance members face particular resource constraints. The most dramatic example is the manpower problem confronting
the West Germans (to which the new Bundeswehr Plan mentioned above is
a first response). Bluntly, the Federal Republic will soon be unable—for
demographic reasons—to fulfil its defence responsibilities within NATO as
it does at present. A couple of figures express the predicament. In 1988 the
number of draftees available to the Federal armed forces was about 250,000
(already below the 300,000-plus of the early 1980s). Five years on, in 1993,
the number will have dropped to around 150,000. The family planning of the
1970s has thus compelled Bonn to undertake a radical revision of force
planning for the 1990s, especially as it affects the army. The authorities have
come up with an elaborate damage limitation scheme. So far as the army is
concerned, its key features are retention of the nominal order of battle,
introduction of a task- and mission-oriented structure for the field forces, and
reduction of the manning strength of that structure's forty-two brigades to
50-70 per cent (present levels being 90 per cent within thirty-six brigades).
For the other Services, straightforward contraction is envisaged: in the air
force from a personnel strength of some 110,000 to nearer 98,000; in the navy
from almost 39,000 to just over 34,000.

For a number of other NATO countries it is the military appetite for
research and development (R&D) resources that is causing most concern. In
both the United States and the United Kingdom, for instance, there has been

official acknowledgement lately of what critics have been asserting for some time; that the commitment of a substantial proportion of a country's scientific and technical talent to military purposes can damage the health of the national economy, by thwarting commercial innovation and thus contributing to loss of international competitiveness. There are difficulties with the logic of this argument, especially when it is alleged that defence pre-empts resources. Moreover, the evidence is ambiguous. Maybe there is more to the explanation of Japan's success in global commerce than the ultra-low proportion of that country's R&D effort that is devoted to defence. Perhaps there is more to the explanation of Western industries' poor showing in product and process innovation than the fact that they have sometimes found it difficult to woo the best scientists and engineers from exciting military work at the far frontiers of technology. Be that as it may, the policy-makers' perception is that there is pre-emption and that 'crowding-out' does occur. Their answer is to allocate fewer R&D resources to defence, more to civilian endeavour.

Against this background of financial and specific resource constraints the question arises: how is NATO to 'maintain and modernize' its capabilities, pending progress in the arms control arena? The answer must be by making more efficient use of the resources that nations are prepared to allot to military purposes, by getting better value for the defence dollar, pound, mark and franc.

Opportunities

How might that be done? It is convenient to distinguish three directions in which more efficient resource use can be sought: within *individual* national defence organizations and services, by the practice of 'good housekeeping'; in *bilateral* arrangements between pairs of countries with particular shared concerns or opportunities for beneficial co-operation; and on an Alliance-wide basis by increased *multilateral or collective* effort, embracing (a) some specialization in the performance of military roles and missions and (b) greater collaboration in procurement (from upstream R&D to actual manu-facture). This third set of possibilities—collective endeavour—is potentially the most important, promising the greatest pay-offs, but the other two are worth brief comment.

Before dealing with them, however, a word on doctrine and concepts of operations is in order. The most inefficient use of resources occurs when money, manpower and matériel are employed for wholly inappropriate purposes. Clearly there is no merit whatever in achieving efficiency in the misuse of resources, no credit due for getting better at doing the wrong things. The point has to be made, though, because NATO is occasionally seized by enthusiasm for a doctrinal innovation or a novel concept of operations, and embarks—or threatens to embark—upon an expensive re-casting of dispositions in accordance with that enthusiasm. The usual result is a damaging distortion of priorities.

This point has to be stressed because latterly the Alliance has been flirting with just such an enthusiasm: for a modified approach to land/air warfare on its Central Front, emphasizing deep strike operations plus massive infusions of so-called emerging technology (ET) weapons. Fortunately this tendency has moderated into a commitment to the improvement of capabilities for relatively shallow Follow-On Forces Attack (FOFA), and to very selective investment in high technology surveillance, communications and weapons systems. It is not out of the wood yet, however. Indeed, the arguments of 1982-87 may have to be gone through again following the appearance of the Report on the Commission of Long-Term Strategy, bearing the title *Discriminate Deterrence* and presented to President Reagan early in 1988. Granted, this is a submission to the American President, not to NATO; and it prescribes priorities for the United States not the Atlantic Alliance. At the same time, it contains strong advocacy of precisely what, in present circumstances, the West should be forswearing: the adoption of a concept of operations encompassing counter-offensives deep into Warsaw Pact territory—not counter-penetration, not counter-attacks, not even counter-strokes, but actual counter-offensive action—and the acquisition of much new technology, even if this means diverting resources from other, more mundane, force improvement programmes. If ever there was a blueprint for squandering resources, not to mention sabotaging the arms control process, this is it.

The hope must be that, as these recommendations of the *Discriminate Deterrence* document are digested, NATO will find it has no stomach for them, and is unwilling to be distracted from the single-minded pursuit of more efficient resource use.

NATIONAL REFORMS

To this end, the individual member states can obviously make an initial contribution by looking each to its own military organization and practice. Defence bureaucracies do have a tendency to become overblown, with rank inflation as pervasive as price inflation. The separate parts of Service organizations also have a tendency to lose their cost-consciousness, especially when centralized accounting and control mean that the careful manager wins no prizes for his parsimony and the spendthrift manager incurs no penalty for his profligacy. As for major systems acquisition, here the relationship between the military customer and the industrial supplier can become so close as to invite conspiracy-theorizing.

It is easier, though, to identify the problems than to prescribe solutions. What one can do is note that when a confident and determined politician or businessman runs the rule over organizational structures and bureaucratic processes, he (or she) can usually find ways of cutting the administration down to size, streamlining its procedures and reviving its competitive impulse. The United Kingdom's Secretary of State for Defence, Michael Heseltine, did as much during the mid-1980s, aided by an outside appointee, Peter Levene, as his Chief of Defence Procurement. The Minister performed major—but thoughtful—surgery on the Defence Department's central organization and encouraged trimming of the support 'tail' throughout the armed forces, using 'privatization' as one instrument. The former defence contractor—poacher turned gamekeeper in some eyes—began, and still presides over, far-reaching reform of the national weapons acquisition process: establishing 'cardinal points specifications' as the norm, insisting on competitive bidding rather than old 'preferred supplier' deals, setting stiffer terms for procurement contracts, and instituting more rigorous project management.

Reform of the procurement process has also paid dividends in the United States, the sure indicator of its success—from the taxpayer's standpoint— being the groundswell of protest that has come from defence-related industry concerning (among other things) allegedly onerous contract terms and the damaging consequences of opening-up the vast American market to international competition. Administrative reform across the board is a feature of the Bundeswehr Plan for 1987-2001. Some common tasks which each branch of the Federal armed forces has hitherto done for itself are to be centrally provided *eg* reconnaissance, telecommunications and air transport. Savings are to be made in performance of the training function by, for example, greater use of simulators. The management of armaments projects is to be tightened, notably by the firm fixing of weapon system specifications at the outset of development and the establishment of fixed cost limits for every stage of the acquisition process.

BILATERAL ARRANGEMENTS

Another route to greater effectiveness for the same money, or the same effectiveness for less money, is through beneficial bilateral co-operation. The recent blossoming of Franco-German co-operation has commanded much attention, mainly because of its general political significance and the particular symbolic importance of the decision to form a joint brigade for service in the Federal Republic. What has attracted less notice is the related commitment to extend reciprocal arms purchases and to build on the two countries' already considerable experience in joint procurement ventures.

More reciprocal purchasing is also one of the expected outcomes of the new interest in Franco-British collaboration that has become evident recently. Each country has undertaken to keep the other informed of evolving requirements and of bidding opportunities as they arise. A programme of conferences has been instituted as a medium for exploring potential joint ventures in particular areas (land systems, naval systems etc.). Even nuclear co-operation has been discussed, with initial emphasis on the practicability of a joint approach to provision of a next-generation stand-off missile for both countries' air forces and with the intriguing possibility of later collaboration on strategic systems.

Nor is it just in these well-publicized instances that bilateralism flourishes. There is much unsung co-operation between the United Kingdom and the Federal Republic, on operational and logistical matters as well as within the framework of collaborative procurement projects like Tornado and the European Fighter Aircraft (EFA). The same could be said of relations between the United Kingdom and Italy, partners in the major EH-101 helicopter programme, while the Italians and the West Germans are beginning to forge new links (following exploratory conversations early in 1988). The smaller NATO countries, too, have been active lately, witness the quiet diplomacy on possibilities for operational co-operation between Dutch and Belgian forces.

COLLECTIVE PLANNING

While NATO nations can do a certain amount individually to get better value for money, and can make further progress to that end by bilateral co-operation with neighbours (or other partners), the most promising opportunities for more efficient use of resources in the Alliance lie in what might be accomplished by a multilateral approach to defence provision.

At present the sixteen nations practise a loose form of joint programming in relation to fielding forces and acquiring arms. Member States make their own decisions about force structures, force levels and force deployments. The role of the international staffs is two-fold: to work out how, from these independent national contributions, there might emerge a coherent whole amounting to more than the sum of its parts; and to devise realistic but challenging goals for future subscriptions. Member States also make their own choices about the weapons systems and matériel they will acquire. The business of Alliance institutions—the Conference of National Armaments Directors (CNAD) and its supporting bureaucracy—is to provide a forum for reviewing national intentions, considering where co-operative effort might be possible, and monitoring progress in existing collaborative ventures.

For a generation these arrangements have suited the Allies. No sacrifice of sovereignty is involved. No central body wields supranational authority. No country has a hard and fast obligation to harmonize its military dispositions or its equipment purchases with those of any other. They have also served the Alliance reasonably well, because within the permissive institutional framework there has been considerable co-ordination of effort.

All this gives some cause for satisfaction but it does not justify complacency. Not to put too fine a point on it, 'business as usual' will not be good enough if NATO is in earnest about maintaining and modernizing its forces under tight resource constraints. New approaches to fielding forces and acquiring arms will have to be examined, in particular the adoption of genuinely collective planning in Alliance decision-making.

The institutional requirements for this are obvious. Where issues of force structure are concerned, there is at present no formal process in NATO for consultation, let alone planning; there is no forum to which member States can submit proposals for change in their force contributions, with a view to learning whether—in the light of what others may be contemplating—one of these might serve (or offend) the collective interest more (or less) than another. Nor is there a mechanism for the Major NATO Commanders (MNCs) to define an ideal force structure, based on individual nations' unique competences, special aptitudes and comparative advantages in different forms of military provision. Yet both deficiencies could be remedied— initially by devising a planners' template of preferred national contributions. Such a template could fulfil an invaluable dual function: offering a point of reference for assessment of the adjustments to their force subscriptions which nations might propose from time to time; and providing the medium for communication by the MNCs of options for change which they themselves might wish to propose with more effective use of resources in mind. (In due course Force Structure Goals could be set in this manner, to stand alongside— perhaps even to supersede—the Force Goals of the present 'planning' process.)

On the procurement side, matters are not quite so haphazard. The CNAD provides a forum to which countries can bring ideas for sharing risk, tech- nology and expense by co-operative endeavour. It is also experimenting with a new Conventional Armaments Planning System (CAPS) whose design features Armaments Goals. Appearances, however, may be deceptive. There is no obvious custodian of the collective interest (other than the Assistant Secretary-General for Defense Support, as overseer of the CAPS trial); and there is no central body responsible for pinpointing areas of potentially beneficial co-operation which may have escaped the CNAD's notice (other than that same Assistant Secretary-General's staff). In particular, there is no planners' roster of preferred acquisition schedules offering a set of procure- ment objectives consistent with the Alliance's Force Goals (and Long-Term Planning Guidelines). Yet such a roster could easily be produced, to serve as a foundation for indicative acquisition planning with efficient resource use in mind.

Can NATO move in these ways beyond joint programming towards collective planning? Is reform feasible in the so-called force planning process—which is currently no more than an elaborate sequence of co-ordinating and cajoling rituals—to allow creative Alliance force structure planning? Is transformation possible in the so-called armaments planning process—until recently just an information exchange and management review apparatus—to allow constructive Alliance procurement planning?

These objectives ought to be attainable. They are certainly coming within reach. Considerable attention has been paid lately—first in the analytical community, later in official and Ministerial circles—to options and prospects for task specialization among NATO members (especially the West European partners). Such interest could easily be harnessed to preparation of the much-needed 'planners' template of preferred national contributions'—in effect, an outline force structure plan for the 1990s.

Likewise there has been much fresh effort recently directed towards fostering more armaments co-operation. A revitalized Independent European Programme Group has been impressively busy, promoting intra-European collaboration in procurement and production. Legislation sponsored by United States' Senators Nunn, Quayle and Roth has enhanced prospects for transatlantic business, some of the Pentagon's funds having been 'fenced off' for joint R&D ventures and side-by-side testing of American and European equipment. The Alliance itself has not only promulgated an ambitious Armaments Co-operation Improvement Strategy; it has actually launched its new CAPS procedure on a two-year trial basis. Moreover, nations are reportedly taking the experiment seriously. This activity presents an opportunity too; it could readily be channelled to the early establishment of NATO-wide planning arrangements, on the CAPS model, incorporating the required 'planners' roster of preferred acquisition schedules'—in effect, a consolidated investment plan for the Alliance.

Prospects

These are the opportunities. What are the prospects? How much of the foregoing can one realistically expect to be transformed into action and institutional innovation? How energetically will countries pursue better value for money in defence, at the national level, in bilateral arrangements and in the potentially most productive area of collective endeavour? Can NATO capitalize on recent achievement—and on what is currently under consideration—in a concerted drive for more efficient resource use?

At the national level, one can be reasonably certain that those governments which have taken steps to slim their bureaucracies, rationalize their organizations and improve their management practices will sustain—perhaps even extend—their efforts. One can be reasonably certain that others will follow suit when resource constraints really bite. Gauging how 'bilateralism' will develop is more difficult. However, some things are clear. First, it is likely that the French connections will mature and multiply as time goes by, if only because the cultivation of these relationships is France's way of drawing closer to her allies, while continuing to do business with the Alliance's integrated military organization only at arm's length (and very selectively). Secondly, Spain will be interested in any new links that offer the prospect of access to technology and make a contribution to the development of its defence-industrial base. Thirdly, Italy also will look favourably on ties which can help strengthen its position in the European arms market, and especially favourably on transalpine affiliations which lessen the country's sense of geostrategic isolation. Fourthly, the Netherlands and Belgium are likely to liaise on a widening agenda of defence matters, impelled by the particular dilemmas which beset small powers in hard times and helped by their long-standing tradition of close co-operation.

Of prospects for the collective approach to fielding forces, based on task specialization, all that can be said is that there may or may not be headway here. Not long ago anyone advocating an Alliance division of labour in fufilment of major tasks used to receive an indulgent hearing, but no more than that. Interest is greater now. In 1983-84 a major study on 'options and prospects' for role specialization in NATO was conducted (by independent analysts). This work confirmed—by practical example—two things: the possibility of useful marginal improvement to the Alliance's conventional posture through specialization by two or more countries in specific shared areas of interest; and the possibility of very substantial benefits from a comprehensive reallocation of roles and responsibilities, through application of the principle of comparative advantage across the board. These ideas were quietly disseminated in 1985. They were then discussed by policy-makers at the first-ever EUROGROUP Seminar in 1986 and by defence planners at various symposia in 1987. They were commended, albeit obliquely, in the comprehensive 'Platform on European Security Interests' published by the Foreign and Defence Ministers of Western European Union (WEU) in October of that year. They were commended, quite explicitly, in the visionary *NATO in the 1990s* document published by the North Atlantic Assembly in the spring of 1988. They have been evaluated in almost every Defence Ministry in the Alliance.

That is the good news. The bad news is that nations remain reluctant to rationalize their force contributions in this way. There are understandable sensitivities about sovereignty. There is a very proper recognition that in some areas of provision 'multinationality'—the number of flags in the line—may be every bit as important as efficiency. There is justifiable concern that some countries might use an exercise in role-sharing as a pretext for role-shedding. All these represent legitimate reservations. What they fail to confront, though, are some harsh realities: that, because of pressure on resources, NATO members are shedding roles anyway and, as a result, arbitrary *de facto* specialization is taking place; that there is no particular virtue in preserving multinationality at the expense of combat effectiveness; and that insistence on sovereign self-sufficiency in security provision is a fundamental contradiction of the very rationale of the Alliance.

Of these realities, it is the evidence of *de facto* specialization that could eventually be decisive, prompting nations to acknowledge that, if an intra-Alliance division of labour is inevitable then 'better by design than by default'. It is then that they will need the 'planners' template' of my earlier formulation.

As for acquiring arms, here too the imperatives of interdependence seem bound, ultimately, to be decisive. Having wrestled with the soaring costs of independent R&D for advanced systems and having discovered what shallow learning curves and small-scale production do for equipment prices, all NATO members—including the United States—now recognize that in military-industrial affairs self-sufficiency is self-defeating. Indeed they are well on the way to a further realization: that even preserving a high degree of self-reliance in weapons development and manufacture is inordinately expensive (and full of risk). All this is impelling them to favour the collective approach to armaments procurement.

Needless to say, governments remain interested in retaining such national technological competence and competitiveness as they can; and most still feel that they must make—and be seen to be making—some effort to accommodate particular Service, industrial and regional interests. Hence their preference, so far, for bilateral or trilateral co-operative projects within which elaborate work-sharing deals can be done; for a sort of 'political carve-up and share-out' model of collaboration. But there are signs that attitudes are changing. The IEPG has arranged a large (and growing) number of Co-operative Technology Projects (CTPs in the jargon). More important, many of the most recent joint ventures have been organized on the basis of competitive bidding among competing transnational consortia, a model of collaboration which involves government-to-government accords on the buying (or procuring) side but relies on industry-to-industry co-operation on the selling (or producing) side and thus makes work-sharing, technology-sharing and risk-sharing matters of commercial rather than political negotiation. Such evolutions augur well for the collective interest and for the success of NATO's experimental CAPS. By the early 1990s the Alliance 'planners' roster' could be a reality.

Conclusion

It is important that NATO keeps its apparatus for deterrence and defence in good repair, and its equipment up to date and up to scratch. The 'daunting challenge' facing Alliance members in the 1990s is how to do this—how to maintain and modernize their forces—despite tight resource constraints, and in the atmosphere engendered by great expectations in the arms control arena.

To meet the challenge they will have to make more effective use of the resources of money, manpower and technical ingenuity that are allocated to military purposes. There are opportunities for doing this. Measures can be introduced at the national level. Things can be done through bilateral co-operation. Most important of all, member nations can opt for a truly collective approach to fielding forces and acquiring arms, applying the division-of-labour principle in the performance of military tasks and to the procurement and production of weapons.

The prospects for more attention to 'good housekeeping' within national defence organizations and more exploitation of beneficial bilateral liaisons are good. What is not so certain is whether countries will be prepared to take the crucial step towards collective planning, which can provide the impetus and the institutional framework for task specialization and for NATO-wide armaments co-operation. They could take it. It is the obvious next stage in the Alliance's evolution. It is also what its fortieth birthday celebrations ought to be about.

SECTION 2
Problems of Defence
Spending—NATO

WHEN asked in June 1980 what Ronald Reagan's promised $20bn. increase in defence spending would mean, the US Defense Secretary Harold Brown replied 'a better grade of parity'. As Walter Goldstein reveals, despite doubling the national debt and contributing to the largest budget deficit in the country's history, the massive defence expenditure of the past seven years has probably made the United States no more powerful than when Reagan came to power.

The Soviet Union, too, has paid dearly for the massive defence expenditure of the 1970s. As Marshal Ogarkov once claimed, all it produced was a force which was poorly trained, inadequately armed and significantly unmotivated (a serious problem in mid-grade enlisted ranks, more serious still in a conscript army). Both powers seem to have forgotten Machiavelli's dictum:

> Money is not the sinews of war, although it is
> generally so considered. . . . It is not gold, but
> good soldiers that ensure success at war.

Stanley Sloan looks at how a United States which thinks itself to be in decline will continue to ask its allies to share the defence burden, a debate which is as old as the Alliance itself. The real problem, of course, is not that burden-sharing would involve a division of labour, or even a division of responsibilities, but a division of power (with which the United States has not yet come to terms). It is hardly compatible with the image of the senior partner which Washington has been so assiduous in promoting since 1949.

CHAPTER 2

Constraints of Superpower Defence-Spending: Military Budgets and Economic Decline

WALTER GOLDSTEIN

Conventional wisdom suggests that the nuclear condominium exercised by the United States and the Soviet Union will probably survive the century. But there is an element of doubt. The relative economic power of both Superpowers has been reduced in recent years as their own allies and trade rivals have surpassed their sluggish gross national product (GNP) growth rates and both powers face some measure of economic distress. Nevertheless, it is assumed that their strategic nuclear duopoly will remain unchallenged. Equipped with 25,000 strategic and tactical nuclear warheads apiece, and with armed forces several million strong, the two countries stand alone as the prime users of coercion in the international order.

When the two world leaders met at the 1987 White House summit 'fiesta', they enjoyed a lordly sense of pre-eminence. The level of confidences exchanged between General Secretary Gorbachev and President Reagan required no third party or *interlocuteur valable*. Both chieftains spoke boldly for their own collective security alliances as they talked about changing the strategic balance and disbanding theatre nuclear forces in central Europe. Each made a formal show of consulting loyal allies after the private feast had concluded, more to display good manners than to acknowledge collegial obligation.

The immediate purpose of the 1987 White House summit was to remove intermediate-range nuclear forces (INF) from central Europe, to negotiate longer-term proposals for the strategic arms reduction talks (START), and to promote a range of détente understandings between the two alliance leaders. The ulterior motives of the summit duo were less visible. Both needed to strengthen their power standoff against their own allies and against the other's global probing. More important was the realization by both sides that neither could afford to maintain current obligations. It was becoming too expensive to maintain (1) the forces needed to police their worldwide spheres of influence; (2) the nuclear arsenals to guarantee an extended and assured deterrence; and (3) the commitments to preserve hegemony in key areas of the Third World. Their own allies in Europe were divided, if not unhelpful, about paying for the modernization of conventional forces. And the two leaders themselves had already had to back down from expensive engagements in Afghanistan and the Gulf, from their endless involvements in the Middle East and in the tropical jungles of Central America, and from the national liberation wars of South-east Asia and sub-Saharan Africa. In fact, the emperors had discovered that they were covered with fewer and fewer clothes; they needed to ask what it was they could do, if they ever managed to collaborate, to restore their ascendancy.

Historians will probably argue in future years about which factor was most instrumental in forcing the Superpowers to modify their global positions in the late 1980s. One school of historians will surely insist that the chief factor prompting change was the vast expenditures incurred by the escalation of the arms race. President Reagan champions this explanation. He emphasizes that his administration spent more than \$2 trillion on military programmes, including a serious plan to develop a space-based defence system, the Strategic Defence Initiative (SDI), which forced the Kremlin to modulate the arms race. A second school will argue that more of the credit is due to Mikhail Gorbachev; he seized power from the old guard bureaucrats and Stalinists in the Kremlin, at considerable risk, to proffer arms control and regional settlements that even President Reagan's stalwart cold warriors could not refuse. A third school is likely to suggest that domestic weariness confronted both societies in the 1980s. The rhetoric of ideological confrontation and cold war enthusiasm had begun to lose its saliency as payments for the arms race multiplied beyond control. Strenuous demands were raised by constituencies ranging from youth and women's groups to angry ethnic minorities and anti-nuclear activists. Critics questioned the call by bemedalled generals to fund new weapons deployments and battle systems in outer space. Instead, they talked about the economic insecurity created by excessive military commitments. They advocated a new phase in the Super-powers' dialogue as they tuned out the doctrinal appeals of Leninist *apparatchiki* or Pentagon freedom fighters.

Unfortunately, the mass media used its colourful glamour to attribute the Superpowers' newfound amity to the personalities of Reagan and Gorbachev. As the oldest President and the youngest General Secretary to command each bloc, they sought to overturn the political power hierarchies and the cold war doctrines that had brought each of them to power. The irony of their personal repudiation of confrontation politics was not lost to the world. Both had risen through the power institutions of the warfare State, insisting that frequent tests of strength should be faced in military confrontation. It was a notable achievement for each leader to accomplish such a historic reversal. Of course, they attributed their ideological conversion to realist calculations rather than to sentimental responses. The suspicion grew, however, that they had become suddenly aware of the thrust of financial pressures and that they listened more attentively to their economic forecasters and planners than to the weapons advice of the Joint Chiefs of Staff and its Soviet counterparts. Both commented on the crash of the stock markets and the turndown in world trade in 1987. They apparently agreed that military threat levels had receded and that the correction of economic drift and decline now claimed a more urgent priority.

The Course of Economic Decline

There are two ways to measure the astronomical costs paid by the Superpowers to maintain their global strength of conventional forces and to modernize their nuclear arsenals. Both approaches are by definition imprecise. The first is to calculate the percentage of GNP and central government expenditures on the armed services, weapons procurement, military research and development (R&D), overseas garrisons, pensions and veterans' benefits. The figure cited for each Superpower, in dollar equivalent terms, is roughly $300 bn. a year. This amounts to roughly 6.7 per cent of the GNP of the United States and more than 15 per cent for the USSR. These figures have been generally accepted in the West, but the Soviet calculations have been contested by angry conservatives in both countries.[1]

Unfortunately, every gauge of military spending is distorted by definitional and denominational ambiguities. Soviet weapons and support costs are usually concealed within other categories of government expenditure, and the numbers of troops or weapons given are not reliable. In the United States and Europe there is no uniform accounting for veterans' pensions, for overseas transfer costs, or for the military portion of the interest payments incurred in carrying the national debt. The conversion of roubles or yen into dollar denominations has been even more misleading, since the dollar's value fluctuated on most currency exchanges in the last few years. It gained nearly 50 per cent after 1982 and then declined 50 per cent after 1985.

The second measure involves calculating the economic opportunity costs incurred by defence spending. This approach tries to estimate the potential benefits sacrificed in order to build military might, and it tries to assess the value of the resources deflected from productive industries to satisfy the manpower and high-technology needs of the armed services. This gauge is subjective, at best, since no estimate of potential benefits or opportunity costs can ever be accurate. Only one example need be cited. The cost to the United States of financing eight years of Mr. Reagan's military build-up came to roughly $2 trillion; in comparison, the US national debt was $1 trillion when he entered office in 1981 and it will be $2.6 trillion when he leaves in 1989. It would be difficult to demonstrate that the military outlays were excessive or that the $2 trillion defence budget would actually have been invested more wisely in export industries or social welfare priorities since no major war took place.

When evaluating opportunity costs it is useful to compare the advantages gained by industrial nations that rigorously restricted their military expenditures with those that did not. For a start, most European members of NATO devoted less than half of the 6.7 per cent of GNP that the US defence presently requires. Japan spent only 1 per cent, compared with the Soviets' contribution of 15 per cent to its military machine. The Soviet Union's economic growth rates have consequently lagged behind those of its own allies. In prior eras, when rearmament drives were labour-intensive, it was held that a valuable boost to the economy could be given by war spending. This notion no longer holds. Nations that spend heavily on armaments, such as the United States and United Kingdom, have forfeited valuable gains in industrial productivity and economic growth. By contrast, their more pacific neighbours invested resources in high-technology industries, R&D, social infrastructure, and capital expansion. West Germany and Japan built powerful export industries to advance their international security, while nations devoting 5 per cent or more of GNP to military purposes resigned themselves to losses in world markets and in the currency's strength.

The Superpowers have forfeited additional benefits overseas by taxing themselves strenuously to rearm. In two years (1983-85) the US capital position switched from that of the leading creditor to leading debtor. By 1988 its foreign debts exceeded $400 bn., and within a decade the deficit on external account could reach $1 trillion. At that point the cost of annual service payments could equal net export revenues, leaving the US financial position in the permanent debtor position of a Third World nation. In its own way, the Soviet Union has also dropped behind in the race for economic 'competitiveness' and solvency. In its recent efforts to raise funding in the offshore money markets, it has had to pay interest rates higher than those facing high-risk borrowers in East Asia. Today the Soviet Union depends significantly on high-technology imports to support its industrial and military systems and a high standard of living, but its exports have never captured a significant share of world markets and its indebtedness is now mounting. Although it remains an impressive *military* giant, the Soviet Union has seen its economic prowess surpassed by Japan and the European Community. It may soon need to counter economic challenges from its allies in Eastern Europe and from the ethnic minorities who condemn the great shortcomings of the Soviet economy.

The High Costs of Military Status

The question of opportunity costs can be rephrased in the light of the Superpowers' poor economic performance: What is the economic utility of creating expensive military capabilities? Is it cost-effective today to invest in additional military might when there has been a steady diminution in industrial prowess? Caution must be used in framing an answer. Comparative costs are formulated in dollar units but are difficult to evaluate accurately because the dollar fluctuates wildly on the money markets. For example, when the yen soared against the dollar it appeared that Japan, the least martial of America's allies, had suddenly become the biggest military spender. Though a limit of 1 per cent of GNP had been placed on Japan's total military spending, its outlays of 3.5 trillion yen exceeded $40 bn. When denominated in current dollars, Japan's defence cost more than the budgeted appropriations of France, the United Kingdom, or West Germany, each of which allocated anywhere from 3 to 5.5 per cent of GNP to the armed services.[2]

Considerable damage would be done to US defence industries if Japan were to procure all of its own aircraft in the 1990s, rather than contracting with the United States, or if it cut back on its offset payments for US forces stationed in East Asia. It is already a matter of dispute that the United States pays heavily for Japan's defence while suffering a trade deficit with Japan of momentous proportions. Both nations fear the trade war tensions that might erupt if the bases were closed or turned over to a Japanese lend-lease agreement, and both have chosen not to fret. A similar problem has emerged over funding the 300,000 US troops currently stationed in Europe. Should the United States tax itself to preserve its regional hegemony in a divided continent and maintain the outposts of its empire indefinitely? Or should it threaten to quit unless the Europeans at last consent to pay for the majority of NATO's expenditures? Strikingly, the Soviet Union faces a comparable set of difficulties in Afghanistan. The cost of supporting large army units, with extensive operation and weapons maintenance, has distorted the budget priorities of the Red Army. No material assistance has been offered by Warsaw Treaty allies. If the Kremlin ever published national account figures, it would appear that the burdens of empire had been just as damaging to the Soviet Union's balance of payments.

A revealing study of the economic burdens of empire, *The Rise and Fall of the Great Powers*, has recently been published by a Yale historian, Paul Kennedy. As the subtitle indicates, his work focuses on 'Economic Change and Military Conflict from 1500 to 2000'.[3] Kennedy suggests that every majestic empire of Europe, from the Hapsburgs in the seventeenth century to the Victorian zenith of the United Kingdom, repeated the mistakes of 'imperial overstretch'. After each had conquered its colonies through war, the European empires inevitably slipped into a course of economic decline. Post-1945 America seems to be repeating the cycle. Kennedy relates the decline in US manufacturing leadership and in its balance of payments position to the 'imperial overstretch' in its military aspirations. The decline has been masked by the pre-eminent status of the United States' economic and military capabilities and by its success in expanding the international influence of its capitalist market and culture. For nearly fifty years the United States has remained the leading power centre of the Western world, and its military might, political weight and cultural influence have not been challenged by China, Japan or the European Community. When necessary, the United States has managed to share its imperial costs either by charging offset expenses against its reluctant allies or by devaluing its currency and forcing European central banks to support the dollar. But the strategies of enforced burden-sharing cannot continue indefinitely. Most of the allies have condemned the relentless piling up of deficits on the domestic and the external accounts, and they have called for a radical restructuring of public finances in the US imperium.

The astronomical expense of maintaining the US military supremacy and its 'spheres of influence' has swollen the size of the national debt. Each year servicing that debt becomes more crippling. Industrial investments at home and overseas have been squandered on wars of peripheral significance or on weapons of dubious utility. In fact, the security that should have been bought with investment in armaments has been imperilled by the excessive strains placed on the US economy. Kennedy could have drawn the comparison between Philip the Second, who ruined Spain's national treasury to build the Great Armada, and Ronald Reagan, who doubled the national debt on his watch and who still dreams of creating an SDI astrodome—an endeavour that would double the deficit yet again. Another historian suggested an epitaph that may be fitting: 'Rome fell; Babylon fell; Scarsdale's turn will come'.

Mr. Gorbachev faces a comparable set of challenges as he struggles with military and bureaucratic factions in the Kremlin to implement *perestroika*. If his restructuring campaign fails, the Soviet Union cannot hope to compete economically with the West, or even with its richer allies in this century. It cannot channel vast resources into exhausting military programmes for another decade if it is also to modernize the low-productivity and the low-technology industries of the Soviet economy. And what benefits could it ever reap if its military power were based on a Third World economy?

Avoiding the pessimistic conclusions voiced by many historians, Kennedy believes that the United States is unique: it is still able to resolve its imperious dilemma, if it chooses, by changing its priorities. While empires of the past were governed by rigid hierarchies, as the Kremlin is today, the political and economic systems of the United States are pluralist in structure and flexible in function. The capacity of each system to change course and shift its values is somewhat unique. It cannot be matched either by today's authoritarian regimes or by the class-bound societies of past empires. The prediction is often made that the United States will emulate the long and painful course of decline set by the United Kingdom, but there is no compelling reason why this must occur. The United States still towers over its allies as the pre-eminent nuclear and military power, as does the Soviet Union within the Warsaw Pact. Their bloc leadership may be challenged in the 1990s, but it will not be replaced. There is no single nation or a regional federation of nations that can usurp the global role and influence exercised by the Superpowers.

As the last round of Reagan-Gorbachev summitry is played out in 1988, a novel vision has been glimpsed: the arms race cannot be funded at increasing levels, or even at present rates, for an indefinite future. It simply must slow down. Though embittered ideologues in both camps have mounted a rear-guard opposition, they are not likely to block further progress on the INF treaties and the START negotiations. It has become evident that the resources to intensify the arms race are no longer available; and that position would not change appreciably, let it be noted, if major social subsidies and welfare programmes were to be cancelled.

A comparison with the relatively unburdened economies of their own neighbours and allies should provide a sharp jolt to the Soviet Union and the United States. The Superpowers are clearly paying too high a price for acting as the world's policemen. It is not a reasonable proposal today to build a first-rate military power base and a second-rate industrial economy. Instead of favouring all the military's outlays, it has become imperative to invest in high-technology industrial sectors, capital formation, good educational and health facilities, and means to lighten debt-servicing payments. High defence spending drains away the growth resources needed by a dynamic society. After forty years of cold war it has become apparent in Washington and in Moscow that 'a policeman's job is not a happy one'.

The Finite Uses of Force

The attitudes of both Superpower leaders toward nuclear war and deterrence have been severely modified in recent years. Neither assumes that nuclear war is likely, let alone inevitable, or that the rapid modernization of arsenals must be achieved at all costs to secure a stable deterrence posture. Gorbachev, for his part, has revised the dogmatic principles of 'scientific socialism'. He no longer insists that class strife and the logic of capitalist destruction will lead to global confrontation. The change in US beliefs followed a similar direction. A report issued by a top-level policy group in the Pentagon concluded in 1987 that strategies based on massive nuclear retaliation were neither credible nor cost-effective and should be replaced with a new doctrine of 'discriminate deterrence'.[4]

The summit manoeuvres of Reagan and Gorbachev reflected this switch from ideological passion to economic calculation. Neither chose to resort to bellicose threats or to accelerate payments for new strategic weapons. Both argued heatedly about 'Star Wars' defence systems and about deploying offensive countermeasures, but their exercises in diplomatic bluffing and crass bargaining were not impressive. Neither could afford to augment defence spending by 10 per cent—and certainly not by 50 per cent—when even the current figures for military spending appeared to be excessive. Military expenditure totals for both Superpowers have been frozen for the last four years at roughly $300 bn. each. On the US side it was striking that

twelve of the thirteen candidates campaigning for the White House refused
to increase—or decrease—the rate of military authorizations. A similar statis
has been detected in the documents and official speeches distributed in
Moscow.

Current rates of military expenditures can be analyzed from another
perspective. The real increase in gross world product (GWP) was measured
at 62 per cent per capita between 1960 and 1987; by contrast, inflation-
adjusted military outlays grew by 146 per cent. During this twenty-seven-
year period, worldwide military spending mounted to a total of $13.8 trillion
(in 1983 dollars), but the increment added to GWP grew by only $8.6
trillion.[5] Annual GWP between 1980 and 1985 rose at a rate of 2.4 per cent
while military spending rose at 3.2 per cent, thus absorbing more than the
total dividend of GWP growth.[6]

Specific data for the Soviet Union cannot be verified, but it is likely to
follow the patterns recorded by Western countries: real growth of gross
domestic product (GDP) is inversely correlated with spending on national
security. In the United Kingdom and the United States military outlays were
particularly generous, but GDP growth was stunted during the 1960s and
1970s. By 1985 the United States' wealth was 47.5 per cent of the total
economic product of the NATO countries plus Japan, but its defence
spending accounted for 70 per cent of their total military outlays; moreover,
with only one-third of the combined population, the United States contributed 40 per cent of allied military and civilian defence personnel.[7]

A further set of comparative data can help advance the argument.

- *Public health and education expenditures* in both the United States and
  the USSR amount to only half of military appropriations. Interestingly,
  the Superpowers rank poorly in all measures of public health, and
  their education systems are demonstratively inadequate.

- *Total military expenditures* on R&D exceeds $75 bn. a year, most of it
  paid for by the Superpowers. SDI and other weapons projects were
  supposed to generate valuable spill-over benefits for civilian R&D,
  but they have largely failed. Productivity gains in what were once
  competitive industries have not materialized at the pace found in
  economies with only small defence burdens.

- *Both nuclear leaders are net debtors* on the world trade and money
  markets. Their balance of payments positions have deteriorated, their
  domestic levels of savings appear to have declined, and their currencies
  have lost value. Their merchandise trade balances are in deficit, and
  an inflow of foreign currency payments is needed to finance their
  investment and security commitments. No reversal of the flow is
  likely to occur for years to come in either country.

Defence spending has become known as 'Keynesianism on steroids'. It is stimulating in the short run, highly addictive, and ruinous in the long run. Though the spree of military spending might have moved the Superpowers toward *détente* during the 1980s, neither can ignore the punishing side effects: deficits become terrifyingly expensive to service every year, interest payments now cost more than investments in infrastructure and industrial modernization, and inflationary pressures have climbed while the purchasing power of each defence dollar has shrunk. A budget of $300 bn. buys less each year while the tax burden of financing it grows heavier. The escalation trend could not continue, and the spending curves have already begun to flatten. In the first years of the Reagan administration (between 1980 and 1985) defence appropriations increased 55.3 per cent; now the rate of annual increment has been decisively halted. Outlays have stuck at roughly $300 bn. for four consecutive years, and it is suspected that they have flattened out in the Soviet Union as well. If allowance is made for the cumulative effects of inflation, the real purchasing by defence agencies has fallen by 10 to 15 per cent.[8]

It is tempting to believe that current and pending arms control agreements will further depress defence spending, but this is not likely to happen. Even if INF and START reductions were quickly effected, present budget levels would be scaled down by less than 5 per cent, since the major share of appropriations still goes to personnel and conventional force strengths. Moreover, the 'bow wave' created by procurement contracts in the last few years has yet to crest. Due to a time lag in actual contract payments, there could even be an increase in military outlays before any significant retrenchment appears. It is estimated that the backlog of appropriated but unexpended funds equals a full year's budget. The FY 1989 budget request goes one step further. It clearly favours weapons modernization and defence industry investments rather than military readiness and personnel; it imposes many of the budget reductions (of $33 bn.) on the latter in order to protect the procurement and research categories.[9]

It is now evident that the five-year appropriation plan submitted by Secretary Weinberger in 1987 has been dismissed as utopian and exaggerated. He proposed to raise the FY 1988 appropriation of $282 bn. to $412 bn. by 1992 and to fund hundreds of new tanks, planes and ships and provide $7 bn. for SDI. The projected increase of 3 per cent a year, after inflation, has been replaced with a more modest scheme, with a 2 per cent real increase, but the projected total would still come to $375 bn. in five years' time, and Congress is not likely to consider it seriously in an election year. Congress has committed itself to the Gramm-Rudman-Hollings formula for slashing the awesome federal deficit by 1990. If Congress is to honour the commitment, one half of the total reduction has to come from the military. But if the inflationary curve should suddenly climb, the Pentagon will have to adjust to austerities of unprecedented severity.

Fiscal Restraints on Military Power

As the power of the two leading adversaries visibly recedes, a number of changes can be identified in their patterns of behaviour. Near-term changes in defence spending are already measurable in the United States, and modifications of comparable patterns in Soviet expenditures are likely to emerge within the 1980s.

1. Deficit reduction programmes will probably take precedence over those for force planning. Secretary Weinberger and the Joint Chiefs of Staff managed to double the military budget between 1980 and 1985, raising expenditures from 4 per cent to 6.7 per cent of GNP. That the increment was deserved or was well used is still a matter of debate. But it is beyond dispute that no further boost can be afforded. It is generally agreed that the cost of carrying the federal deficit is too burdensome, given the weakness of the dollar and the high interest rates that US industry consequently has to meet. Draconian cuts will have to be made in non-defence as well as military outlays, and taxes will eventually have to be raised, no matter what the Presidential candidates promise before a general election. If these steps are not taken, the vigour of the US economic recovery programme will be thwarted and a serious recession could hit the business world.

2. The scope of the Soviet Union's buildup has been questioned lately in the United States, and even the CIA has reduced its estimates of Soviet military spending since the late 1970s. Assumptions about rouble conversion rates, hardware costs, personnel pay, R&D outlays, weapons acquisitions, and other budget outlays have been questioned by *The Wall Street Journal*, the Joint Chiefs of Staff and British authorities.[10] It has at last been realized that Soviet defence costs cannot be converted into US prices. It is silly to price high-technology weapons, garrison bases, or conscripts' pay at US standards. Military pay averages $20,000 a year in the United States, and it cannot be compared with the average of non-volunteer armies of the Soviet Union. Neither can estimates of Soviet defence work with US operational assumptions. It is reported that Soviet submarines and aircraft are frequently kept off-station to save fuel and maintenance bills and that their performance efficiency is not impressive. Moreover, since many Soviet divisions are considerably under-strength, their combat readiness has been critically reappraised.[11]

3. Poor planning in the US Defence Department is likely to intensify the scrutiny given to future programmes. The Weinberger game plan has been criticized as 'spending without strategy'. What good was a 600 ship navy, which included 15 separate aircraft carrier fleets, when an emergency blew up in the Gulf and there were no small minesweepers to be found? And what was the combat status of the US army in Germany if it lacked ammunition and training? In the meantime defence lobbyists and service chiefs clamoured for the MX and the Midgetman missiles, for the B-1 and the Stealth bomber, for the Strategic Defence Initiative, and for major additions to conventional force strengths, especially in Europe. There was evidence that their lobbying was too successful. Strategic missions were either duplicated or overfunded, and the less glamorous requirements of conventional defence were shortchanged. An élite group convened in 1987 to review the lopsided build-up of the 1980s. In their official report, *Discriminate Deterrence*, they sharply noted that the two most expensive items—European theatre and strategic nuclear components—were the two force structures that were least likely to be used.[12] Why, was it then asked, should a five-year budget for another $2 trillion place a major emphasis on aircraft carriers and expensive fighter bombers, when munitions and spare parts were already in short supply? And in any case, was it possible that a qualitatively better defence could be purchased for only $1.5 trillion?

4. Castigation for procurement waste and cost overruns proved that neither defence contractors nor the Pentagon itself could dismiss congressional scepticism. Public opinion was shocked by news reports of toilet seats or screwdrivers sold to the Pentagon at outrageous prices by 'Fortune 500' companies—many of which are now operating under criminal indictment for padding their invoices. Everyone agreed the profligacy had to stop. Multibillion dollar cost overruns had accumulated for the B-1 bomber and the M-1 tank. The poor engineering of armoured vehicles and tactical artillery systems wasted hundreds of billions of dollars, and weapons often had to be aborted once the funding was blown. The confidence of the US Congress receded as the armed services showed more skill at fighting each other in appropriations skirmishes than in battlefield combat.

5. Domestic political pressures mounted as inter-service rivalries and legislative manoeuvring intensified. Lobbying pressures on Capitol Hill began to deflect strategic doctrine choices, and the Pentagon began to rely on 'quick fixes' and false savings in place of long-term planning schedules. Congress was blamed for the disorder, but it alone was not at fault. Cuts in procurement budgets often resulted in greater waste and more protracted outlays, and Congress was deeply divided over financing SDI, the MX and Midgetman missiles. The indecision of the executive branch was confusing to Congress, to NATO allies, and to the adversary. No one was sure which budget priorities were dispensable or which had to be taken seriously. For a start there was the $26 bn. appropriations request for the SDI programme. It was mainly contested on financial grounds and not because of technical feasibility or strategic necessity. As the 1980s rolled forward, the President changed the weapons targets and the strategic functions of the space-based 'Star Wars' system. After he did so, the Senate whittled it down and then the House chopped its annual funding in half. It had become clear that many existing programmes would have to be abolished if the full SDI funding were ever approved. In the end, SDI funding proposals withered slowly on the vine. Despite the proselytizing of the President, congressional hawks and the official science establishment, the SDI venture began to unwind. If only it had been a political coalition of industrial lobbies and State delegations, its funding might have been endorsed by Congress.

6. *Most disconcerting of all*, the doubling of the defence budget produced few of the anticipated gains in procurement and deployment. To some extent, the lavish budgets had weakened organizational and managerial procedures, leaving US security demonstrably depleted. Procurement budgets had increased by 25 per cent in each of the early Reagan years, but it appeared that ammunition stocks had severely run down and that pay increases for the volunteer army had failed to keep pace with inflation. It was not clear what benefits had been gained from the $2 trillion military outlays of the Reagan administration or where the cost containment process should begin.[13]

A critical question emerged from the confusion over defence priorities and missions. How much capability was needed for containment purposes and flexible response strategies, especially in Europe? A major concern with the Middle East had been announced, but the 'rapid deployment force' had been suddenly abandoned, and at great cost. Modernizing the war-fighting capabilities of the NATO forces assumed a new urgency once the INF treaty was initialled, but the NATO allies disagreed about the high-technology weapons that should be bought and who should pay for them. As the Weinberger budgets kept rising, the weapons list became strategically incoherent.[14] There were no clear guidelines for multi-year acquisitions of weapons under development or to clarify strategic doctrine. Did the US weapons budget imply that it was about to raise or to lower the threshold of nuclear engagement? Was it going to concentrate on global rather than regional defence needs, and was it likely to reduce its overseas garrison strength in Europe and South Korea? More troubling was the confusion resulting from the President's battle with Congress to fund the SDI projects. At some point he decided to build the administration's entire defence programme on the issue of accelerating the space defence race with the Soviet Union. He retreated when he met resistance, not from Gorbachev but from the budget-choppers in Congress.

The Economic Distress of the Superpowers

There is a danger of exaggerating the economic difficulties facing the leadership élites in the United States and USSR. Neither country's industrial structure is bankrupt, nor is its economy nearing the point of collapse. But both systems are seriously over-extended. They cannot command the resources needed to fulfil the onerous responsibilities to which they have committed themselves. For entirely different reasons, both have overdrawn their investment capital and their overseas accounts, and both have failed to match the competitive spirit of their successful allies and trade rivals. At home they face urgent demands to raise consumption standards and capital funds, but they cannot hope to do so while a major portion of GDP and of central government expenditure is siphoned away for military purposes.

Despite the sharp differences between their political systems, there are two choices that the Superpowers can pursue as they try to resolve their common dilemma of 'imperial overstretch'. Depending on their success in improving their bilateral relations and the confidence-building arrangements between Moscow and Washington, they can move toward one of two long-term goals:

1. To phase out nuclear and conventional defence commitments in order to lower tension levels in central Europe or troubled Third World regions; or,
2. To create a global management system and devote at least as much attention to multilateral forms of economic and financial stability as to the security or deterrence concerns of alliance blocs and treaty partnerships.

There is no simple dichotomy between these two choices. Any course of action will involve both unilateral and multilateral decisions. But the options can be usefully categorized, first in terms of levels of economic or military co-operation required; second, by the degree to which the Superpowers will have to act with their allies, adversaries, and outsiders—rather than on their own.

What is remarkable is the fact that basic choices will actually have to be made in the near future; they cannot be evaded or once again postponed. For nearly half a century the two bloc leaders were able to buy peace and to preserve a relatively stable hegemonic order at a cheap price. Except in a few cases, their bipolar concentration of power went largely unchallenged. They were able to mask the signs of economic deterioration that were slowly cracking open the foundations of their military ascendancy. Now the masquerade is over. Neither has an extra $1 or $2 trillion to modernize its nuclear deterrent, or to strengthen its conventional capabilities, and certainly not to do both together. Their intercontinental and sea-launched ballistic missile squadrons are still formidable symbols of power, but the industrial expansion that both societies need is truly in peril. They cannot afford it under present conditions.

The option of negotiating a cutback of force structures and deployment is the more practical of the two and is therefore, ironically, the most resisted of the solutions at present available. Soviet leaders cannot easily walk out of Afghanistan, Kampuchea, and the inconclusive wars in Africa, and they pretend to drag their heels when they enter negotiations to dampen down the arms race. For a different set of reasons, US leaders disclaim any great enthusiasm to scale down the Pentagon's budget, military commitments in the Gulf of Nicaragua, or the awesome cost of maintaining 300,000 troops in Germany. Various proposals are advanced to economize in these high-priced ventures, but they eventually fall by the wayside. In most cases they require a unilateral force withdrawal or a risky cutback in strategic deterrence or a diplomatic loss of face that no Superpower can easily accept. The principle of bloc leadership has helped preserve nuclear stability and bipolar order as well as the *amour propre* of the leaders. Each Superpower has guaranteed the security of its allies and protectorates; in return, the dependents acknowledged the political pre-eminence and the global leadership of their protector. In retrospect, the condominium of the Superpowers was built on both threat and exchange relationships that proved to be remarkably durable and inexpensive.

On the US side it is clear that the appeal for military solutions 'as usual' must soon change. Japan and the European allies are worried about how the failing dollar will affect their own currency reserves and transactions. If the US defence budget and the federal deficit grow, inflation will spread world-wide. They fear that the next administration will bring home some of the US garrisons stationed in Europe or Asia or that Congress will be so irritated by their 'free rider' refusal to share the common defence burden of a collective security alliance that it will resort to trade sanctions or policy reprisals.[15] Unofficial suggestions to lighten US costs in Europe, or to 'decouple' US strategic forces from European tactical forces, have prompted nervous and irate responses from European parties both on the Left and the Right. In the last resort, neither wants to disrupt the hegemonic balance. Hence the Europeans have agreed to co-operate with the arms control deals that were negotiated over their heads in the Reykjavík or Washington summit meetings, and they also volunteered to support the exchange value of the dollar.[16] But at some point they will demand that the post-Reagan regime should either restore a vigorous bloc leadership or, alternatively, correct its overstretched positions in order to strengthen its economic power base.

The second choice available to the Superpowers is more ambiguous and challenging. It also requires a departure from established principles of inter-state behaviour. The status ascendancy of the bloc leaders would be opened up to challenge; their nuclear duopoly and political dominance could also be diminished as nations turned increasingly toward multilateral action and away from bipolar hierarchies. It is likely that the military security pacts would survive, but greater concern would be invested in building institutions for global management rather than confrontation. And the new arrangements would better correspond to economic forms of pluralism rather than thermonuclear duopolies of power.

The chief obstacle to change would probably come from the Superpowers themselves. Their pretences of power and invulnerability would have to be considerably trimmed. The USSR would fall to third and soon to fourth or fifth place in the world order if it were ranked by national wealth or industrial product rather than by military firepower. The standing of the US economy would also be impaired. It accounted for more than half of the world's wealth in manufacturing product in 1945, but its share had fallen to 31.5 per cent by 1980 and it is likely to decline to 20 per cent by the end of the century.[17] More important, US financial assets and industrial investments overseas had once been the dominant factor in world trade and credit flows. Today the United States owes so much to foreign holders of dollar securities that its external account is in disrepair and it is increasingly vulnerable to threats by foreign lenders to liquidate their holdings. Unless it can manage to reduce its consumption standards or its defence budget, the administration that follows President Reagan's will be more sensitive to tremors in the Eurodollar market than in the Superpower standoff. The current trade-off requires the allies in Europe and Asia to lend the United States sufficient money to pay for most of their own defence. This arrangement will come apart if the credit markets continue to weaken. At that point, the United States might have to threaten to withdraw the 400,000 troops deployed overseas, and the threat would create powerful tensions among allied governments.

The conclusion remains that the great power game cannot survive for long in its current form, and neither can the bipolar division of strategic power. No sudden or dramatic change is likely to topple the old order. Nor will the pressures to change in Washington be as strenuous—or threatening—as those exercised in Moscow. It is reasonable to predict that both Superpowers will have to shed the illusions and expenses of empire, though for entirely different reasons and on entirely different time schedules. Within the century they will probably experience a common fate: the purchase of hegemony 'on the cheap' will no longer be within their grasp. The days of the American Century or of the Soviets' Commonwealth are not finished, but the Superpowers' economic distress denies them the range of diplomatic coercion, military initiatives, and nuclear contingency plans that they once commanded. It was the United Kingdom's fate to lose an empire and its world role. It may be that the *Pax Atomica* will also come apart, not because new challengers emerge to unseat the old but simply because the two hegemonical powers become too debilitated to cut their losses and change their strategic doctrines.[18]

This chapter was first published in the SAIS Review 8:2 Summer-Fall, 1988. SAIS Bologna Centre, Italy.

Notes

1. Most of the comparative data on military personnel, weapons spending, GNP growth rates, productivity gains, and capital investment ratios cited here has been drawn from *The Military Balance 1987-1988* (London: International Institute for Strategic Studies, 1987) and from the *Budget of the U.S. Government, FY 1989* (Washington, D.C.: Government Printing Office, 1988). Also see Hugh Mosley, *The Arms Race: Economic and Social Consequences* (Lexington, Mass.: Lexington, 1985); and Lloyd J. Dumas, *The Overburdened Economy* (Berkeley, Calif.: University of California, 1986).

2. *The Economist*, 23 January 1988, 28; and 13 February 1988, 66.

3. Paul Kennedy, *The Rise and Fall of the Great Powers: Economic Change and Military Conflict from 1500 to 2000* (New York: Random House, 1987).

4. See Mikhail Gorbachev, *Perestroika: New Thinking for our Country and the World* (New York: Harper & Row, 1987); and the U.S. Department of Defense, *Discriminate Deterrence* (Washington, D.C.: Government Printing Office, 1988).

5. Economic data on GDP levels, defence budgets, and dollar conversions were drawn from Ruth Leger Sivard, *Survey of World Military and Social Expenditures* (Leesburg, Va.: World Priorities, 1987); and the *SIPRI Yearbook 1986: World Armaments and Disarmament* (New York: Oxford University Press, 1986).

6. *SIPRI Yearbook 1986*, 210.

7. See Caspar Weinberger, *Report on Allied Contributions to the Common Defense* (Washington, D.C.: Department of Defence, 1987), 5.

8. Useful data is compiled in the *Statistical Abstract of the United States 1988* (Washington, D.C.: Department of Commerce, 1987); on Soviet spending see *The Military Balance 1987-1988*, 27-33.

9. On the 'bow wave' spending of backlogged funding, and also for an expert analysis of the FY 1989 budget request, see Stephen Cain, *The FY 1989 Defence Budget* (Washington, D.C.: Center on Budget and Policy Priorities, 1988).

10. *The Wall Street Journal*, 21 August 1987; *The Military Balance 1987-1988*; and Carl G. Jacobsen, "Soviet Military Expenditure and the Soviet Defence Burden," *SIPRI Yearbook 1986*, 263-73.

11. For a technical reappraisal, see Joshua M. Epstein, *Measuring Military Power—the Soviet Air Threat to Europe* (Princeton, N.J.: Princeton University Press, 1984); and Steven L. Canby, "Military Reform and the Art of War," *International Security*, vol. 7, no. 3 (Fall 1982).

12. See the feature articles analyzing *Discriminate Deterrence* (note 4 *supra*) in *The New York Times*, 13 January 1988, and *The Economist*, 16 January 1988, 21-22; see also *The FY 1989 Defense Budget*.

13. See the analysis of William W. Kaufmann, *A Reasonable Defense* (Washington, D.C.: The Brookings Institution, 1986), 9-12. He also quotes from Churchill's memory of a Cabinet meeting before World War I. Churchill had asked for six new dreadnoughts, but Lloyd George insisted on limiting expenditure to four, so the Asquith Cabinet compromised at eight.

14. For an extensive list of policy criticisms, see Joshua M. Epstein, *The 1987 Defense Budget* (Washington, D.C.: The Brookings Institution, 1986), 8-12; and Lawrence J. Korb, "Spending Without Strategy," *International Security*, vol. 12, no. 1 (Summer 1987): 166-75.

15. On the threat to withdraw US troops or to resort to trade sanctions, see David P. Calleo, *Beyond American Hegemony: The Future of the Western Alliance* (New York: Basic Books, 1987).

16. See Robert E. Osgood, "Europe's Dependence on American Protection," in Walter Goldstein, ed., *Clash in the North: Polar Summitry and NATO's Northern Flank* (Washington, D.C.: Pergamon-Brassey's, 1988).

17. Paul Kennedy, "The First World War and the International Power System," *International Security*, vol. 9, no. 2 (1984): 36-39.

18. Calleo, in *Beyond American Hegemony*, writes an excellent theoretical chapter on the loss of hegemonic authority. He examines the historical record of the United Kingdom and then the United States before asking why they lost power. Was it the hegemon that weakened its political and economic clout, or was it the hegemonic order that was transformed from a unilateral to a plural structure? The author concludes on a prophetic note (see page 126): '(W)hereas Soviet expansionism is reasonably contained, American fiscal and monetary disorder is not. ... (The U.S. roles of) containing Soviet military power and maintaining a viable world economy seem increasingly incompatible.'

CHAPTER 3

The Burden-sharing Debate: Revising the 'Transatlantic Bargain'

STANLEY SLOAN[1]

The equitable sharing of burdens and benefits has been an issue between the United States and its NATO allies from the earliest days of the Alliance. The terms of the North Atlantic Treaty signed on 4 April 1949 reflected a compromise between the European desire for strong commitments by the United States to the defence of Western Europe and pressures within the United States, particularly in the US Congress, to limit the extent of those commitments. The 'transatlantic bargain' that largely shaped the Alliance we know today was not consummated until 1954, after the failure of the European Defence Community initiative left NATO's multilateral defence arrangements heavily dependent on a substantial and continuing US role in West European defence, including the American nuclear 'guarantee'. From that point forward, the structure of alliance political and military relationships virtually guaranteed that the sharing of defence burdens would be a recurrent issue among the allies.[2]

In truth, 'burden-sharing' is more than an issue. The term today is almost universally understood as an implicit or explicit American complaint about the relative defence efforts made by the United States as compared to those of its West European allies. The complaint grows out of the fact that the American commitment to participate in the defence of Europe was not originally intended to be as open-ended as it has become. American administrations have consistently defended the fact that a substantial US commitment to the defence of Europe has continued far beyond what most post-war architects of the NATO alliance foresaw. The US Congress, however, a not-so-silent partner in the transatlantic alliance between North America and Western Europe, has remained convinced that, following recovery from the destruction of World War II, the West European countries have not done all that is possible to shift the burden of defence efforts in the Alliance. The burden-sharing complaint has largely emanated from US Senators and Representatives who, for a variety of reasons and at a variety of points in NATO's history, have argued for actions to readjust the burden of defence efforts in the Alliance.

The burden-sharing complaint, of course, has not arisen in isolation. It has been given prominence over the years by the shifting fortunes of politics, economics, and international security relationships. The Soviet Union has played an important role in determining these shifts. The extent of both US and European defence efforts has been substantially influenced by American and West European perceptions of the threat to Western interests posed by the Soviet Union. The fact that the allies have never seen the threat through exactly the same eyes also plays an important part in the burden-sharing issue. The status of the United States as a global Superpower has imposed its own terms on the debate. And the vicissitudes of international trade and economics have helped determine the ebb and flow of the burden-sharing question.

For those who have followed this debate for many years, there is more continuity than change in the contours of the issue. The relationship between West European and US defence efforts in the Alliance is deeply rooted in the structure of the security relationship between Western Europe and North America. The US complaint is generally expressed as a *critique* of all West European NATO members as a group. But a fundamental explanation for why there is a burden-sharing problem is that the West European NATO members are not a 'group', at least not enough of a group to accomplish what an effective response to the American complaint would require.

An important question in 1988 is whether the defence burden-sharing issue will remain the rather sterile accounting exercise it has largely been, particularly since the NATO allies in 1978 adopted the goal of increasing defence spending by 3 per cent annually in real terms, or if it will be transformed into a more fundamental discussion of the Alliance relationships that determine how the burdens and risks of Alliance membership are shared. The natural tendency of governments is to avoid such fundamental debates, and to continue to 'manage' the problem. The ability of NATO governments to continue to deal with the burden-sharing problem within this familiar context, however, may be called into question by some important underlying shifts in economic relationships and political perceptions which may be so profound as to put the problem beyond the reach of standard Alliance management techniques.

This Chapter summarizes the history of the burden-sharing issue (or complaint, if you will), looking in particular at the events that may be shifting the focus of the burden-sharing question. It closes with a discussion of the current status of the issue and its future implications for the NATO alliance.

Origins and Evolution of the Burden-sharing Complaint[3]

At the end of World War II, the United States began a rapid withdrawal and demobilization of its troops from Europe. The US disengagement ended, however, with the breakdown of co-operation between the Western allies and the Soviet Union. By 1947, US policy was focused on the need for strengthening

Western Europe to counter Soviet political and military strength. The Marshall Plan became the vehicle to provide assistance for European reconstruction and recovery, and the United States encouraged the Europeans to develop regional economic co-operation to use the aid more effectively. The United States accepted the lion's share of the effort to defend Western Europe in the early years but anticipated that European recovery and a regional security organization in alliance with the United States would eventually provide the basis for West European military security.

On 11 June 1948, following the Communist takeover in Czechoslovakia, the US Senate overwhelmingly passed the Vandenberg resolution, which expressed support for American participation in regional collective security arrangements established in accordance with Article 51 of the United Nations Charter. The resolution laid the groundwork for negotiation of the North Atlantic Treaty with the governments of Belgium, Canada, Denmark, France, Iceland, Italy, Luxembourg, the Netherlands, Norway, Portugal and the United Kingdom. The treaty was signed in Washington on 4 April 1949. Greece and Turkey acceded to the treaty on 18 February 1952 and the Federal Republic of Germany became a member on 9 May 1955.

The focus of US policy was not a build-up of West European national forces. Secretary of State Dean Acheson, testifying before the Senate Foreign Relations Committee in 1949, described the US attitude in the following terms:

> ... (Economic) recovery is a prior necessity; therefore the size of the European forces must be such that they do not interfere with recovery. And it looks as though (they) will continue to be quite small for some time.

THE KOREAN WAR AFTERMATH

The Korean war, following the Soviet explosion of a nuclear device in 1949, convinced American planners that the West would have to prepare to defend against a possible Soviet attack in Europe. On 9 September 1950, President Truman announced the assignment of four additional US divisions to Europe, and in December he authorized General Eisenhower to serve as Supreme Allied Commander, Europe (SACEUR). On 4 April 1951, the Senate endorsed the President's decisions, but qualified its support in Resolution 99. This Resolution expressed the 'sense of the Senate' that, among other things, the US Joint Chiefs of Staff should certify that the European allies were making a realistic effort on behalf of their own defence; the European partners should make the major contribution to allied ground forces; and provisions should be made to utilize the military resources of Italy, West Germany and Spain.

The defeat of the European Defence Community in 1954 was the first great burden-sharing disappointment for the United States, frustrating the hopes of many in the US Congress that such a community would eventually make it possible for the United States to withdraw most of its ground forces from

Europe. As a consequence of the decisions of 1954, including the decision by the Eisenhower administration to adopt a policy of 'massive' nuclear retaliation against the Soviet Union to deter Soviet attacks on the West, the military strategy of the Alliance came to rest heavily on the US nuclear guarantee and a substantial American military presence in Europe both to strengthen conventional defence and to help make the nuclear guarantee credible.

As the Alliance settled into a framework heavily influenced by US military power and political leadership, mechanisms were established to scrutinize the defence efforts of NATO members. In particular, a defence review procedure was established so that any changes in a member's defence contributions could be reviewed and criticized by other members—in theory, in advance of the final decision by the country involved. Cost-sharing formulas were also arranged in the early 1950s to finance NATO infrastructure costs—the expense of facilities, services, and programmes regarded as of common benefit to the Alliance members. The cost-sharing programme has operated essentially on the 'ability to pay' principle. In the early days, the United States agreed to pay the largest share of infrastructure expenses. In subsequent years the US share has been progressively reduced until it now constitutes approximately 27 per cent of infrastructure costs.

THE 1960s AND 1970s

The administration of President John F. Kennedy in the early 1960s sought to revive the concept of a European pillar in NATO to yield a greater European contribution to Western defence. Its policy advocated an Atlantic partnership with shared responsibilities between the United States and eventually a united Europe. The Kennedy period also witnessed the beginning of the financial arrangements between the United States and West Germany designed to offset the costs of stationing US forces in that country. In 1962, the United States and West Germany agreed to an offset programme whereby West Germany would purchase military equipment in the United States to compensate for US military expenditure in West Germany. These agreements were renewed and expanded in the Johnson and Nixon administrations to include German purchases of US treasury bonds and, in the 1970s, repair of barracks used by US forces in Germany. (German offset payments to the United States had totalled about $10 bn. when the agreement was allowed to expire in 1975.)

US involvement in Vietnam, French withdrawal from the integrated military structure of NATO in 1966, and US economic problems diminished support in the Congress for US overseas troop commitments in general during the 1960s and led the Johnson administration to press the Europeans to increase their defence efforts. This period saw a strong Congressional movement, led by Senator Mike Mansfield, to cut US forces in Europe.

Senator Mansfield, a Democrat from Montana, introduced the first of the Mansfield Resolutions on 31 August 1966. The resolution judged that 'the condition of our European allies, both economically and militarily, has appreciably improved since large contingents of forces were deployed'; the commitment by all members of the North Atlantic Treaty is based upon the full co-operation of all treaty partners in contributing materials and men on a fair and equitable basis, but 'such contributions have not been forthcoming from all other members', 'relations between the two parts of Europe are now characterized by an increasing two-way flow of trade, people and their peaceful exchange'; and 'the present policy of maintaining large contingents of United States forces and their dependents on the European Continent also contributes further to the fiscal and monetary problems of the United States'. The Senate was asked to resolve that 'a substantial reduction of United States forces permanently stationed in Europe can be made without adversely affecting either our resolve or ability to meet our commitment under the North Atlantic Treaty'.

Senator Mansfield sought to restructure the Alliance by substantially reducing the US role, rather than to fine-tune Alliance burden-sharing relationships. His approach posited fundamental changes in East-West as well as West-West relations. He reintroduced the Resolution in 1967, 1969, and 1970. When it emerged on 25 January 1970, it had obtained the signatures of 50 co-sponsors—for the most part, Senators regarded as political liberals. But these Resolutions and efforts to attach troop reduction provisions to defence legislation up to 1974 failed to win final passage.[4]

The administration of President Richard Nixon, which came into office in 1969, was concerned about US balance-of-payments problems, but its initial efforts to get the Europeans to pay for the US presence in terms of new offset deals, trade or monetary concessions made little headway. The allies objected to the prospect of American troops becoming little more than mercenaries in Europe, and argued that the US troop presence was, after all, in America's, as well as Europe's, interest.

The Nixon Doctrine, first enunciated in an Asian context in Guam in 1969 and subsequently applied globally, brought a turn away from intensive US efforts to get the Europeans to redress financial imbalances caused by the presence of US troops. American policy was re-focused almost exclusively on encouraging the allies to use available resources to make improvements in their own defence capabilities. In December 1970, addressing the North Atlantic Council in Brussels, President Nixon elaborated on the US commitment:

> NATO's conventional forces must not only be maintained, but in certain key areas strengthened. Given a similar approach by our allies, the United States will maintain and improve its own forces in Europe and will not reduce them unless there is reciprocal action from our adversaries. . . .

All subsequent US administrations—Democratic and Republican—have taken essentially the same approach.

The main success of the new US approach was to encourage the European allies to intensify the work of the so-called EuroGroup. The EuroGroup started as an informal caucus of European defence ministers, which met for the first time in 1968. The first major EuroGroup project was the European Defence Improvement Programme, announced in December 1970. This programme represented about $1 bn. in European defence improvements over a five-year period. It included specific national force improvement above and beyond planned expenditures and increased European contributions to the NATO infrastructure fund to build additional aircraft shelters and to introduce the NATO Integrated Communications System.

A prominent Congressional action relating to US force levels and the European defence effort in the early 1970s was the so-called 'Jackson-Nunn' amendment to the Fiscal year (FY) 1974 Department of Defence (DoD) Authorization Act, 1974 (PL 93-155), under which the Congress required that the European allies offset the balance-of-payments deficit incurred by the United States as a result of the 1974 costs of stationing US forces in Europe. Failure to offset would have resulted in automatic reductions in US force levels. On 2 June 1975, President Ford, in the final quarterly report to Congress on the European offset effort, reported that the deficit had been more than fully offset and that the troop reduction provisions of the Jackson-Nunn amendment would not have to be implemented.

A combination of events in the mid-1970s decreased Congressional pressure for unilateral US troop reductions in Europe. The talks on Mutual Force Reductions, which opened between NATO and Warsaw Pact delegations in Vienna in 1973, exercised a major influence. The Nixon administration, and the successor administration under President Ford, argued that chances of getting the Warsaw Pact countries to reduce their forces would be undermined if the United States reduced unilaterally. In addition, reports of Warsaw Pact force improvements tended to weaken the case for unilateral Western troop reductions. On the financial front, the US balance-of-payments improved considerably in 1975, lessening pressure from that quarter.

The Congress, in this period, increasingly focused on making US and allied contributions to the Alliance more effective, requiring a reduction of the ratio of support forces in the US presence in Europe and encouraging the inter-operability and standardization of NATO equipment. In an amendment to the FY 1975 DoD Authorization Act, the Congress required that US support forces in Europe be cut by 18,000 men, authorizing the Secretary of Defence to increase combat personnel in Europe by an equal number. In 1975, Congress required preparation of a study of the costs of NATO's past failure to standardize. In the so-called 'Culver-Nunn' amendment, Section 814 of Public Law 94-106, the Secretary of Defence was required to report to Congress the initiation of any procurement action of any major new system not consistent with the standardization of NATO forces.

President Carter basically continued the policy approaches of the Nixon and

Ford administrations. His initiatives focused on encouraging improvements in European forces, promoting efficiencies in Alliance defence co-operation, and continuing to improve US forces committed to NATO. At a summit-level NATO meeting in London on 11 May 1977, President Carter proposed a new 'Long-Term Defence Programme' for the Alliance. An important part of this programme was a pledge by all NATO countries to increase defence expenditures in real terms 3 per cent above inflation during the life of the programme. Defence ministers of the thirteen NATO countries participating in the integrated command structure produced the required guidance on this and other aspects of the programme a week later, specifying that:

> This annual increase should be in the region of 3 per cent, recognizing that for some individual countries economic circumstances will affect what can be achieved; present force contributions may justify a higher level of increase.

Another summit-level NATO meeting held in Washington in May 1978 approved the programme of defence improvements that had been developed during the preceding year, including the 3 per cent commitment.

Intensification of Burden-sharing Concerns

In 1979-80, a number of factors created renewed concern about European defence efforts. One of the products of the debate over SALT II was a consensus in support of major increases in US defence expenditures. The failed attempt to rescue the US hostages in Iran and the Soviet invasion of Afghanistan late in 1979 reinforced this consensus in the United States.

But most Europeans did not interpret the Soviet invasion of Afghanistan or the revolution in Iran as direct threats to Europe and were, therefore, reluctant to see it as requiring additional defence efforts. Furthermore, economic growth slowed in most European countries in 1980-81, making real increases in defence spending particularly difficult.

In 1979-80, Congress showed increasing impatience with the defence efforts of the allies. An 'allied commitments report' amendment to the FY 1981 Department of Defence Authorization Act (PL 96-342, Section 1006) required the Secretary of Defence to report on allied progress toward meeting the 3 per cent spending objective, to describe cost-sharing arrangements within NATO and with Japan, and to explain efforts being undertaken to 'equalize' the sharing of defence burdens with NATO allies and Japan. The provision also expressed the sense of Congress that the President should seek increased support from host nations for the costs of stationing US forces there.

The Reagan administration transmitted the first required allied commitments report to the Congress in March 1981. The report found that, on average, the allies had failed to meet the 3 per cent objective in each of the three years of its existence. The non-US average showed real increases of

42 STANLEY SLOAN

2 per cent (1978), 2.5 per cent (1979) and 2 per cent (1980). The report said that failure of the allies to meet the spending commitment could be seen by the Soviet Union as 'a weakening of our collective resolve' and could 'result in widespread shortfalls in meeting NATO force goals'. But the report also said that 'fixed percentage contributions from Allied governments are an issue of somewhat lesser importance than development of a mutually-agreed, coherent effort to counter the Soviet challenge'. It concluded that, based on quantitative indicators developed for the report, the allies as a group appear to be shouldering at least their fair share of the NATO and Japan defence burden, with some allies carrying somewhat more than their 'fair share' and others less. With slight variations, the Department of Defence has reported essentially the same conclusion in annual reports to the Congress every year since then.

By March 1982, negotiations begun during the Carter administration on wartime host nation support had led to an agreement with West Germany on additional facilities and services which the Germans would provide to support the arrival of American reinforcements in an emergency. This would include various logistics support, maintenance, hospital and other facilities to reduce the logistics 'tail' required to be brought from the United States or supported by the United States in Germany.

Throughout its two terms the Reagan administration continued to lobby the allies to encourage increased defence spending. US officials at the same time told the Congress that European contributions to Western defence were more substantial than often portrayed, arguing that the NATO allies made important contributions that were not directly measured by standard quantitative measures. The administration has pointed out that items such as allied host nation support, West German support for Berlin, and earmarking of civilian assets for defence are not included in standard calculations of defence efforts.[5]

Congress, however, convinced that the administration had not done enough to promote greater European defence efforts, has demonstrated its concerns in various ways in recent years. When the Congress approved the FY 1983 continuing appropriations for defence in December 1982, funds for the American contribution to the US-West German host nation support agreement (under which the Federal Republic would commit men and matériel to support arriving US reinforcements in wartime) were deleted, as were funds for two POMCUS (pre-positioned material configured in sets—*ie* ammunition and supplies in Europe for reinforcing American units) planned for the Netherlands and Belgium (PL 97-377). The Congress also passed a 'speciality metals' clause, a 'buy American' provision, that would have made purchase of European-made weapons systems virtually impossible. The Reagan administration succeeded in reversing this action as well as restoring funds for the West German host nation support agreement and partial funding for the POMCUS programme in the FY 1983 supplemental defence appropriation (PL 98-63).

In 1982, the displeasure of members of Congress about European attitudes towards the Soviet Union, in combination with the general Congressional desire to allocate limited resources among growing commitments, produced the most serious effort in a decade to legislate reductions in US forces in Europe. Senator Ted Stevens sought a cut of approximately 20,000 in the number of troops the Reagan Administration intended to station in Western Europe in FY 1983; and the Senate Sub-committee on Defence Appropriations, chaired by Senator Stevens, approved such a limitation by a 12-1 majority. When the appropriations bill was passed by the Congress in December 1982, the amendment was modified to limit US troops in Europe to the September 1982 level of 315,600. The amendment as adopted, a compromise worked out between Senators Stevens and Nunn, allowed the President to waive the ceiling for national security reasons—an option the President took in June 1983, to allow the additional stationing of 1,380 personnel associated with the planned deployment of ground-launched cruise missiles.

A variety of reasons led members of Congress to support the cap on US forces. Some apparently hoped that the measure would signal to the Europeans that the Congress was not prepared to devote additional resources to European defence unless the allies demonstrated equal willingness. Others, however, may have simply wanted to begin the process of containing US expenditures for NATO.

In 1983, Senator Nunn proposed that the cap be continued in the next year. The proposal, incorporated in the FY 1984 Department of Defence Authorization Act, carried forward the previous cap of 315,600 but allowed growth to 320,000 to account for cruise missile programme personnel, if the administration would submit a series of detailed reports and certification to the Congress concerning allied defence efforts (PL 98-94).

When the Reagan administration submitted the required allied commitments report of March 1984, it summarized the record of allied performance in defence spending over the five-year term of the 3 per cent commitment. The weighted average increases for all non-US NATO allies was 2.6 per cent in 1980, 2.8 per cent in 1981, 2.3 per cent in 1982, and between 1.9 per cent and 2.1 per cent for 1983.

The fact that the trend in allied spending had moved steadily away from the 3 per cent goal (while the trend in US spending was moving substantially above the goal) galvanized concern in the Senate about allied defence efforts. If the allies were performing so poorly with the existing 3 per cent objective, what would happen if the goal were allowed to expire?

THE NUNN AMENDMENT

On 20 June 1984, Senator Nunn, joined by Senator William Roth and sixteen other co-sponsors, offered Amendment 3266 to the FY 1985 Department of

Defence Authorization bill (S. 2723). The amendment expressed the view that
NATO 'should improve its conventional defence capability so as to lengthen
the time period that Western Europe can be defended adequately by conventional forces without the necessity of resorting to the early use of nuclear
weapons in the event of a non-nuclear attack on any NATO member country'.

As an incentive for the allies to make improvements, the amendment
proposed a 'permanent ceiling' of 326,414 on US forces 'assigned to permanent
duty ashore in European member nations of NATO'. The amendment stipulated that: 'Beginning on 31 December 1987, and ending 31 December 1989,
the permanent ceiling ... shall be reduced effective 31 December each year
by 30,000. ...' The troop reduction requirement could be waived, however,
if 'during the previous calendar year, member nations of NATO, other than
the United States, have increased their defence spending by an aggregate
average of 3 per cent, after inflation, as measured in the annual report of the
Secretary of Defence on the allied contribution to the common defense...'.

The amendment's principal requirement, therefore, focused on the 'input'
objective of 3 per cent real growth in defence spending. But the proposal
offered another avenue for the allies to prevent cuts in US troop levels under
the amendment. The amendment would have permitted the Secretary of
Defence to waive the reduction required for any calendar year by certifying
to the Congress that the allies had accomplished three 'output' objectives:

1. Placed firm orders or accepted delivery of an increase in the supply
   of air and ground munitions 'so as to reduce, on an average, 20 per
   cent of the gap between the goal, as established in NATO Ministerial
   Guidance, of thirty days supply and the level of such munitions
   available in the central region of NATO as of 1 January 1985';
2. Increased the number of 'minimum essential and emergency operating
   facilities and semi-hardened aircraft shelters in Western Europe so as
   to reduce, on an average, 20 per cent of the gap between the number
   of such facilities available on 1 January 1985 and the number required
   by NATO Ministerial Guidance...';
3. Improved NATO's conventional defence capacity to an extent which,
   in the certified opinion of the Supreme Allied Commander in Europe,
   'contributes to lengthening the time period between an armed attack
   on any NATO country and the time the Supreme Allied Commander
   would have to request the release and use of nuclear weapons'.

According to the proposed amendment, if the non-US NATO allies met all
three objectives in any given year, the administration could waive the entire
30,000 troop cut scheduled for that year. Meeting two of the three would
have waived all but 10,000 of the cut; meeting only one of the three would
have waived all but 20,000 of the scheduled reduction. The amendment also
stipulated that the Department of Defence should provide a variety of reports
on allied defence efforts.

In response to European complaints that Europe buys many times more weapons from the United States than the United States is willing to buy from European manufacturers, the amendment would have authorized up to $50 m. 'to acquire certain types of weapons, sub-systems, and munitions of European NATO manufacture ... for side-by-side testing with comparable United States manufactured items'. Finally, the amendment included an escape clause 'in the event of a declaration of war or an armed attack on any NATO member country' and permitted the President to waive the requirement 'if he declares an emergency and immediately informs the Congress of his action and the reasons therefore'. Senator Nunn's initiative caught many observers by surprise. Neither the Reagan administration nor the European allies had anticipated that the Senate would involve itself in a major debate on NATO in 1984. Furthermore, most observers were additionally surprised that it was Senator Nunn, long regarded as a friend of NATO, who had proposed the initiative.

In debate on the Senate floor on 20 June Senator Nunn explained that his intent was not to question the validity of NATO or to challenge continued American participation in the Alliance. The Senator said that 'this is not a petition for divorce. . . . This is a petition for the Alliance to carry out its vows that have been made over and over again but have since not been carried out'. He focused particularly on the need to increase the length of time that NATO could expect to sustain a non-nuclear defence on Europe, pointing out that it made no sense for the United States, by itself, to 'increase a munitions supply in NATO when we already have twice the amount that our allies have in their 5-year plans. . .'. The Senator concluded by arguing that 'when our allies have problems, they will determine, as the weakest link in the chain always does, how long we can fight'.

Senator Roth, in support of the amendment, expressed his distress that European officials had 'made it clear that there is no prospect for additional significant real growth' in European defence budgets in the near future. He contrasted this outlook with President Reagan's plans for continued expansion of US defence spending. Senator Roth said: 'There are strong voices, respected voices, in the United States calling for reform of the Alliance, for the re-allocation of the burdens and responsibilities'.

To make a reallocation of burdens possible, Senator Roth observed, 'The requirement for a 3 per cent real increase in European defence spending contained in this amendment is reasonable and well within European capabilities'. Echoing a familiar Congressional warning to Europe, he argued that 'the people of this country simply will not continue to spend large amounts of US tax revenue for the defence of Western Europe if Europe itself is not willing to join in the effort'.

Senator John G. Tower, Chairman of the Senate Committee on Armed Services, led the opposition to the Nunn-Roth amendment. Tower asked his colleagues to 'understand. . . why we are in Europe in the first place', observing: 'We are not there just to defend the blue-eyed Europeans', but because 'it is in our national interest to be there'. He applauded Nunn's objective of improving NATO's non-nuclear defences, but argued that 'this is the wrong way, the wrong time, to try to achieve through this means the kind of result we seek. ... When the President of the United States says "We must not do this", when the Secretary of State says "Don't do it"; the Secretary of Defence says "Don't do it", then the burden of proof is on those who can legislate something here and walk away from it'.

Senator Tower maintained that the European allies had just gone through a difficult political struggle to deploy new long-range American nuclear missiles on their territory against strong popular opposition. 'We would kick our friends in the teeth' by passing the amendment, the Senator suggested, embarrassing 'the Margaret Thatchers, the Helmut Kohls of this world that have stood fast for what they thought was right and gone ahead with deployments'.

In conclusion, Senator Tower contended that troop cuts could leave residual US forces exposed: 'The troops that will remain will be in greater hazard as a result of our having pulled 90,000 troops out over a 3-year period of time'.

Senator William S. Cohen offered a substitute amendment, adopting the same objectives, in the same language as the Nunn-Roth amendment, requiring detailed reports from the administration on European defence efforts, but deleting the provisions concerning US troop reductions.

Following the debate, and after an intensive lobbying effort by the Reagan administration, the Senate voted 55-41 to table the Nunn-Roth amendment. Senator Cohen's substitute amendment was then called for a vote. Prior to the vote on Cohen's amendment, Senator Nunn took the floor to comment that the Cohen amendment was 'certainly better than nothing', observing that although the 'teeth' had been removed from his proposal, the Cohen amendment still retained a ceiling on US troops in Europe and funding for side-by-side testing of European weapons systems. He urged adoption of the Cohen amendment. The vote on the Cohen substitute found ninety-four Senators in favour and only three opposed. The provision was ultimately adopted in conference with the House of Representatives (which had no such language in its bill) and was signed into law by President Reagan as part of the FY 1985 Omnibus Defence Authorization Bill (PL 98-525) on 19 October 1984.

The European reaction to the Nunn proposal was, on balance, predictably negative. Many European officials and experts agreed with the intent of the proposal, and some privately welcomed whatever push it might give to European defence efforts; but virtually all objected to what they viewed as its coercive approach. The West German Minister of Defence, Manfred Woerner (a Christian Democrat and reserve *Luftwaffe* pilot who became NATO's Secretary General in 1988) later told reporters in Washington: 'Threatening is not the method with which you can treat an ally.... We ought not to be treated this way with a stick.'

In addition, many European commentaries pointed out that the West

European allies already carry a substantial share of the defence burden in Western Europe, that the real costs of defence efforts could not be measured simply in terms of direct monetary inputs and that the real costs of defence for many European countries were underestimated because they drafted military personnel, and therefore spent less on manpower than the United States.

In spite of the negative European reaction to the amendment, however, there was widespread recognition that Senator Nunn's proposal represented an important trend in American attitudes toward the Alliance to which the allies would have to react. US Ambassador to NATO, David Abshire, said: 'A Nunn Amendment that didn't make it might be a good message. A Nunn Amendment that made it would be a bad methodology'—suggesting that although the Reagan administration had opposed the amendment, it may have wanted the message to get across in Europe. By all appearances, the message—or at least *a* message—had begun to get across to Europe. The result was an undramatic but clearly discernible move toward a more cohesive European contribution to European defence.

One week after the defeat of the Nunn-Roth amendment, former West German Chancellor Helmut Schmidt proposed that Germany and France effectively merge their armed forces and reduce their reliance on the American nuclear guarantee. Schmidt's proposal was received sceptically in Paris and met a lukewarm reception in West Germany. But the allies were sensitive to the mood in the Congress which inspired support for the Nunn-Roth amendment and, partly in response to this mood, had already planned a major new initiative to revitalize the moribund Western European Union.

REVITALIZATION OF THE WESTERN EUROPEAN UNION

The Western European Union (WEU) had been created in October 1954, following the failure of the European Defence Community, as part of the structure of alliance relationships discussed earlier. The main role of WEU was to provide a framework for monitoring West German rearmament. Its control function for a long time made the West Germans reluctant to regard it as a viable candidate for the organization of West European defence efforts. While the WEU hovered for many years near institutional irrelevance, Paris, nonetheless, kept a few embers burning so that the fire could be rekindled when the time was right.

On 27 October 1984, the defence and foreign ministers of France, West Germany, Italy, the United Kingdom, Belgium, the Netherlands and Luxembourg agreed in Rome to revitalize the Union. The ministers decided that similar combined ministerial meetings would be held twice a year in the future, and that their discussions would include a wide variety of defence and security topics, including arms control. Their purpose would be to build a greater European consensus on security issues. In addition, the ministers agreed that henceforth the Western European Union would promote co-operation in the production and procurement of advanced armaments. They said, in the Rome accord, that the WEU would encourage the activities of the broader Independent European Programme Group (IEPG), to include all NATO European allies and designed to promote European arms collaboration, with the aim of producing more West-bound traffic on NATO's transatlantic 'two-way street' in armaments trade.

FROM STICKS TO CARROTS IN THE CONGRESS

In 1985, Congressional action on defence burden-sharing moved away from sticks and toward more carrots designed to create a positive political environment for improvements in NATO's conventional forces. The FY 1986 Department of Defence Authorization bill included a number of incentives for conventional force improvements and transatlantic defence co-operation. Turning away from the main focus of his 1984 legislative efforts, Senator Nunn proposed an amendment to the FY 1986 Defence Authorization bill to include $200 million for co-operative research and development projects with one or several NATO allies. The programme was approved and subsequently continued in the FY 1987 Defence Authorization Bill and broadened to include other non-NATO US allies.

In addition, the FY 1987 Defence Authorization also reallocated funds the administration had requested for the Strategic Defence Initiative (SDI) to promote research into conventional defence technologies—thereby originating a 'balanced-technology initiative'. Not less than $300 m. was fenced off to fund research on advanced conventional defence technologies and not less than $153 m. for enhancing the defence technology base. The co-operative development programme was funded in the FY 1988 defence appropriations bill, with $150 m. for NATO Co-operative Development programmes and $43 m. for the NATO Co-operative Development Testing Programme. Of these funds, approximately $15 m. was designated for a co-operative programme with Israel. A further $16 m. was specifically allocated for a joint programme with the United Kingdom and other interested countries to develop new methods for surveillance of ocean waters with radar to enhance anti-submarine capabilities.

The Europeans have strongly welcomed these defence co-operation initiatives. On the other hand, they have been well aware of the continuing sentiment in Congress that the allies should 'do more'. This awareness has been intensified by the general political acceptance in the United States that the defence build-up of the Reagan administration has come to an end and that the next US administration will be required to reduce the growth in defence spending in order to help reduce the American budget deficit.

Towards Restructuring the Burden-Sharing Debate?

The events surrounding the US deployment of intermediate-range nuclear (INF) missiles in Europe and the US-Soviet treaty eliminating all such US and Soviet missile systems appear to have had a significant impact on prospects for European defence co-operation. The many barriers to European defence co-operation—material, military, historical, political and psychological—have for most of the last forty years been the source of substantial inertia among European governments. The last eight years of experience with the issue of INF, however, appear to have provided the critical mass required to begin to push the process of European defence co-operation ahead. These dynamics may have been instrumental in moving the burden-sharing issue toward some more fundamental decisions.

In 1979, when NATO decided to deploy new intermediate-range nuclear missiles, very few observers would have imagined that the INF story, as it unfolded, would stimulate both the Left and the Right in Europe to support intensified defence co-operation. The Left coalesced first, in opposition to the deployment of the new INF missiles. One important symbol of the effect of the deployment on the Left was the formation of the 'Scanlux' grouping of European socialist and social democratic parties. Beginning in 1981 as a low-profile consultation on security policy among Left parties in the Scandinavian and Benelux NATO countries, the group was transformed into a forum including 'observers' from other West European socialist parties. Throughout the 1980s, the Scanlux group has been a central focus for shaping common perspectives on security policy issues among Western Europe's socialist parties. One of the points of general consensus has been that the European countries should have greater influence over NATO's policies.

It is particularly ironic that the US 'zero-option' proposal, originally vilified by the Left as non-negotiable with the Soviet Union, ultimately, under new Soviet leadership, provided the basis for US-Soviet agreement, producing an outcome that the European Left has to regard as far better than it could have reasonably hoped for in the early 1980s.

On the other hand, the INF outcome disturbed many on the political Right in Europe. For these observers and politicians, the 'zero-option' approach had been ill-conceived in terms of NATO's strategic interests and the accord demonstrated that Europe's strategic interests were not at the top of the American political agenda. The American attitude had been signalled by US actions at the Reykjavik summit meeting in October 1986, where not only the INF 'zero-option' was agreed in principle, but where President Reagan proposed eliminating all ballistic nuclear missiles. This surprise initiative stunned Europeans, who believed that ballistic missiles would continue to be the most reliable vehicle for American and European deterrent capabilities for the foreseeable future. More out of regret than anger, the political Right in Europe turned toward European defence co-operation as a necessary insurance policy against what became increasingly seen as 'inevitable' further US reductions in its contribution to European defence.

The movement was particularly evident in co-operation between France and West Germany. Bonn and Paris intensified consultations at many levels and agreed to form a European brigade and, in September 1987, the two countries conducted major joint military exercises in Germany with combined French and German forces operating under French command. This first-ever major French-German military exercise had been in planning for several years, but the timing tended to highlight the clear trends in political thinking.

Perhaps most notably, the WEU countries in October 1987 issued a 'Platform on European Security Interests' which constituted the most explicit and far-reaching European statement to date on common approaches to European security issues. The document emphasized the continuing importance for Western security interests of both nuclear weapons and American involvement in European defence. The West Europeans also used WEU consultative and decision-making procedures to help co-ordinate their enhanced naval contributions to the Western presence in the Gulf in 1987.

Because European fears of a Soviet military attack are certainly not on the increase with Mikhail Gorbachev in the driver's seat in Moscow, it would appear that the recent governmental steps toward European defence co-operation are more in response to the perceived American threat of a reduced commitment to European defence than to any concern about an imminent Warsaw pact invasion. (For that matter, the apparently growing perception in the United States that the Soviet Union does not intend to attack Western Europe is used by some Americans to argue that the United States can afford to reduce its presence there, clearly demonstrating the perverse effect that Soviet policies can have on the burden-sharing issue!)

The official American reaction to greater European defence co-operation in 1987 appears to have changed substantially from a somewhat more sceptical attitude expressed by some American officials in the mid-1980s. In a number of major speeches delivered late in 1987 and early in 1988, President Reagan explicitly supported the process of European defence co-operation and the construction of a European pillar in the Atlantic Alliance.

In a speech entitled 'The Agenda of US-Soviet Relations' delivered to the cadets of the US Military Academy at West Point on 28 October 1987, Reagan observed that

> ... we have seen the emergence among some of our European allies of a willingness, even an eagerness, to seek a larger, more closely co-ordinated role for Western Europe in providing its own defence. We Americans welcome this.

Reagan went on to note that the United States had for many years been the 'senior partner' in the Alliance, but that 'now the alliance should become more and more among equals, indeed, an alliance between continents'. The communiqué issued by the NATO summit meeting in March 1988 explicitly endorsed steps toward European defence co-operation, tending to confirm the earlier trends in West European and US policies.

There was further evidence of American and European political support for the directions suggested by President Reagan's new line. In May 1988, a special committee of US Senators and Representatives and Canadian and European parliamentarians issued a report calling for a new political mandate for NATO that would explicitly endorse the construction of a 'real West European pillar' in the Alliance. The committee was chaired by Senator William V. Roth, Jr. and included Senator Sam Nunn, two of the key participants in recent Senate action on NATO issues. While the committee could not totally agree on the best ways to construct such a pillar (partly due to differences among European members about the future role of the WEU), the principle and ideas for a number of 'building blocks' were accepted by Democrats and Republicans on the US side and by European conservatives and social democrats alike.[6]

In spite of these signs of movement toward basic changes in the Alliance, some Congressional activity remained strongly focused on the burden-sharing complaint, and frustrated by the evolutionary process of change that this implies. Attempting to reduce the federal budget deficit and irritated by trade deficits with key allies, many members of Congress appeared tempted to return to the use of 'sticks' to influence the relationship between the United States and its allies.

Congressional hearings early in 1988, which focused on European security and burden-sharing issues, revealed a strong sentiment for the European allies to take on a greater role in NATO. At the same time, there continued to be no apparent consensus on how US policy could best encourage such a trend while still ensuring US security interests. Hearings by the House Armed Services Committee panel on defence burden-sharing chaired by Representative Pat Schroeder reflected the still-conflicting perspectives. The hearings saw sharply contrasting approaches taken by panel members and Reagan administration witnesses. While witnesses from the State and Defence Department testified that the administration was keeping burden-sharing 'at the centre' of the dialogue with the allies, a number of panel members and private witnesses 'suggested that a lack of diplomatic will has led the United States to shoulder a disproportionate share of the cost of Western defense'.[7]

The next American administration could play a crucial role in shaping the future of the burden-sharing debate. If past history is a guide, the next administration will be tempted to defend its right to manage relations with the allies, with the benefit of Congressional advice but without direct Congressional involvement. Most members of Congress may be willing to support such an approach *if* the administration is able to convince them that it is encouraging trends that will alter current burden-sharing relationships. To do so, the administration will require evidence from the European side that the apparent movement toward a more cohesive European effort in the Alliance is more than a cosmetic change. Given the constraints on resources likely to be available for defence over the next few years, more serious and successful co-operative efforts will be required than those that have been attempted in the past. If the building blocks for a European pillar are not evident in a few years' time, the burden-sharing debate could become a much more severe challenge to alliance cohesion than at any time in the past.

Notes

1. The views in this Chapter are those of the author and do not necessarily represent those of the Congressional Research Service or the Library of Congress.
2. For more detailed discussion of the political dynamics shaping the 'transatlantic bargain', see: Stanley R. Sloan, *NATO's Future, Toward a New Transatlantic Bargain'*, National Defense University Press, Washington (1985), Macmillan, London (1986), p. 3-31.
3. This historical discussion is based on work previously published in the Congressional Research Service report entitled 'Defence Burden-Sharing: U.S. Relations with the NATO Allies and Japan'.
4. For a detailed treatment of this period and a thorough overview of the United States Senate's involvement in alliance policy, see: Phil Williams, *The Senate and US Troops in Europe*, (Macmillan, London, 1985).
5. Richard Perle, who in his capacity as Assistant Secretary of Defence for International Security Policy oversaw preparation of these reports for most of the Reagan administration, said that the reports had attempted to put the best face on 'pretty dismal figures'. (See George Leopold, 'Study Rekindles Heated Burden-Sharing Debate, Challenges Congress' Assertions', *Defence News*, 28 March 1988, p. 13.)
6. *NATO in the 1990s*, Report of the North Atlantic Assembly's Special Presidential Committee on NATO in the 1990s, May 1988.
7. Dan Beyers, 'US diplomats brush off criticism, insist burden-sharing at "top of agenda"', *Defense News*, 21 March 1988, p. 6.

SECTION 3
Problems of
Defence-Spending—
Warsaw Pact

THE role of the East Europeans in the Warsaw Pact offers an interesting point of comparison. Keith Crane suggests that historically the Europeans have spent as little as possible on defence; Michael Checinski that their role is likely to increase in the years ahead.

No-one should minimize the problems confronting the Soviet Union. So far it has been able to produce SU 27 fighters, T 80 tanks and Mig 23s at the same rate as before because the production capacity to support defence procurement was already in place when Gorbachev came to office. The crunch will come in the 1990s if he attempts to reduce defence-spending by asking the Soviet Union's allies to contribute more.

The historical record, alas, is not encouraging. If they, too, are pursuing perestroika *programmes of their own, they will doubtless recall that both the 1953-57 and 1965-70 periods of economic reform were followed by periods of economic stagnation. Burden-sharing for Eastern Europe may involve a measure of power-sharing as well, which, in turn, may threaten the measure of control the Soviet Union has exercised since the Warsaw Pact was first created in 1955.*

CHAPTER 4

The Determinants of Spending in Eastern Europe: Defence Expenditure in the Non-Soviet Warsaw Pact

KEITH CRANE

In politics and military might, Eastern Europe plays second fiddle to the Soviet Union within the Warsaw Pact. In terms of numbers, however, non-Soviet Warsaw Pact (NSWP) armies field 859,000 men, more than the 565,000 Soviet forces in the region.[1] NSWP air forces provide substantial contributions to Soviet forces.[2] NSWP air defences are firmly integrated with Soviet operations in the area.

Despite the numerical importance of East European soldiers and military equipment, little is known in the West of the size of expenditures on these forces nor what induces East European leaders to commit these resources to the military. This Chapter is directed towards partially filling these gaps. It concludes by extrapolating from these findings to speculate on the future course of military spending in the region.

Reported Military Expenditures

All the East European countries currently report budget figures for aggregate military spending, except Bulgaria, which ceased to do so in 1970 (*Table 1*). However, the detail is generally minimal. Czechoslovakia, Hungary and Poland also report realized expenditures in the statistical yearbooks. Czechoslovakia provides a further breakdown into expenditures by the Czech lands, Slovakia, and the federal government.

The GDR published no figures on defence spending until 1960 when the percentage of the national budget allocated to defence and security was published. Actual budgetary totals for defence and security have been published since 1968; separate defence figures have been published since 1977.[3] The figures in *Table 1* are estimates of defence-spending for the years before 1977 and the official published statistics for subsequent years.

Hungary provides only a single figure for defence-spending and another for

55

TABLE 1
Reported East European and Soviet Military Spending Budgets
(Millions of domestic currencies or 1970 = 100)

Year	Czechoslovakia (crowns)		The GDR (marks)		Hungary (forints)		Poland (zlotys)		Romania (lei)		USSR (roubles)	
1960	8783	58.9	1000	17.5	3100	31.5	14920	41.8	3392	48.0	9,300	52.0
1961	9512	63.8	1000	17.5	3376	34.3	17019	47.6	3639	51.5	11,600	64.8
1962	10854	72.8	2700	47.3	4913	49.9	18379	51.4	3924	55.5	12,600	70.4
1963	11332	76.0	2800	49.0	6500	66.0	20695	57.9	4134	58.5	13,900	77.7
1964	10217	68.5	2900	50.8	6163	62.6	21881	61.2	4346	61.5	13,300	74.3
1965	10125	67.9	3100	54.3	5757	58.5	23255	65.1	4735	67.0	12,800	71.5
1966	10841	72.7	3200	56.0	5219	53.0	25213	70.6	4927	69.7	13,400	74.9
1967	12385	83.0	3600	63.0	5433	55.2	26438	74.0	5146	72.8	14,500	81.0
1968	13189	88.4	4814	84.3	6440	65.4	30332	84.9	5751	81.4	16,700	93.3
1969	14268	95.6	5229	91.5	7644	77.6	33519	93.8	6319	89.4	17,700	98.9
1970	14919	100.0	5712	100.0	9848	100.0	35724	100.0	7067	100.0	17,900	100.0
1971	15943	106.9	6019	105.4	9891	100.4	37684	105.5	7424	105.1	17,900	100.0
1972	16770	112.4	6217	108.8	9430	95.8	39490	110.5	7710	109.1	17,900	100.0
1973	17647	118.3	6571	115.0	9488	96.3	42290	118.4	7835	110.9	17,900	100.0
1974	18071	121.1	6746	118.1	10564	107.3	46353	129.8	8744	123.7	17,700	98.9
1975	19728	132.2	7154	125.2	11811	119.9	50204	140.5	9713	137.4	17,400	97.2
1976	20365	136.5	7613	133.3	11671	118.5	54242	151.8	10575	149.6	17,400	97.2
1977	20130	134.9	7868	137.7	12607	128.0	60932	170.6	10963	155.1	17,200	96.1
1978	20808	139.5	8261	144.6	14983	152.1	63255	177.1	11713	165.7	17,200	96.1
1979	21380	143.3	8674	151.9	16200	164.5	68192	190.9	11835	167.5	17,100	95.5
1980	22900	153.5	9403	164.6	17700	179.7	71572	200.3	10394	147.1	17,100	95.5
1981	23099	154.8	10145	177.6	19060	193.5	80560	225.5	10503	148.6	17,100	95.5
1982	24560	164.6	10776	188.7	20200	205.1	186180	521.2	11339	160.4	17,100	95.5
1983	25261	169.3	11401	199.6	21900	222.4	201380	563.7	11662	165.0	17,100	95.5
1984	26276	176.1	12222	214.0	22700	230.5	263400	737.3	11888	168.2	17,100	95.5
1985			13041	228.3			325170	910.2				

Sources: Czechoslovakia and Hungary—Statistical Yearbooks; Poland—Statistical Yearbook, National Budgets and Alton et al., 1980;
The German Democratic Republic—Alton et al., 1980 Statistical Yearbooks; The Soviet Union—Becker, 1985, p. 4.

defence incomes, presumably payments by enterprises for labour supplied by the military.

Poland publishes budget figures for current military spending and spending on military investment. These figures for military investment are probably limited to military construction. Half of this figure is spent on military housing;[4] the remainder is so small that it patently excludes procurement; it may cover construction costs of military bases. Like Hungary, Poland also publishes figures for military earnings.

Alton argues that since 1972 Polish military investment expenditures have not been included in realized expenditures reported in the statistical year-book.[5] Figures for expenditures by the Ministry of Defence are greater than those reported for national defence in the yearbook by roughly the amount budgeted for military investment since this date. For this reason, my post-1972 estimates of total military spending were constructed by adding budgeted spending for military investment to the military expenditure figure given in the yearbook.

In recent years Romania has been more forthcoming concerning military expenditures than the other countries. It has provided the United Nations with breakdowns on military expenditures by service category (air force, navy and army) and by expenditure category (procurement, operations and maintenance, personnel and military research and development). However, with this exception, the East Europeans provide very little information on the size of their military expenditures.

RELIABILITY OF BUDGETS

Not only is there a paucity of data on East European expenditures but one questions whether the reported expenditures actually reflect real resource flows to the military, or whether the budgets may be falsified. The Soviet budget, for example, has omitted important military expenditure categories for years. In 1987, a message from Mikhail Gorbachev to a disarmament conference stated that military procurement, construction and R&D expenditures have not been included in the published defence budget, but are inserted elsewhere in the USSR state budget.[6] The same may be true for Eastern Europe.

Checinski (1974) and Loebel have argued that actual East European military expenditures are much higher than those reported in the official defence budgets. Loebel, who was a department head of the Czechoslovak National Bank in Bratislava, set up a group to trace military expenditures during the Prague Spring. The group concluded that resource flows to the military were three times those reported in the national budget. Loebel is reported to have said that the unreported expenses of the military were covered by price subsidies to arms manufacturers. The subsidies covered losses that were planned by the central authorities to reduce military budget figures.

Unfortunately, his work remained in Czechoslovakia when he departed after the Soviet invasion in 1968.

Loebel's work leaves some unanswered questions. Price subsidies on domestically-purchased armaments should be included in the defence budget, but price subsidies on arms exports, a major item for both countries, should not. If the subsidies were lumped together, the conclusion that actual defence expenditures exceeded reported expenditures by three times would be exaggerated. Loebel's figures are also puzzling because, according to his own figures, procurement would account for about 80 per cent of total military spending. This ratio is very high.

Checinksi (1974) argues that armaments production has been subsidized in Poland through the system of granting priorities and through subsidies to military equipment manufacturers. He also claims that military production receives a hidden subsidy because indirect costs in Poland have been allocated by labour inputs.[7] He argues that in plants producing both military and civilian goods, military production is more capital-intensive, because the machinery is designed for these products; production of civilian goods on these machines uses relatively more labour inputs. Consequently, indirect costs fall disproportionately on civilian goods. Checinski cites a study of seven Polish armaments producers showing that a re-allocation of indirect costs would have raised military equipment prices by up to 200 per cent.

The evidence Checinski cites to support his arguments is somewhat mixed. For example, he notes that in 1958 a circular was sent to all Polish armaments factories *forbidding* them to allocate indirect costs from military to civilian production, indicating that this type of subsidization was not official policy.[8] He notes that because of accounting systems, factory managers found it impossible to disaggregate costs, implying that the degree of indirect subsidization is difficult if not impossible to measure. The argument that civilian goods have a higher labour content than capital goods in armaments plants is also open to question. Priority production for hard currency exports, for example, is more labour-intensive than lower priority production in Poland. Consequently, civilian goods production is unlikely to be much more labour-intensive than the production of high priority military goods in these plants.

COMPATABILITY WITH BUILDING BLOCK ESTIMATES

Other evidence indicates that if the military is cross-subsidized from other budget categories, these subsidies are a fraction, not a multiple of military spending. Thomas Clements, a Defence Intelligence Agency analyst, has constructed military expenditures series for the East Europeans using the building block method.[9] Clements identifies the physical elements of the NSWP armed forces and then multiplies them by domestic prices or US prices converted at purchasing power parity exchange rates to Eastern

European prices. The sum of these costs equals total military expenditures in domestic currencies.

Clements's estimates for Czechoslovakia, Hungary, Poland and Romania average only 15 per cent above the reported budgets, a difference he attributes to possible differences in coverage between the reported budgets and his estimates.[10] He found the reported East German budget exceeded his estimates by a wide margin. Clements notes the difference may be due to payments for the support of the Group of Soviet Forces-Germany.

He concludes that the reported military budgets are useful for measuring nominal military spending trends. Both the magnitude and rates of increase of the reported budgets are roughly consistent with his building block estimates. He also notes that steady growth and the absence of abrupt changes in the size of the Polish and Czech budgets indicate that coverage has probably remained the same since the 1940s when detailed, inclusive budgets were first published.

Other evidence indicates that the East European military budgets cannot be as easily dismissed as those of the Soviet Union. All East European budgets have steadily increased in nominal terms over the past two decades, in contrast to the budget reported by the Soviet Union (*Table 1*).

The size of the budgets also seems reasonable as a share of net material product, considering the size and composition of the East European forces (*Table 2*). They run 2-6 per cent of Utilized National Income (UNI), ratios that would be somewhat lower if gross domestic product (GDP) was used as the divisor. Although UNI is less than GDP, the share differences in the case of Hungary are only about 0.2-0.6 percentage points, indicating that the reported military budgets as a share of total output are roughly on a par with those of many countries in Western Europe.

NON-MILITARY BUDGET CATEGORIES

If the military budgets are deliberately under-reported, these expenditures must be hidden elsewhere in the national budget. Unfortunately, the East European budgets are often short of detail and the extent of reporting of the national budgets varies from country to country and over time. So it is difficult to test this hypothesis using the reported budgets for all these countries.

A close analysis of the Polish budgets indicates that they provide little room for unreported military expenditures, except for military R&D financed through the Ministry of Science and Technology. Elsewhere, subsidy categories that are likely to cover military expenditures are fairly well accounted for. The East Germans, Czechs and Hungarians have some room to hide expenditures under subsidies to enterprises. Whether this is the case is an open question. The East German budget also contains an unexplained residual between total reported budgetary expenditures and the sum of

TABLE 2
Military Budgets as a Percentage of Utilized National Income

Year	Czechoslovakia (UNI)	Poland (UNI)	Hungary (UNI)	(GDP)	GDR (UNI)	Romania (NMP)
1962	6.32	4.32	2.88	2.59	3.7	3.59
1963	6.84	4.53	3.57	3.26	3.8	3.45
1964	6.21	4.52	3.20	2.92	3.8	3.27
1965	5.97	4.41	3.06	2.77	3.8	3.24
1966	5.70	4.45	2.61	2.25	3.7	3.07
1967	5.51	4.43	2.43	2.20	3.8	2.98
1968	5.22	4.63	2.78	2.29	5.0	3.12
1969	5.00	4.88	3.03	2.45	5.0	3.18
1970	4.96	4.88	3.48	2.96	5.1	3.32
1971	5.09	4.48	3.07	2.73	5.2	3.08
1972	5.06	4.15	2.93	2.40	5.1	2.91
1973	4.96	3.80	2.77	2.19	5.0	2.67
1974	4.65	3.57	2.66	2.32	4.9	2.65
1975	4.83	3.45	2.75	2.45	5.0	2.68
1976	4.81	3.20	2.57	2.19	5.1	2.64
1977	4.83	3.34	2.52	2.15	5.0	2.54
1978	4.76	3.22	2.63	2.38	5.2	2.52
1979	4.70	3.41	2.80	2.38	5.3	2.37
1980	4.79	3.49	2.96	2.45	5.1	2.04
1981	5.06	3.63	2.96	2.44	5.5	1.98
1982	5.18	3.97	2.93	2.38	6.0	1.80
1983	5.21	3.45	3.04	2.44	6.3	1.77
1984		3.71	2.94	2.32	6.6	1.68

Source: Statistical handbooks of Czechoslovakia, the German Democratic Republic, Hungary, Poland and Romania.

Notes: Utilized national income (UNI), the goods consumed within the country, was employed rather than NMP, because it is a measure of the resources domestically available to the national governments. The Hungarian GDP measure was used as a point of reference for Western measures. The GDR does not publish values for UNI so these values were estimated. See Crane (1987) for details.

specified expenditures. It averaged 6.8 per cent of the total budget between 1979 and 1985. It is unclear what this residual is spent on. Part may be devoted to foreign trade subsidies, but these could also be located in the category of government expenditures on industry. The increases recorded in the latter category over the past five years are more consistent with the decline in the profitability of GDR exports and the concomitant need for the State to subsidize them. This residual could also be used to pay for Soviet forces stationed in East Germany, subsidize industrial production or investment, cover some other expenses or go toward military spending. If the last is the case, this category could provide an increment of over 100 per cent to the military budget.[11]

George Stahler has found evidence supporting Loebel's argument that a large part of Czechoslovakia's military expenditures is financed outside the reported military budget. In the 1968 Czech statistical yearbook, the 1967 budget was disaggregated by government office, as well as category, a much finer breakdown than provided in other years. In this yearbook the reported military budget fell under the government departmental 'Other Headings,' which was financed from the category, 'Financial Expenditures'. Small parts of the expenditures of several other government departments were financed from this category but only one, entitled 'General Administrative Expenditures' was entirely financed in this way.

Expenditures in this section comprised 128 per cent of the reported military budget. In the 1969 yearbook this category was eliminated and various components scattered among other categories, but most were included in 'Services and Expenditures of a Non-Productive Character'.[12] This category rose from 2,314 m. crowns in 1967 to 29,511 m. crowns in 1968. 'Financial Expenditures' were 28,992 m. crowns in 1967. This category covers net subsidies for foreign trade and may cover general government administration costs but may also hide additional military expenditures. It may be the category Loebel refers to in his work. If so, this category provided a potential source for military spending that averaged 142 per cent of the reported military spending between 1968 and 1983.

SOCIAL EXPENDITURES

Alton *et al.* (1980) have shown that certain military expenditures on personnel are included in budgetary categories other than defence-spending. Transportation of soldiers to their first tour of duty and during leave is at least partly paid for by the national railroads or bus services, which in turn usually receive government subsidies for operating costs.[13] Pre-entry physicals are paid for by the national health service. Enterprises pick up the wage bill for reservists on manoeuvres, and the national pension and welfare offices pay the pensions of retired military officers, as well as disability insurance and child support allowances for all military personnel. Military education may also be included in the education budget, although Polish defence budgets from the late 1940s include an item for military academies.[14] The sum of these costs is not insignificant, running at 12-17 per cent of the reported budgets, but about half of these extra costs accrue from military pensions paid by the State.[15]

These costs are not multiples of the reported budgets, nor do they indicate that the military budgets are purposefully understated for propaganda reasons. Pension and child support benefits for all occupations, including the military, are handled by a central administration in these countries. Concessionary fares on public transportation are also normal parts of the system.

CONSISTENCY WITH OTHER DATA

Elsewhere, I have attempted to reconstruct East European military spending on personnel, operations and maintenance, procurement of military durables and R&D, using cost of living, input-output, industrial production, budgetary and trade data.[16] Where possible, I attempted to use more than one technique to estimate each expenditure category. These reconstructed military budgets provide another indication of the reliability of the reported budgets. Between 1969-83 my annual estimates averaged 106.3 per cent of the reported Czech budgets, 104.0 per cent of the Hungarian budgets, and 107.2 per cent of the Polish budgets. Estimates of East German operations and maintenance expenditures together with personnel costs average 56.1 per cent of reported expenditures.

Given the margin of error in my estimates, I believe they provide a fairly close fit with the reported budgets. These estimates provide support for the proposition that the reported budgets record the bulk of actual military expenditures on personnel, operations and maintenance, and procurement.

Although the evidence is not complete, a reasonable working hypothesis is that, with the possible exception of Czechoslovakia, the reported defence budgets contain the major components of military spending: personnel costs, procurement, operations and maintenance, and construction. In the case of Czechoslovakia, military construction costs appear to be covered under the investment rather than the military budget.[17] Czech procurement costs may also be subsidized through other budgetary categories. The reported budgets for all countries except Romania appear to omit military R&D expenditures, some personnel expenditures identified by Alton et al. (1980) covered by ministries other than the Ministry of Defence, most notably military pensions and family support costs, and some direct subsidies for military producers. Estimates of these apparently unreported costs run 12-17 per cent of the reported budgets for personnel costs and 1-7.5 per cent for R&D.[18] I have been unable to locate or quantify the extent of direct subsidies to military producers. Close perusal of the Polish budgets failed to provide evidence that they are more than a few per cent of the reported budgets. In the case of Czechoslovakia, Loebel states that they have been multiples of the military budgets; Stahler has identified a budgetary category that could cover these expenditures.[19]

Although all these measures reduce the size of the reported military budget, some were probably not adopted for purposes of deception. In particular, the provision of military pensions and family support through the social security administrations of these countries appears to stem from the universal nature of pensions and family support grants in centrally-planned economies, rather than a conscious decision to hide military spending. In short, in contrast to the Soviet budget, and with the possible exception of Czechoslovakia, military expenditures reported by the East Europeans probably cover major expenditure categories except for military R&D and pensions.

Determinants of Military Spending

The preceding discussion assessed the validity of the officially reported East European defence budgets. What, however, determines the levels of these expenditures? In other nations, government decisions on the size of the military budget depend on the existence and extent of threats of invasion, the wish to threaten, fears of revolution, the need to placate generals (often an important interest group) and pressure from dominating powers. They are constrained by competing demands from other claimants on resources and by economic output as well as what the country can beg, borrow, or steal from its neighbours. In the case of Eastern Europe, however, many have argued that the Soviet Union plays the deciding role because of its proximity, military strength and influence.[20] East European leaders, on the other hand, claim military spending decisions are made independently, after collegial discussions with other members of the Warsaw Pact, in response to anticipated NATO aggression.

Apart from the reports of a few emigrés,[21] we know little of how such decisions are actually made in the NSWP. However, the pattern of NWSP military expenditures should reflect the effects of these various influences. These patterns provide a means to test the relative importance of different incentives and constraints. Below several hypotheses concerning the determinants of military spending in the NSWP are presented. Subsequently, a model of military spending decision-making is developed and estimated to assess the relative validity of the hypotheses in explaining observed patterns of military spending.

SOVIET PRESSURE

After the 22-23 November 1978 meeting of the Warsaw Pact Political Consultative Committee (the highest political body in the Warsaw Pact), Nicolae Ceausescu, First Secretary of the Romanian Communist Party, openly complained of Soviet pressure to increase military spending.[22] According to Ceausescu, the Soviet Union pressed the NSWP to increase military expenditures in response to the May 1978 NATO agreement to raise expenditures by 3 per cent annually in real terms. Other countries, notably Hungary and Poland, also reportedly complained privately of Soviet pressure.[23] If Soviet pressure is an important determinant of NSWP military expenditures, post-1978 NSWP spending should have increased in response to the 1978 Soviet request.

ECONOMIC WHEREWITHAL

The opportunity costs of military expenditures are a compelling reason for NSWP governments preferring lower levels of military spending than those

C-DA—F

desired by the Soviet Union. The East Europeans have been much less successful than the Soviet leadership in instilling support for the existing systems through ideology. Consequently, they have based much of their political legitimacy on economic performance. Because central control of the economy is so strong, Communist Parties and their governments are held responsible, and often take responsibility, for consumer supplies and changes in living standards. Because military spending is a budget item, whether hidden or overt, the top party leadership must be well aware of the opportunity costs of spending more on the military than on housing or consumer goods subsidies. Because economic problems have often led to civil disturbances and, subsequently, regime changes in Eastern Europe, party leaders may feel that spending on civilian subsidies increases their job security far more than increased military spending.

Not surprisingly, East European leaders appear to have little inclination to increase military spending. Hungarian and Polish officials have indicated that they have been unable to accelerate spending increases because of economic problems.[24] After the renewal of the Warsaw Pact in 1985, Hungarian Minister of Defence Lajos Czinege stated that Hungary would meet its obligations to the Alliance only 'in proportion to the capabilities of our national economy and our realistic possibilities'.[25] However, the extent to which economic wherewithal determines military spending levels is unknown.

DOMESTIC UNREST

Since World War II, East European history has been punctuated by mass outbursts against the Communist authorities. The local military establishments have not been immune to these developments. The Hungarian army disintegrated during the Soviet invasion in 1956; only one unit appears to have supported the Soviet forces.[26] The Czech officer corps contributed to political liberalization in 1968 through its criticisms of Warsaw Pact doctrine regarding Czech national interests.[27] Ciaston notes that Polish defence expenditures declined in 1957 and 1958 because of the domestic situation.[28] This period marked the reinstatement of Gomulka and the dismissal of Soviet officers from the Polish military. Some Polish soldiers reportedly agitated for independent trade unions within the military during the Solidarity period. However, Polish soldiers fired upon striking workers in 1970 in Gdansk, and Jaruzelski was able to rely on army support when he used the police to quell Solidarity in 1981 and 1982. Because the military has been so closely involved in these events, political crises are likely to affect decisions on military expenditures levels in these countries.

EXTERNAL THREATS

The East European and Soviet leaderships ascribe the need for military spending to an external threat, specifically NATO. Erich Honecker, First Secretary of East Germany's Communist Party, summed up this view:

> Faced with imperialism's increasing aggressiveness and its counter-revolutionary practices, we must systematically improve our national defence. ... Our armed forces must be continuously vigilant toward the changing, increasingly dangerous imperialist methods of class stuggle ... developed by the enemy to unleash and carry out aggression.[29]

This rationale has been repeated by every other member of the Warsaw Pact at various times.

If these statements represent real fears of war (or fears that external threats could weaken the position of the local leadership), one would expect to see a decline in the emphasis given to the military during a period of better relations with potential adversaries. *Détente* was such a period. Poland, Czechoslovakia and East Germany (GDR) signed treaties with the Federal Republic of Germany (FRG)—purportedly their greatest external threat—in 1970, 1972, and 1973, respectively. The FRG established diplomatic relations with Romania in 1967; and with Czechoslovakia, Hungary and Poland in the early 1970s. It also created a new framework for relations with the GDR at the same time. Not only did political relations between NSWP countries and the FRG change dramatically, but commercial, cultural and political relations with the rest of NATO also improved greatly. If external relations greatly affect military expenditure decisions in the NSWP, changes in expenditure in this period should reflect this improvement.

The Model

Because the NSWP tends to be acted upon, rather than an actor, I have constructed a model of military spending incorporating the assumptions that NSWP leaderships weigh Soviet pressure, available resources, the domestic political situation and external threats when deciding how much to spend on the military. The model is linear, implying that each of these forces enters the decision-making process independently, adding to or substracting from overall spending levels.

The dependent variable, military spending in constant prices, was assumed to equal reported military expenditures deflated by a price index. As argued above, NSWP countries' reported military expenditures probably encompass the bulk of actual expenditures on personnel, procurement, and operations and maintenance, and so are probably close to total military spending. Reported expenditures were deflated by price indexes for non-consumer goods and services for Czechoslovakia, Hungary and Poland and an estimated Net Material Product (NMP) deflator for the GDR. Romanian statistics are unusually poor: the Romanians do not publish price deflators. An implicit deflator for NMP was calculated and used for the years 1980-84. Nominal expenditures were assumed to equal real expenditures for earlier years because of the lack of an appropriate deflator. This may be less of a problem for Romania than for other countries because many prices were frozen for long periods in the 1960s and 1970s. Because Bulgaria does not publish any statistics on military expenditures, it was excluded from the analysis. Expenditures were converted to index numbers (1970 = 100). The index ran from 1960 to 1985 for all countries except the GDR. Reliable estimates of GDR military spending begin only in 1962.

Indices for UNI in constant prices were used as proxies for available resources for all the countries except Romania, where NMP was used. UNI was considered superior to NMP because the latter measures only the production of material goods, not consumption. UNI better reflects what is available to policy-makers for military spending. Some thought was given to using Western estimates of GNP for these countries. Since East European policy-makers presumably rely on their own statistics when making budget decisions, not Western recalculations of GNP, the East European figures for UNI were considered a better reflection of what policy-makers consider when making these decisions.

In this model, NSWP relations with the Federal Republic of Germany were used as a proxy for a potential Western threat. The FRG was chosen because, as well as the United States, it is consistently branded the potential aggressor in bloc propaganda, and the FRG is the only NATO member that has stated a desire to alter its present borders at the expense of the NSWP (albeit peacefully). The dramatic change in NSWP-FRG relations, signalled by the establishment of relations in the early 1970s, provided a convenient demarcation for a probable change in East European leadership perceptions of a NATO threat. Consequently, a dummy variable was used to differentiate between the periods before and after the signing of treaties and the normalization of relations between the FRG and these countries. The dummy took on a value of one the year after a treaty was signed or diplomatic relations established.

A dummy variable was also used to assess the effect of domestic disturbances on military spending. In the case of Poland it was given a value of one during any year of a violent disturbance—1970, 1976, and 1980-82—and the following year. The period of 1968 to 1971 was selected for Czechoslovakia because the Czech officer corps was purged at this time. Normalization was asssumed to be more-or-less complete by 1972. The Polish armed forces do not seem to have suffered the same loss of confidence during the Polish crisis, so the effects on the military were not assumed to be so long lasting.

A dummy variable was also used as a proxy for changes in Soviet pressure to spend. The variable took on a value of one after the 1978 decision by Warsaw Pact members to respond to higher NATO spending with more spending of their own. The analysis ends in 1984, the year before Gorbachev came to power. Thus I assume that greater Soviet pressure to increase military spending was relatively constant in the 1979-84 interregnum period. The Soviet Union has probably varied the level of pressure in other periods as well, but no other well-documented instance of an increase or decrease in pressure was found. This variable should provide a fair test of the efficacy of Soviet pressure to increase spending in the late 1970s and early 1980s.

The Results

EASTERN EUROPE

The results of the regressions are presented in *Table 3*. They indicate that UNI has been the most important determinant of military spending in Eastern Europe. The primary force driving expenditures in these countries, both as a group and individually, has been available resources.

The model indicates that domestic disturbances had no discernible effect on military expenditures in Czechoslovakia and Poland. This result probably does not extend to expenditures on security forces. It may reflect the fixed nature of many military costs (food and clothing for personnel, operations

TABLE 3
Factors Affecting Military Spending in Eastern Europe

Czechoslovakia   F = 166.0   No. of observations = 22
MILINR = 33.9 + .69 × UNIR* − .87 × SOVPRESS − 2.45 × GERM − 1.75 × DOM
    (6.41) (10.44)   (−.29)   (−0.48)   (−0.58)

GDR(a)   F = 134.4   No. of observations = 23
MILINR = −61.3 + 1.58 × UNIR* + 23.14 × SOVPRESS* − 13.76 × GERM
    (−3.12) (6.97)   (2.86)   (−1.16)

Hungary   F = 39.97   No. of observations = 25
MILINR = 24.5 + .59 × UNIR* + 10.28 × SOVPRESS* − 1.12 × GERM
    (2.02) (3.74)   (1.79)   (−.12)

Poland   F = 4.585   No. of observations = 25
MILINR = 35.00 + .46 × UNIR* − 1.29 × SOVPRESS + 8.47 × GERM + 4.09 × DOM
    (4.56) (4.84)   (−.26)   (1.04)   (1.02)

Romania   F = 134.84   No. of observations = 25
MILINR = 28.00 + .53 × NMP* − 31.6 × SOVPRESS + 15.2 × GERM
    (5.66) (8.90)   (−3.92)   (2.28)

Total   F = 77.38   No. of observations = 120
MILINR = 45.9 + .36 × UNIR* + 8.57 × SOVPRESS* + 20.6 × GERM + 2.02 × DOM
    (9.18) (6.44)   (1.75)   (3.94)   (.36)

Where MILINR = Reported military budgets in constant prices, UNIR = Utilized National Income in constant prices, SOVPRESS = a dummy variable for Soviet pressure to increase military spending after the 1978 Warsaw Pact meeting, GERM = dummy variable for years following the signing of the treaties between the FRG and the East Europeans in the early 1970s, and DOM = a dummy variable for years of or following violent domestic political conflicts. T statistics are given in parentheses.

* Starred variables indicate the null hypothesis could be rejected at a 5 per cent level of significance.

(a) Military budget estimates for the GDR begin in 1962.

and maintenance of existing equipment, purchase commitments for some types of military equipment, etc.) or may indicate that the priority of military spending for East European leaderships remains insulated from domestic disturbances.

The estimates also indicate that *détente* had no discernible effect on NSWP military spending. None of the estimates of the co-efficients for the dummy variable for improved relations with the FRG were significantly less than zero at the 5 per cent level. The external threat of West Germany does not seem to have been an important factor in determining military expenditures in these four countries during the 1960s, 1970s or early 1980s.

The Soviet Union appears to have had limited success in inducing the East Europeans to spend more on the military. The hypothesis that post-1978 Soviet pressure had no effect on military spending levels could be rejected at the 5 per cent level for Hungary, the GDR and the NSWP group as a whole. The estimates for the other countries were insignificant. In the case of Romania, Soviet pressure appears to have been counter-productive.

NATO

To test this model for generality, a similar regression was run for several members of NATO. Defence expenditures deflated by the GDP price deflator were regressed against UNI in constant prices (GDP minus the current account balance), dummy variables for *détente* (assumed to begin in 1971), and the 1977 NATO agreement to increase military spending by 3 per cent annually in real terms. Regressions were run for Belgium, Denmark, France, the Federal Republic of Germany, Italy, Luxembourg, the Netherlands, Norway and the United Kingdom.

With the exception of the United Kingdom, the estimate of the co-efficient for UNI is highly significant for all countries (*Table 4*). More surprising is the significance of the dummy variable for the 3 per cent agreement. Except for Belgium, West Germany and Norway, these countries appear to have devoted relatively more to military spending after this agreement than before, taking economic performance into account. Although these countries may not have reached the full 3 per cent specified in the agreement, they appear to have responded to the spirit of the initiative. In contrast, the co-efficient for the dummy variable for *détente* was insignificantly different from zero at the 5 per cent level for all countries. Although the West Europeans may have made a political commitment to *détente*, they apparently have not felt secure enough to let it affect their military spending.

DIFFERENCES IN UNI PERCENTAGE ON MILITARY SPENDING

The above model was designed to test various hypotheses concerning the reasons spending levels change from year to year within each country.

TABLE 4
The Determinants of Military Spending in NATO

Belgium   F = 525.34   No. of observations = 24
MILINR = 4. 92 + .97 × ABSORB* + .27 × DÉTENTE + 3.85 × AGREE
(.81) (13.19)   (.08)   (1.27)

Denmark   F = 50.63   No. of observations = 23
MILINR = 10.93 + .70 × ABSORB* − 5.27 × DÉTENTE + 11.03 × AGREE
(3.53) (5.19)   (1.01)   (2.61)

France   F = 108.6   No. of observations = 24
MILINR = 61.19 + .46 × ABSORB* − 5.07 × DÉTENTE + 17.83 × AGREE*
(8.52) (5.12)   (1.11)   (5.16)

West Germany   F = 24.63   No. of observations = 24
MILINR = 56.76 + .53 × ABSORB* + .96 × DÉTENTE + 2.73 × AGREE
(3.77) (2.88)   (.14)   (.48)

Italy   F = 59.46   No. of observations = 24
MILINR = 54.29 + .47 × ABSORB* + 7.76 × DÉTENTE + 9.97 × AGREE*
(5.36) (3.58)   (1.22)   (1.99)

Luxembourg   F = 15.8   No. of observations = 24
MILINR = 61.4 + .74 × GDP* − 19.8 × DÉTENTE + 28.3 × AGREE*
(2.06) (2.05)   (.99)   (1.96)

Netherlands   F = 157.53   No. of observations = 24
MILINR = 49.38 + .54 × ABSORB* − 2.05 × DÉTENTE + 5.60 × AGREE*
(9.00) (7.62)   (.62)   (2.16)

Norway   F = 99.22   No. of observations = 24
MILINR = 15.78 + .82 × ABSORB* − 8.51 × DÉTENTE − 5.14 × AGREE
(1.77) (7.72)   (1.40)   (1.08)

United Kingdom   F = 24.65   No. of observations = 24
MILINR = 85.39 + .22 × ABSORB + 2.72 × DÉTENTE + 11.93 × AGREE*
(6.41) (1.52)   (.54)   (3.99)

Where MILINR = Reported military budgets in constant prices, ABSORB = absorption (utilized national income), GDP = Gross Domestic Product in constant prices, DÉTENTE = a dummy variable for better Western European-Warsaw Pact political relations assumed to begin in 1971, and AGREE = a dummy variable for the years following the 1978 NATO agreement to increase military spending by 3 per cent annually.

* Starred variables indicate the null hypothesis could be rejected at the 5 per cent level of significance.

Another question is why levels of effort vary over time and across countries. In this case a common measure of military effort is needed. To avoid the issue of differing levels of development and the problems of converting military expenditures into a common currency, I have used the percentage of military spending in UNI as a measure of effort in this model. Otherwise the regression equations are the same as in the first model, except for the inclusion of a dummy variable for geographical location.

This variable, TIER, differentiates the Northern Tier countries that either border West Germany or straddle Soviet lines of communication to the Central region, from those that lie on the periphery and have no borders with NATO countries. TIER was given a value of one for Northern Tier countries and zero for Hungary and Romania.

The results of this model, shown in *Table 5*, are not robust. The model indicates some response by Czechoslovakia to Soviet pressure. The estimates of the co-efficient for the dummy variable, SOVPRESS, are positive and significantly different from zero using the 5 per cent level for Czechoslovakia and the group as a whole. However, estimates for the other countries were insignificantly different from zero. Estimates of the co-efficients for the dummy variables for an external threat were insignificantly different from zero, with the exception of the GDR. The co-efficients for domestic unrest were also insignificantly different from zero.

The role of economic growth in military spending decisions takes on a different aspect in this model. The percentage of UNI going to the military appears to *decline* as the economy grows for Czechoslovakia, Poland, Romania, and the group as whole. Military spending is income-inelastic for these countries. In other words, in hard times military spending is not reduced proportionately to UNI, and in good times it does not rise as rapidly as consumption in other areas.

TABLE 5
The Percentage of UNI Devoted to Military Spending

Czechoslovakia   F = 68.8   No. of observations = 24
$$MILPER = 7.15 - .02 \times UNIR + .45 \times SOVPRESS^\star + .24 \times GERM - .32 \times DOM$$
$$(21.5)\ (-4.30) \qquad (2.30) \qquad\qquad (.72) \qquad\quad (-1.60)$$

GDR(a)   F = 21.7   No. of observations = 23
$$MILPER = .87 + .04 \times UNIR^\star + .38 \times SOVPRESS - .87 \times GERM^\star$$
$$(1.17)\ (4.29) \qquad (1.24) \qquad\qquad (-1.95)$$

Hungary   F = .5   No. of observations = 24
$$MILPER = 2.5 + .004 \times UNIR - + .14 \times SOVPRESS + .31 \times GERM$$
$$(5.41)\ (.71) \qquad\qquad (.62) \qquad\qquad (-.39)$$

Poland   F = 14.6   No. of observations = 24
$$MILPER = 5.0 - .008 \times UNIR - .009 \times SOVPRESS - .29 \times GERM + .22 \times DOM$$
$$(19.67)\ (-2.45) \qquad (-.05) \qquad\qquad (-1.05) \qquad\quad (1.63)$$

Romania   F = 123.08   No. of observations = 25
$$MILPER = 3.73 - .006 \times NMP - .200 \times SOVPRESS + 0.06 \times GERM$$
$$(48.96)\ (-7.05) \qquad (-1.61) \qquad\qquad (.61)$$

Total   F = 5.03   No. of observations = 121
$$MILPER = 4.92 - .01 \times UNIR + .51 \times SOVPRESS^\star + .08 \times GERM + .56 \times DOM$$
$$(16.6)\ (-3.19) \qquad (1.77) \qquad\qquad (.26) \qquad\quad (1.71)$$

Total   F = 59.75   No. of observations = 121
$$MILPER = 3.68 - .009 \times UNIR + .33 \times SOVPRESS + .20 \times GERM + 1.74 \times TIER^\star$$
$$(18.0)\ (-4.11) \qquad (1.84) \qquad\qquad (1.02) \qquad\quad (13.93)$$

Where MILPER = Reported military budgets as a per cent of UNI, UNIR = Utilized National Income in constant prices, SOVPRESS = dummy variable for Soviet pressure to increase military spending after the 1978 Warsaw Pact meeting, GERM = a dummy variable for years following the signing of the treaties between the FRG and the East Europeans in the early 1970s, DOM = a dummy variable for years of or following violent domestic political conflicts, and TIER = a dummy variable for Northern Tier states. T statistics are given in parentheses.

★ Starred variables indicate the null hypothesis could be rejected at the 5 per cent level of significance.

(a) Military budget estimates for the GDR begin in 1962.

The estimate of the co-efficient for TIER was positive and highly significant. Unfortunately, this variable is too crude to differentiate between the hypothesis that the Hungarian and Romanian leaderships prefer to spend less than other NSWP members on the military, that geographical location is an important determinant of military spending, or that the Soviet Union applies more pressure on the Northern Tier countries to spend on the military than on Hungary or Romania. Any or all of these hypotheses could be correct.

Additional Tests

SOVIET PRESSURE

Because of the conflicting results of the two models concerning Soviet pressure, I conducted additional tests of the hypothesis that the Soviet Union has been able to induce NSWP countries to spend more on the military. Assuming that budget changes are a good reflection of total actual expenditure changes, the record of East European military expenditures after the 1978 Warsaw Pact agreement provides a test of the extent of Soviet influence on spending levels in Eastern Europe. The results, recorded in *Table 6*, indicate that, with the exception of the GDR, the East Europeans failed to accelerate the rate of increase in their expenditure levels. The figures for real spending (nominal spending deflated by the price index for non-consumer goods and services) show average annual growth rates of 1 per cent or less for all countries except the GDR, which is considerably lower than the NATO targets of 3 per cent. In real terms these increases were less than half the rate of the previous seven-year period for all countries, again with the exception of the GDR.

Apart from Romania, increases did exceed 3 per cent in nominal terms. However, inflation in Czechoslovakia and Hungary, not to mention Poland, accelerated in these years, so the nominal figures are a poor reflection either of increases in the burden of defence or of absolute increases in spending. Moreover, rates of inflation were so high that policy-makers must have been well aware of them when they were drawing up budgets. These countries appear to have given consumption or debt service a higher priority than military spending, despite Soviet pressure.

SOVIET SUBSIDIES

Reisinger (1983) argues that the Soviet Union has induced the NSWP to increase military spending by applying economic leverage. Soviet economic leverage is determined by benefits bestowed on the East Europeans; the greater the benefits, the higher the percentage of GNP the East Europeans are expected to spend on their militaries.

TABLE 6
Annual Percentage Increases in Reported Military Budgets
(Per cent)

Year	Czechoslovakia		GDR		Hungary		Poland		Romania
	Nominal	Real	Nominal	Real	Nominal	Real	Nominal	Real	Nominal
1972	5.2	5.3	3.3	3.3	0.4	−1.1	4.8	4.4	3.9
1973	5.2	5.1	5.7	5.7	−4.7	−6.4	7.1	5.3	1.6
1974	2.4	2.6	2.7	2.7	0.6	−2.3	9.6	6.3	11.6
1975	9.2	9.3	6.1	5.5	11.3	7.8	8.3	5.9	11.1
1976	3.2	3.0	6.4	6.4	11.8	1.1	8.0	−5.0	8.9
1977	−1.2	−5.9	3.4	3.3	−1.2	−5.5	12.3	−1.2	3.7
1978	3.4	3.2	5.0	5.0	8.0	5.9	3.8	0.1	6.8
1979	2.7	2.4	5.0	5.0	8.1	5.8	7.8	5.6	1.0
1980	7.1	5.1	8.4	0.8	9.3	−5.3	5.0	−1.8	12.2
1981	0.9	−3.8	7.9	7.9	7.7	1.3	12.6	−7.1	1.0
1982	6.3	−1.2	6.2	6.2	6.0	1.4	131.1	1.3	8.0
1983	2.9	3.2	5.8	5.8	8.4	2.6	8.2	−7.3	2.8
1984	4.0	−3.9	7.2	7.2	3.6	− .6	30.8	15.2	1.9
1985			6.7	6.7			23.4		
Average 1972-78	3.9	3.2	4.6	4.6	6.4	2.2	7.7	2.3	6.7
Average 1979-present	4.0	0.3	6.8	5.7	7.2	.9	31.3	1.0	.2

Notes: Increases in real expenditures were calculated by deflating nominal expenditures by the price index for non-consumer goods and services for all countries but the GDR, where an NMP deflator was constructed.

Reisinger tests his hypothesis by comparing the rank order of East European countries by military budgets as a percentage of GNP with their rank order by the value of trade subsidies given them by the Soviet Union, as computed by Marrese and Vanous (1983). He finds the two series are positively correlated. The null hypothesis that they are uncorrelated can be rejected in most cases at the 5 per cent level of significance (*Table 7*).[30]

Reisinger's model appears to be incorrectly specified. He correlates an absolute measure, the dollar value of the subsidy, with a relative indicator, military expenditures as a percentage of GNP. The absolute measure seems unwarranted. If a subsidy as a percentage of national income is large, the leaders of a small country may value it more highly than the leaders of a larger country, even if the subsidy is smaller in absolute terms.

I have rerun Reisinger's hypothesis test, substituting the rank orders of the value of the subsidies as a percentage of GNP for the absolute values.[31] My results are markedly different. In no case can the hypothesis that the two series are uncorrelated be rejected using a 10 per cent level of significance. In most years there seems to be little correlation between the two series. In short, this test provides no support for the hypothesis that the East Europeans increase the share of output devoted to the military in exchange for trade subsidies from the Soviet Union.

TABLE 7
The Relationship Between Military Spending and Soviet Subsidies

	1970	1971	1972	1973	1974	1975	1976	1977	1978
Reisinger's Results									
Tau	.81	.73	.62	.75	.79	.79	.77	.81	.88
P-Value	.014	.031	.064	.026	.017	.018	.023	.014	.006
My Results									
Tau	.47	.47	.33	.20	.20	.33	.33	.33	.47
P-Value	.189	.189	.348	.573	.573	.348	.348	.348	.189

PRESSURE FROM THE MILITARY-INDUSTRIAL COMPLEX

Even though there are many *prima facie* reasons why most members of NSWP leaderships may not wish to increase military spending, one would expect their military establishments to hold an opposing view. The prestige, degree of power and salaries of the military depend in part on the size of the military budget. In the normal course of events one would expect the military to lobby for more money.

The military has several avenues through which it can present its case. First, in 1985 the Minister of Defence or senior commanders had seats on the Politburos in Bulgaria, the GDR, Poland and Romania.[32] The most notable example in this case is Poland where several members of the armed forces, past and present, are in the Politburo or the Council of Ministers, and where General Jaruzelski is First Party Secretary. These individuals are in a position directly to represent the military's interests. It is probable, however, that some of these individuals, such as former Defence Minister Ustinov in the Soviet Union, may merely represent the Party's domination of the military.

A second avenue is through ties to Soviet commanders. Former members of the Polish political and military élites say that Polish officers complained to their Soviet comrades if they believed the domestic political leadership was denying their needs. The Soviet commanders would then complain to the Kremlin, which in turn would apply pressure on the Polish leadership. These statements, however, imply somewhat more voluntarism in both the political systems and the military than is often assumed in Eastern Europe.

Volgyes (1982) argues that heavy industry is an important ally of the military. For Czechoslovakia or Poland, where the arms industry appears to be of some importance, this may be true. For the GDR and Hungary, however, the linkage seems weaker, because the military is probably not an important customer for these groups. As ministers in charge of heavy industries in Bulgaria and the GDR have seats on the Politburos, however, if a military-industrial lobby exists, it is represented on the top decision-making bodies in these countries. In 1985, the country with the highest percentage of UNI devoted to the military, the GDR, had both the Minister of Defence and a minister in charge of a heavy industry in the Politburo. Only in Bulgaria and Poland is the military-industrial complex also so heavily represented.

During the period of analysis (1960-84) the position of the military changed most radically in Poland. In 1981 Defence Minister Wojciech Jaruzelski became Premier, then First Party Secretary; subsequently he initiated a military crackdown, during which many officers took important positions in the Polish government. If General Jaruzelski and his military associates have a greater preference for military spending than their civilian counterparts and if they have successfully imposed these preferences on the government, the rise in military spending should be detectable.

Military spending does not appear to have been affected. The percentage of Polish UNI devoted to the military has risen by only 0.1 percentage point, from an average of 3.61 per cent of UNI during the Gierek era to 3.71 per cent between 1982-84.

Conclusions

This analysis indicates that the primary determinant of military spending levels in the NSWP is available resources—UNI. Although increases in UNI appear to lead to increases in military spending, with the exception of the GDR, the percentage of military spending in UNI has fallen as these countries have become richer.

Neither domestic unrest nor changes in relations with the Federal Republic of Germany appear to have affected military spending levels. The evidence that Soviet pressure since the 1978 Warsaw Pact decision to accelerate spending has led to significant increases in military spending is mixed. The first model indicates that Hungary and the GDR may have responded to this pressure. Budgetary data, however, indicate that all the countries, with the exception of the GDR, slowed rather than accelerated spending after the 1978 decision.

The evidence that the "military-industrial complex" in these countries has been able significantly to affect spending levels is also mixed. In 1985, the GDR, the country with the highest percentage of UNI devoted to the military, had both the Minister of Defence and a minister in charge of a heavy industry on the Politburo. Only in Bulgaria and Poland is the military-industrial complex so heavily represented. Poland, the country where the role of the military in the government has changed most dramatically, has not recorded dramatic increases in military spending in recent years. The share of the military budget in UNI was roughly the same in 1985 as it was in 1981.

Because economic wherewithal is such an important determinant of reported spending levels, future expenditures are likely to follow output growth in these countries, although probably at a slower rate, if the future mirrors the past. Thus economic forecasts should provide a good indication of future military spending.

Current economic forecasts indicate growth will be slow. Hungary, Poland and Romania are all suffering from slow growth, partly due to problems in servicing their hard currency debts. Hungary's and Poland's problems show no signs of abating. Utilized national income fell in Hungary in 1988 and is expected to grow slowly over the next few years, leaving little room for increases in military expenditures. Poland is also unlikely to show rapid rises in either UNI or reported military spending in the immediate future. Romania, on the other hand, has repaid much of its debt, but the resulting costs in terms of reduced investment and privation are likely to mark the country's economy for the next few years.

East Germany and Czechoslovakia suffered a marked deceleration in reported economic growth in 1987, despite the absence of hard currency debt problems. The capital stock of both countries has aged, both face severe problems in marketing manufactured goods, especially machinery on Western markets, and both have had to incur increased ecological and monetary costs in order to maintain energy output, primarily by trying to extract the same amount of coal and lignite as in the past. These factors are likely to continue to reduce economic growth and consequently increases in military spending.

As noted above, with the exception of the East Germans, the East Europeans have displayed a notable lack of enthusiasm for increasing military expenditures. If, in fact, conventional arms control talks with NATO are initiated and are fruitful, these countries may take the opportunity to reduce military spending, accelerating the decline in the share of military spending in utilized national income.

Notes

(*Full details of works cited appear in the Bibliography which follows.*)

1. *The Military Balance, 1983-1984*, pp. 18-23.
2. Lewis, 1982, p. 112; *The Military Balance, 1983-1984*, pp. 18-23.
3. Alton *et al.*, 1980, p. 3.
4. *Zolnierz Wolnosci*, 24 June 1976, p. 3, as cited in Alton, 1982, p. 420.
5. Alton *et al.*, *op. cit.*, 1980, p. 4.
6. "More on Petrovoskiy Speech", Moscow, *Izvestiya*, 27 August 1987, p. 4 as published in FBIS-SOV-87-169, 1 September 1987, p. 2.
7. Checinski, 1974, pp. 17-18.
8. Checinski, 1974, p. 20.
9. Clements, 1985, p. 463.
10. For example, as noted by Alton (1980), some military personnel costs are absorbed by ministries other than the Ministry of Defence. Clements's estimates may also differ from the budgets reported by the East Europeans because his prices were estimated in dollars and then converted to East European currencies via purchasing power parity exchange rates. The dollar price estimates or the purchasing power exchange rates may have been inaccurate.
11. Between 1981 and 1985 the residual ranged from 128 to 96 per cent of the recorded defence budgets and averaged 113 per cent. The residual declined over time as a percentage of the recorded military budgets.
12. *Statisticka rocenka CSSR 1969*, p. 165.

13. Military personnel receive concessionary prices on railroad and bus tickets in these countries.
14. Clements, 1985, p. 457.
15. Alton *et al.*, 1980.
16. Crane, 1987.
17. Alton *et al.*, 1968.
18. Alton *et al.*, 1980, Table 9; Crane, 1987.
19. Personal communication.
20. Checinski, 1974, p. 24.
21. Checinski, *op. cit.*
22. Patrick Moore, 'The Ceausescu Saga', *RAD Background Report*, no. 275, Radio Free Europe Research, 20 December 1978.
23. Simon, 1985, p. 126.
24. Budapest Domestic Television Service, 19:25 Greenwich Mean Time, as cited in *FBIS, EE,* 19 December 1978, p. F4; Bernard Marguerite, *Le Figaro*, 11 December 1978, p. 3.
25. Radio Free Europe Research, *RAD Background Report*, No. 143, 20 December 1985.
26. Mackintosh in Holloway and Sharp, 1984, p. 46.
27. Johnson, Dean and Alexiev, 1982, p. 115.
28. Ciaston, 1969, p. 31.
29. Honecker, 1979, pp. 49-50.
30. Reisinger, 1983, p. 152.
31. Trade subsidy ratios were calculated in constant prices from the same data sources Reisinger used.
32. Radio Free Europe Report, 7 June 1985, Part III.

Bibliography

Alton, Thad, Frank Bandor, Elizabeth M. Bass, and Jaroslav Dusek, *Financial and Fiscal Systems of Czechoslovakia*, United States Arms Control and Disarmament Agency, Washington, DC, 1968.

Alton, Thad, Gregor Lazarcik, Elizabeth M. Bass, and Krzysztof Badach, 'East European Defense Expenditures, 1965-82' in Joint Economic Committee, *East European Economies: Slow Growth in the 1980s*, Vol. 1, Washington, DC, 1985.

Alton, Thad, Gregor Lazarcik, Elizabeth M. Bass, and Wassyl Znayenko, 'East European Defense Expenditures, 1965-78' in Joint Economic Committee, *East European Economic Assessment*, Washington, DC, 1981.

Alton, Thad, Gregor Lazarcik, Elizabeth M. Bass, and Wassyl Znayenko, *Military Expenditures in Eastern Europe, Post World War II to 1979*, OP-63, L.W. International, New York, 1980.

Alton, Thad, Gregor Lazarcik, Elizabeth M. Bass, and Wassyl Znayenko, *Military Expenditures in Eastern Europe, Working Papers*, L.W. International, New York, 1977.

Becker, Abraham S., *The Burden of Soviet Defense: A Political-Economic Essay*, R-2752-AF, The Rand Corporation, Santa Monica October 1981.

----, *Sitting on Bayonets: The Soviet Defense Burden and the Slowdown of Soviet Defense Spending*, JRS-01, The Rand Corporation, Santa Monica, 1985.

Checinski, Michael, *A Comparison of the Polish and Soviet Armaments Decisionmaking Systems*, R-2662-AF, The Rand Corporation, Santa Monica, California, January 1981.

----, 'The Military-Industrial Complex: Planned and Non-Planned Consequences of CMEA Defense Spending', paper for the NATO Economic Colloquium 1982 'The CEMA Five-Year (1981-1985) Plans in a New Perspective: Planned and Non-Planned Economies'.

----, 'The Costs of Armament Production and the Profitability of Armament Exports in Comecon Countries', Research Paper No. 10, The Soviet and East European Research Centre, The Hebrew University of Jerusalem, November 1974.

Ciaston, Stanislaw, *Ekonomiczne Aspekty Obronnosci*, Wydawnictwo Ministerstwa Obrony Narodowej, Warsaw, 1969.

Clements, Thomas W., 'The Costs of Defense in the Warsaw Pact: A Historical Perspective', in Joint Economic Committee, *East European Economies: Slow Growth in the 1980s*, Vol. 1, Washington, DC, 1985.

----, *A Dollar Cost Comparison of NATO Europe and Non-Soviet Warsaw Pact Defence Programs, 1970-76*, (U), DDB-1910-2-78, Defence Intelligence Agency, August 1978, Declassified December 31, 1984.

Crane, Keith, *Military Spending in Eastern Europe*, R-3444-USDP, The Rand Corporation, Santa Monica, 1987.

Czirjak, Laszlo, and George Pall, *Financial and Fiscal Systems of Hungary*, United States Arms Control and Disarmament Agency, Washington, DC, 1968.

Feiwel, George R. and Alexej Wynnczuk, *Recent Developments in the Polish Financial System*, US Arms Control and Disarmament Agency, Washington, DC, 1971.

Gabriel, Richard A., ed., *Fighting Armies: NATO and the Warsaw Pact, A Combat Assessment*, (Greenwood Press, Westport, Connecticut, 1983).

Glowny Urzad Statystyczny, *Rocnik Statystyczny (RS)*, Glowny Urzad Statystyczny, Warsaw, various years.

Herspring, Dale R., 'The Soviet Union and the East European Militaries: The Diminishing Asset', mimeo, 1985.

Herspring, Dale R., and Ivan Volgyes, eds., *Civil-Military Relations in Communist Systems*, (Westview Press, Boulder, Colorado, 1978).

Holesovsky, Vaclav and Claus Wittich, *Financial and Fiscal Systems of Poland*, US Arms Control and Disarmament Agency, Washington, DC, 1968.

Holesovsky, Vaclav, Alexiej Wynnyczuk and Jaroslov Pusch, *Recent Developments in the Czechoslovakia Financial System*, US Arms Control and Disarmament Agency, Washington, DC, 1971.

Holloway, David, and Jane M. O. Sharp, eds., *The Warsaw Pact: Alliance in Transition?*, (Cornell University Press, Ithaca, New York, 1984).

Honecker, Erich, *The German Democratic Republic: Pillar of Peace and Socialism*, (International Publishers, New York, 1979).

The Military Balance, International Institute for Strategic Studies, London, various years.

Johnson, A. Ross, Robert W. Dean, and Alexander Alexiev, *East European Military Establishments: The Warsaw Pact Northern Tier*, (Crane Russak, New York, 1982).

Johnson, A. Ross, 'Soviet-East European Military Relations: An Overview', WN-8957-PR, The Rand Corporation, Santa Monica, CA, January 1975.

Koezponti Statisztikai Hivatal, *Agazati Kapcsolatok Merlege, 1970-1979*, Koezponti Statisztikai Hivatal, Budapest, 1981.

Lewis, William J., *The Warsaw Pact: Arms, Doctrine, and Strategy*, (McGraw-Hill, New York, 1982).

Marer, Paul and George Pall, *Recent Developments in the Hungarian Financial System*, US Arms Control and Disarmament Agency, Washington, DC, 1971.

Marrese, Michael and Jan Vanous, *Soviet Subsidization of Trade with Eastern Europe*, Institute of International Studies, University of California, Berkeley, 1983.

Nimitz, Nancy, *Soviet Expenditures on Scientific Research Since 1928*, The Rand Corporation, Santa Monica, California, RM-3384-PR, January, 1963.

Radio Free Europe, RAD BR/143 20 December 1985 Vol. 10, No. 51.

Reisinger, William M., 'East European Military Expenditures in the 1970s: Collective Good or Bargaining Offer?', *International Organization*, Vol. 37, no. 1, Winter 1983.

Rice, Condoleezza, 'Defence Burden-Sharing', in *The Warsaw Pact: Alliance in Transition?*, David Holloway and Jane M. O. Sharp, eds., (Cornell University Press, Ithaca, New York, 1984).

Simon, Jeffrey, *Warsaw Pact Forces: Problems of Command and Control*, (Westview, Boulder, Colorado, 1985).

Stachow, Leszek K., 'Poland' in *Fighting Armies: NATO and the Warsaw Pact, A Combat Assessment*, Richard A. Gabriel, ed., (Greenwood Press, Westport, Connecticut, 1983).

Statistical Office of the United Nations, Department of Economic and Social Affairs, *A System of National Accounts and Supporting Tables, Studies in Methods*, Series F, No. 2, United Nations, New York, 1953.

Statistical Office of the United Nations, Department of Economic and Social Affairs, *Basic Principles of the System of Balances of the National Economy* Studies in Methods Series F, No. 17, United Nations, New York, 1971.

United Nations—General Assembly, *Report of the Secretary General: Reduction of Military Budgets—Military Expenditures in Standardized Form Reported by States*, A/40/313, 20 May 1985.

Volgyes, Ivan, *The Political Reliability of the Warsaw Pact Armies: The Southern Tier*, Duke University Press, Durham, North Carolina, 1982.

----, 'The Warsaw Treaty Organization in the 1980s: Can Internal Differences be Managed?', 20 April 1982, mimeo.

CHAPTER 5

Comecon and The Warsaw Pact: The Economic Implications of Greater Burden-Sharing

MICHAEL CHECINSKI

In the autumn of 1987, a conference sponsored by the Alerdink Foundation was held in Budapest to discuss East-West relations in the context of the economic and political changes in the USSR. Summarizing the discussion, the participants acknowledged that a way could be found out of the very critical situation the Comecon countries faced by using one of four options:

(1) Continuing the existing policy at home and abroad and strengthening the autarchic line of development, an approach advocated by the so-called fundamentalists, who still represent the view of the large decision-making élites in the Comecon countries. These influential groups believe that the only way to guarantee the economic security of Eastern Europe is to pursue a policy of economic autarchy at home.

(2) To ensure the policy of the first option, the integration process in Comecon has to proceed faster and more rigidly, and must be focused above all on the most modern areas of technology. This should help to create a base independent of the West for restructuring Comecon industry.

(3) Establishing a more open economy, better linked with the world market, and finding ways to expand economic and technological relations with the West. This view was supported by the majority of the Comecon discussants. They argued that this is the only real way to overcome the deep crisis which has confronted the economies of the East European countries since the early 1980s.

(4) Using international institutions such as the United Nations and also international agreements to guarantee the economic security of socialist states.[1]

A careful reading of Mikhail Gorbachev's book[2] will reveal that the Soviet leader is trying to accomplish the third option, while not totally ignoring the other three. Being realistic, Gorbachev understands that, without Western technologies and credits, the USSR and Comecon as a whole will not be able to stop their economic decline. In the search for large-scale economic support from Western countries, the role of the smaller socialist states has been emphasized more persistently than ever before in the recent writings and speeches of Gorbachev and other Soviet leaders.

The policy of the USSR, and of the non-Soviet Warsaw Pact countries, aimed at shattering the Cocom (Western co-ordinating committee controlling the export of strategically sensitive technology to Communist countries) trade barriers and developing more enterprises in hyper-modern, defence-related areas based on joint ventures between Comecon and Western companies, is nothing more than an attempt to implement the third option. *Perestroika* should also modernize the industries of all Comecon members and make for more efficient economic links between them. The problem, however, is that there are 'no ready-made answers . . . and nobody has offered anything cohesive' to solve this knot of conflicts. Gorbachev acknowledges that 'negative accretions in the relations have not been examined with a sufficient degree of frankness, which means that not everything obstructing their development and preventing them from entering a new, contemporary stage has been identified'. The Soviet leader argues that the negative trends within the Comecon countries started only at the end of the 1970s, when 'contacts between leaders of fraternal countries became more and more for show than for real business'. Now, under his leadership, everything must be improved. Towards this end, 'over the past two-and-a-half years the Soviet Union and its friends in the socialist community have jointly carried out great work. . . . The entire range of political, economic and humanitarian relations with the socialist countries is being cast anew'.[3] These are promising words and in many respects echo similar statements made by Nikita Khrushchev. Yet, a simplistic comparison between the two leaders may be misleading, not because they are different people but because the domestic and international situation of the USSR today and its situation in the Khrushchev era are not comparable. Gorbachev has different problems to solve than had Khrushchev thirty years ago. Gorbachev's programme and the role of the NSWP countries can only be correctly assessed in the context of the economic and political situation in which the Soviet Union finds itself.

Perestroika, Brezhnev's *Nedostroika* and the Implications for USSR-NSWP Relations

In the early 1970s, the USSR began an unprecedented military build-up in an attempt to make itself stronger than NATO. The Soviet political leadership, and the military élite exploited technologies borrowed, legally and illegally, from the West and used the great stream of hard currency earnings boosted in those years by rising prices for oil, gas, and gold—products exported in large amounts by the USSR—primarily to build a tremendous arms arsenal. The military acquisition programme absorbed all the resources that were badly needed to modernize the machine-building industry and heavy industry in general. Probably, the Soviet leaders believed that, with the creation of superior military might, they would be free to act throughout the world without any need to worry about Western interests or a military threat from NATO. Being militarily strong, they could divert more resources to the basic and military industries in order to modernize and meet the technological revolution of the coming century. With this in mind, they sacrificed not only light industry, agriculture and the economic infrastructure— the Achilles heel of Soviet policy for decades—but also many industrial branches of crucial importance to the Soviet armed forces.

New military technologies introduced in NATO in the 1980s, in particular the SDI programme, once it had gained support and was in progress, aroused in the Soviet military élite the fear that its expensively-developed armed forces would very quickly become impotent. All this took place at the outset of a new, large-scale Soviet procurement cycle and arms reconstruction programme,[4] a process difficult to stop without endangering important elements of war-readiness and without abandoning very costly investment by the military industry and long-term research projects of the defence-related R&D establishments and design bureaux. Yet, the modernization of the entire military-industrial sector is held back and limited by obstacles inherent in the socio-economic system of the USSR and its East European allies. Despite the tremendous amount of money allocated for R&D in the Comecon countries, their share in the world's knowledge intensive industry is insignificant, as *Table 1* illustrates.

In the years of the greatest military build-up in history, between 1970 and 1980, the socialist countries exported licences to a value of $10 m. less than the developing countries. More alarming was the value of imported licences. In 1980, the developing countries imported licences to a value four times as high as all the socialist countries, including China. These figures are only one indicator of the profound crisis into which Soviet technological development began to sink in the early 1970s. As a result, Brezhnev's grandiose arms policy faced an *impasse*. With entirely new technologies being developed in the West, the USSR started the 1980s with an out-moded industrial base, an under-developed R&D infrastructure and a backward agriculture. The offspring of the over-invested arms sector was a military giant backed by an economy of *nedostroika* (under-accomplishment). This is why Gorbachev started his programme of *perestroika* and the policy of 'new political thinking'. It is, first, a correction of Brezhnev's mistakes and, second, an inevitable compromise between the requirements of long-term defence goals and the urgent need to modernize the Soviet economy, especially the defence industry.

The slogan of military 'sufficiency', first proclaimed in early 1987, is, in fact, a new phrasing of arguments used by Brezhnev in the era of *détente*, such as 'the USSR is spending for defence no more than is absolutely necessary'. In the 1970s, the policy of *détente* was exploited primarily as a cover for extending the *quantity* of Soviet arms. In the new 'sufficiency programmes' the emphasis is on *quality*, not quantity. According to General

TABLE 1
The World Turnover of Licences in the Years 1970-1980
(In $Millions)

Years		1970	1975	1980	Percentage of world total, 1980
Socialist Countries	E	20	50	50	0.4
	I	350	500	650	5.0
Development Countries	E	35	60	60	0.5
	I	761	1600	2600	20.9
Developed Countries	E	3506	7050	12750	99.1
	I	2540	5150	9550	74.1

E = Export, I = Import
Source: Ryszard Rapacki, *Miedzynarodowy handel licencjami* The International
Trade with Licences), *Handel Zagraniczny*, 1987, No. 8, p. 24

V. Varennikov, a first deputy chief of the Soviet General Staff, 'a new period in the development of the Soviet armed forces (has begun) in which the main distinguishing feature will be the growth of quality'.[5] More resources absorbed by the defence sector should now be used for modernizing the economy. 'No doubt', General Shabanov has stated, 'the defence burden is heavily felt by the socialist economy. Disarmament will help to develop our economy faster'.[6] This means that Soviet defence policy and that of the whole Warsaw Pact will be somewhat modified in the coming years, while a new approach will be adopted to keep the Warsaw Pact forces in a state of full war-readiness.

The policy of using the resources allocated for defence for modernizing primarily the arms arsenal could not, therefore, omit the NSWP members. Although in these countries the process of modernizing the arms sector will be quite different from that in the USSR, its implications for their status in the Warsaw Pact and Comecon may be considerable.

The arguments of the NSWP leaders for using defence funding not only to increase the quantity of arms but in a more rational way, were expressed in the early days of Gorbachev's leadership, immediately after Chernenko's funeral and during the meeting of East European leaders in Warsaw at which the extension of the Warsaw Pact Treaty for a further twenty years was approved on 26 April 1985.[7] With the loudly-proclaimed policies of *glasnost* and 'sufficiency', there should be more real freedom for the East European leaders to express their views and requirements. The impact of this increased margin of freedom and of the new Soviet arms strategy on foreign, economic and defence policy will, however, be stronger within Comecon than within the Warsaw Pact for a variety of reasons. To assess correctly the possible development of the entire complex of relations within the Comecon/Warsaw Pact community in the era of *perestroika*, the economic and military-political relations between members of the two institutions must first be examined at greater length.

Mechanical Unity Or Functional Ties?

The Soviet Union and the other members of the Warsaw Pact are bound together by formal (institutional) and political-economic ties. As institutions, the Warsaw Pact and Comecon are primarily instruments of Soviet policy, useful for maintaining the unity of the Soviet bloc. But political-economic links do play some independent role within them. The other members of the Warsaw Pact are interlocked with the Soviet Union out of practical common military-political interest. This is why the Warsaw Pact is a body without a common spirit. There are more conflicting than integrating national factors in relations between Poland and the GDR,[8] between Poland and the USSR, between Hungary and Romania, and between Czechoslovakia and the GDR. Neither West Germany nor the GDR today represent any real threat to the Soviet Union, but both German states remain a serious problem for Poland and Czechoslovakia.

As a military organization, however, the Warsaw Pact plays an important role for the USSR in the process of political negotiations with NATO; it is used as an exchange coin, which could be paid in exchange for the disbandment of NATO.[9] Comecon is used in the same way, to facilitate economic relations between the USSR and the European Community. It is unrealistic, therefore, to speculate whether the Soviet Union will be ready to dissolve either organization in the foreseeable future. On the other hand, there are many indications that most Warsaw Pact and Comecon members would like to be free of both organizations, or at least see their conditions of membership radically changed. In the Warsaw Pact, such views will meet with sharp Soviet disapproval, but in Comecon they will encounter a less rigid Soviet stance.

This difference in the Soviet approach can be attributed to two factors. The Warsaw Pact is concerned with defence and foreign affairs, issues kept firmly under Soviet control and having no direct impact on East European domestic life. Comecon's activities are concerned with the national economies, and everything that happens in this field has far-reaching and immediate implications for the stability of Soviet policy in Eastern Europe, a fact that can no longer be ignored by the Soviet leadership. Furthermore, the members of Comecon have played, and will continue to play, a crucial role in the transfer of Western technology and credits. Eastern Europe's 'integration' with the USSR is guaranteed by the fact that today the members of Comecon are to a great degree dependent on the USSR as a supplier of energy, raw materials and military hardware. The Soviet Union is also the largest customer for industrial goods exported by the East European countries. In contrast to the Warsaw Pact, Comecon is an institutional expression of the very real and deep-seated economic ties between the USSR and its East European neighbours.

A few statistics will illustrate this point. In 1980 the members of Comecon exported 54.1 per cent, and in 1985 60.7 per cent, of their total exports to

other members of the community. The corresponding figures for imports
were 53.3 per cent in 1980 and 61.8 per cent in 1985. In 1985, Western
developed countries accounted for 10.8 per cent of exports and 4.8 per cent
of imports.[10] The Comecon share in the total foreign trade of its individual
members in 1986 was as follows:

Bulgaria	78.7 per cent
Czechoslovakia	74.6 per cent;
Hungary	71.6 per cent;
Poland	71.7 per cent;
the GDR	65.0 per cent;
and the USSR	61.1 per cent.[11]

The volume of foreign trade is not the only indicator of economic interdependence. The structure of Comecon's internal trade is also impressive.
While the NSWP members have for many years been dependent on Soviet oil,
gas and raw materials, since the late 1970s another extremely important trend
has been the growing dependence of the Soviet Union on Comecon's industrial
production. Many important manufactured goods, such as machinery,
chemicals, optical and electronic goods, means of transportation and communications, and a variety of consumer goods (not necessarily of the highest
quality) are exported to the USSR. Between 1976-80 Comecon supplied the
Soviet Union with 26 per cent of its railway carriages, 13 per cent of its buses
and as much as 50 per cent of telephone equipment.[12] In 1986, Comecon
members provided the USSR with 70 per cent of its machinery imports,
which represented 36 per cent of current Soviet investment in equipment,
installations and instruments.[13] Even so backward a country as Bulgaria
exports far more machinery to the USSR than it imports from it. In 1985,
machinery accounted for 21 per cent of all Soviet exports to Bulgaria but 51
per cent of Soviet imports from it.

The corresponding figures for other East European countries are no less
impressive: Czechoslovakia—10 per cent and 60 per cent respectively; the
GDR—12 per cent and 69 per cent; Hungary—13 per cent and 52 per cent;
Poland—12 per cent and 50 per cent; and Romania—19 per cent and 40 per
cent. In the 1988 trade agreement between Poland and the USSR, the Soviet
Union agreed to remain primarily a supplier of energy and other raw materials,
and Poland an exporter of machinery, and communications equipment.[14]

The interdependence of the members of Comecon is, therefore, based on
a solid economic substructure. In addition, the USSR is able to keep a firm
grip on its trading partners through the established currency and price
system. There is no doubt that, without the artificial transferable rouble and
its very backward foreign trade pricing system, the volume of trade between
Comecon's members and the USSR, and their economic interdependence
could decline very rapidly indeed.

ECONOMIC AND POLITICAL IMPLICATIONS OF COMECON'S
PRICE AND CURRENCY SYSTEM

The internal Comecon currency and price system has little in common with
that operating on the world market. For many years East European economists
and senior officials have been calling for its abandonment. The problem first
arose at a session of Comecon in 1971, when the so-called Complex Programme
of Economic Integration was discussed and approved. A firm proposal for introducing a genuine transferable currency was put forward by Poland and
Hungary. Eighteen years later, it is clear that the transferable rouble is incapable
of satisfying even the Soviet Union and is at variance with the elementary needs
of its Comecon partners in their conduct of foreign trade. This was acknowledged by Ivan Ivanov, a deputy chairman of the Soviet Foreign Trade Commission, during the Davos Symposium held in Geneva in February 1988.[15]

Whereas the Soviet Union is thinking in terms of a ten-year period in which
to change the existing Comecon currency system, its allies are pressing for
an immediate change, starting with at least partial convertibility of the East
European currencies, in particular of the artificial transferable rouble. In a
book recently published in Czechoslovakia, the author argues that no real co-
operation or joint venture is possible without a new pricing system. Yet this
view is firmly opposed by Yu. Sychev, a leading Soviet Comecon official[16]
and even Gorbachev and Soviet Prime Minister N. I. Ryzhkov have addressed
the issue. At the 43rd Comecon Session in Moscow on 13-14 October 1987,
there was a dramatic discussion on means of solving the problem. While
Ryzhkov agreeed that the price and currency problem must be resolved, he
argued that it would require a longer, unspecified, period of time. Other East
European leaders showed impatience and pressed for an immediate solution,
if only a partial one. It is worth citing some of the statements made by the
leading participants in this Comecon session:[17]

N. Ryzhkov (Soviet Prime Minster): 'We are supporting the agreement
of the majority to introduce the convertibility of national currencies and of
the transferable rouble. ... We need more time for this, however, and it
will be necessary first to make serious changes in the economic mechanism
and in the principles of co-operation of the (Comecon) countries'.

K. Grosz (Prime Minister of Hungary): 'It is impossible to develop
economic integration without a radical reconstruction of the existing
financial-currency and credit system of co-operation. Even in the short
term it would be possible to achieve decisive progress if even partial
convertibility of the transferable rouble were introduced. ... We really
regret that the section of the decisions of the CMEA session devoted to
currency-financial issues contains so few concrete elements'. (It should
be noted that similar arguments were used in an interview with Miklos
Nemeth, a secretary of the Hungarian Party Central Committee, published
in the Soviet Central Committee weekly paper *Ekonomickeskaya gazeta*.)[18]

Z. Messner (Prime Minister of Poland): 'Commodity prices should be brought closer to world market prices. . . . My suggestion is to have two main proposals discussed at the next session of the Comecon Council—on currency-financial mechanisms and on our trade prices.'

L. Strougal (Prime Minister of Czechoslovakia): 'We should agree that the mechanism of socialist integration has never worked in its entirety, and in many areas integration is only in the first stage of development. This is particularly true of the currency-financial system, the existing methods of which are an obstacle rather than an incentive to international co-operation.'

A special report prepared by a group of Polish economists for General Jaruzelski, which was subsequently chosen for incorporation in the 'Second Stage of Poland's Economic Reforms', contains a clear-cut demand for the replacement of the existing price and currency system by an internationally comparable and acceptable currency.[19] The author of one published analysis concluded that the advantages of a fully convertible currency system clearly outweighed the disadvantages.[20]

Why, therefore, is the Soviet Union so inflexible and unwilling to make radical changes in the existing money and pricing policy? Nobody can ignore the important economic obstacles in the way of immediate change but this is perfectly clear to the other Comecon members. Closer analysis of the consequences of replacing the artificial transferable rouble with a convertible currency will show that Soviet resistance to such changes is not so much economic as political. The transferable rouble, an artificial international currency, makes it very difficult to trade on the world market beyond Soviet control. Tied to this currency as they are, the East European countries *must* trade first and foremost with the USSR and each other, even if they are interested in selling attractive commodities and services elsewhere for transferable roubles or in holding these roubles in the Comecon banks as financial reserves. Another problem is that foreign trade cannot be correctly calculated with the existing currency and price system.[21] Such calculations may look realistic to some Western analysts, but they are totally misleading for East European economists, who know both the advantages and disadvantages of trading with the Soviet Union.[22]

Bound to the artificial transferable rouble, therefore, East Europeans have little option in the matter of their foreign trade and no real opportunity to co-operate with Western companies. But the artificial currency and price system has also begun to be a tremendous obstacle to the Soviet Union's own economic development. Until the mid-1980s, the Soviet leaders believed that they could meet the Western technological challenge by using their traditional methods—the stepped-up theft of foreign technology and concentration of resources and efforts on selected, defence-related areas. Faced with a new and complex technological revolution, they found these methods no longer of value. The only way to keep track of the rapid progress in technology was to integrate their own economy—and, subsequently, the economies of the Comecon countries—with the world market. As a leading Soviet economist put it:

> Our economic mechanism has also turned into a serious brake on genuine socialist integration. It has hindered the organic interweaving of economic interests in the basic units of the economies of the Comecon countries— between worker collectives. Integration has only affected the upper echelons of power, in an administrative-bureaucratic way. It has been of an extremely artificial, superficial nature. We have found ourselves very far from realizing the ideal of socialism—direct contact between the peoples in the socialist commonwealth. And how could such contact be achieved when our previous system fenced us off from our partners in Comecon with currency, administrative, visa and other barriers? . . . The rouble ceased to be an accounting unit in external relations. The Soviet economy was in a state of self-isolation, fenced off from the outside world by currency, structural, organizational-administrative and other barriers. And this at a time when the level of economic and scientific-technical development of a modern state is directly dependent on the level of its participation in international division of labour and its involvement in international co-operation . . . [23]

To illustrate how damaging is the absence of convertible currencies, let us take the most recent experiences with joint enterprises and joint ventures. In 1986, the Soviet and Polish governments signed an agreement to build joint enterprises in both countries. Accordingly, twelve major projects were selected for implementation over two or three years. Following the first experts' report, however, only a single joint enterprise was salvaged, and then only after high-level administrative intervention by the Polish and Soviet governments. This single enterprise, Pollena-Miraculum, will produce cosmetics. The other eleven projects, all of much greater economic importance, have had to be abandoned because of the 'absence of convertible currencies'.[24]

The Soviet Union is thus confronted with one of its most difficult economic problems. Any solution is fraught with unpredictable economic and political consequences for its status as a Superpower and dominant state within Comecon and the Warsaw Pact. If the existing pricing and currency system is not changed, there is no way of arresting, let alone reversing the negative trends in the Comecon countries. If a really convertible currency were introduced in the East European economies, the entire complex of economic relations within Comecon would be revolutionized. It would then be very hard for Comecon to control and manipulate the development of the East European national economies in line with the interests and goals of the Soviet Union. With convertible currency at their disposal, East European countries would prefer to buy modern rather than old technologies, more competitive expertise, better-quality industrial products and cheaper materials by using the bargaining procedures established on the world market in place of the bureaucratic and inflexible Comecon-Soviet trade system.

Moreover, these are not the only consequences that introduction of a freely exchangeable currency would entail. A pricing system comparable with that of the world market and national economies open to trade agreements and international investments would undermine the entire system of the centrally planned and directed socialist economy.[25] In the long term, this could destroy the backbone of Eastern Europe's economic and political relations with the USSR. It would also be in direct conflict with the war-economy policy enforced by the USSR in all the Warsaw Pact states, as a more detailed examination will illustrate.

The Comecon War Economy and Eastern Europe's Future Role

Much has been written about *perestroika* both in the USSR and Eastern Europe but little attention has been paid to its impact on the war-economy policy of the Warsaw Pact members. Perhaps one of the reasons that Western analysts have ignored this phenomenon is the lack of a common approach by NATO and the Warsaw Pact to how to use their entire economic potential for defence purposes. Any common approach is in fact impossible because of the extremely different socio-economic systems of the two blocs. A state-owned and centrally planned national economy creates unique conditions for developing a war economy even in peacetime.

As a component of the broader concept of military doctrine and strategy, a war economy addresses the question of how the entire national economy can supply the requisite combat capability of the country. To achieve this goal, all economic branches and sectors are integrated under the umbrella of the Military Department of Gosplan and are co-ordinated by the Military-Industrial Commission.[26] According to the *Soviet Military Encyclopedia*,

> The war economy is closely tied to the civilian economy; it is based on the economic strength of the state. . . . The basic branches of the national economy exercise a decisive influence on the war economy . . .[27]

The extent of the structural integration of the war and national economies should dispel any notion that the Soviet military élite would resist allocation of resources from the military-industrial sector to the civilian sector, should this be necessary to increase economic growth. For decades all military commanders have been taught that the basis of military might is the economic potential of the state and, in particular, the technological level of industry. As the Soviet Deputy Defence Minister V. Shabanov recently remarked:

> The might, fighting ability, and combat-readiness of the armed forces are determined to a great extent by the qualitative state of the country's economy. One can say that the level of technological equipment of the army and navy, and the outlook for their development, are directly dependent on the economic potential of the state . . .[28]

In the Soviet Union, the development of military technology and the arms acquisition programme are part of a more complex system of war-economic planning that encompasses the entire country and most social and political aspects of its development. It is, therefore, pure fantasy to think that *perestroika* can ignore the scope of military-economic planning. In proof of this thesis, the Soviet military élite's expectations from the Twelfth Five-year Plan, which will be fulfilled in the era of *perestroika* should be noted:

> There will be an enhancement of the degree of readiness of the country for economic mobilization and—should the need arise—for switching the national economy at short notice from a peacetime to a wartime footing, and of its ability to satisfy economically the requirements of the armed forces both in peacetime and time of war.[29]

Obviously, such complex defence planning could not be accomplished by the Soviet armed forces alone, only by the highest political decision-making bodies of the state. This is why Soviet military commanders never doubt that the Politburo and the Defence Council are the most suitable institutions to outline the main directions of the state's defence policy. This tenet is deeply engrained in Soviet military-political thinking, its system and history. It is no coincidence that a Soviet writer recently noted:

> The rich experience of the Council for Labour and Defence (STO, created in April 1920) was exploited in World War II in the work of the State Committee for Defence (GKO) and played a crucial role in achieving victory over fascist Germany and imperialist Japan. Today, according to Paragraph 121 of the Soviet Constitution, *in the country and in the armed forces* the Defence Council created by the Presidium of the Supreme Soviet is in charge and wields great authority on important state, military-political, and economic matters.[30] (*Emphasis added.*)

Perestroika was thus outlined first by the Politburo and the Defence Council and only then declared by Gorbachev to be the 'new political thinking'. This new thinking is nothing less than the product of the Soviet regime's seventy years' experience of how to confront the next technological revolution in the best interests of defence. Gorbachev's policy is, in fact, an adaptation of Mikhail Frunze's concept of the homogenous military-technological-economic policy of the Party that was first developed in the early 1920s.[31]

'The homogenous military-technology policy of the USSR remains in line with the defence direction of its military doctrine', Deputy Defence Minister V. Shabanov has written.[32] This policy is an important sphere of activity of the Soviet Union and its Warsaw Pact allies. It is aimed at co-ordinating all fields of science and technology and employing their achievements to strengthen national defence. This includes the standardization of civilian and military technologies to make the conversion of industry to a war-time footing easier. According to one Soviet view:

> The powerful military-scientific and military-economic potentials that the USSR and the countries of the socialist community have at their disposal enable them successfully to realize a homogenous military-technology

policy and to ensure that the joint armed forces have everything necesary to fulfill their responsible tasks and duties.[33]

Nobody in the Soviet leadership, nor any member of the Warsaw Pact military élite today doubts that the centre of gravity of the military-political competition between NATO and the Warsaw Pact has moved to the area of technology. Gorbachev's willingness to enter into far-reaching political compromises with the US and NATO is dictated by the need to close the technological gap between Comecon and the West. Careful reading of his book will explain why he is convinced that such compromises are unavoidable. Recalling the period immediately after the October Revolution, when a peace treaty with Germany was objected to by many members of the Central Committee, Gorbachev argues:

> Lenin, however, kept calling for peace because he was guided by vital, not immediate, interests, the interests of the working class as a whole, of the Revolution and the future of socialism. To safeguard them, the country needed respite before going ahead. Few realized that at the time. Only later was it easy to say confidently and unambiguously that Lenin was right. And right he was, because he was looking far ahead; he did not put what was transitory above what was essential. The Revolution was saved.[34]

Today, the Soviet Union and the Warsaw Pact in general similarly need a great respite 'to save the Revolution and the future of socialism'. On such crucial issues as technological progress, what is adequate for the Soviet Union must be adequate for its Warsaw Pact allies. Of course, entering into compromises with the 'imperialists' does not necessarily mean allowing them the same concessions. Nonetheless, it is politically difficult to separate Soviet behaviour towards the West from the analogous relations of the East European countries with the capitalist world. Indeed, a socialist community that is more open to the West can demonstrate that the Soviet 'new political thinking' is a serious undertaking, not just a tactical manoeuvre.

As I have already pointed out, it would create for Comecon much better opportunities for a wider flow of credits, technical expertise and technologies from the West. At the same time, such openness could be fraught with dire consequences for the future of the war-economy policy in the USSR and Comecon in general. The integrated Warsaw Pact war economy includes not only the co-ordination of arms production plans but also harmonized R&D programmes, the standardization of civilian technologies and their close orientation on defence needs, prior development of defence-related logistics, common civil-defence projects, and many other Warsaw Pact war-economy programmes. Such common Warsaw Pact-Comecon programmes were easy to carry out when political motives were dominant. This will inevitably change, however, in the era of *perestroika*. Economic calculation and efficiency will have to be given priority, and economic decisions will have to be made on the lower, enterprise level, with the main goal being profit. In addition, political and economic openness towards the West could develop its own dynamic, with unpredictable implications for the internal relations of the Warsaw Pact members.

The Soviet leadership is aware that uncontrolled developments of this sort may occur. This is why it is trying to substitute other forms of control of a formal or informal nature for the margin of freedom surrendered to national governments in Eastern Europe. In the past, three main forms of Soviet control were used: (1) administrative-organizational; (2) economic; and (3) informal (or secret). Over the decades, each of them has undergone manifold evolution.

Immediately after the October Revolution, the USSR developed every form of international relationship—diplomatic, cultural, economic and military—with capitalist states. After World War II, such customary links and institutions were employed in establishing relations between the USSR and the semi-independent countries of Eastern Europe. What distinguished Soviet-East European relations was the Communist Party superstructures which were absent from universally recognized models of international relations. This in itself signifies the blurring of the border between formal and informal inter-state relations, since the Party is formally a political movement representing not the government but a small fraction of society.

Party relations between the Warsaw Pact states, however, are, in a sense, also formal, since they are often covered by specific inter-Party agreements, formalized links between the Parties' bureaucracies, and accepted Communist principles (equal rights, Communist internationalism, etc.). In the pre-war era (1918-43), Communist tasks, principles and obligations were outlined by the Comintern. After World War II, this role was to some extent fulfilled by the Cominform. When that disappeared in the mid-1950s, the split inside the world Communist movement became more profound and irreversible.[35] Never again was the USSR able to establish such a tight Communist international institution under its control. Unity of ideology also disappeared from relations between Moscow and the East European Parties. Step by step the power of Communist arguments was replaced by arguments of power.

Stalin and his successors—including Gorbachev—have never believed in the effectiveness of ideology alone. That is why, immediately after World War II, the Soviet Union planted a large number of 'advisers' in the East European armed forces and security services, and developed a wide range of informal links and means of control. The main beneficiaries of these informal links and channels of influence were the KGB and the Soviet military command. Soviet military planners used the Warsaw Pact institutions established in 1955 in many areas. The KGB primarily used its 'invisible' secret agent network in the most sensitive and important decision-making institutions—Politburos, Party Central Committees, governments, and military commands—of the East European Countries.[36] At critical junctures these informal channels of influence were of even greater importance to the Soviet Union than the formal ones.

Gorbachev is trying to develop another form of control and co-ordination. In the first year of his leadership, he began to arrange regular meetings of all Comecon Central Committee secretaries responsible for specific areas of activity—the economy, ideology, foreign affairs, etc. In addition, meetings between parliamentary commissions, armed forces, chief editors of Party journals and newspapers, and many other Party and government institutions have been arranged.[37]

The major factor determining changes in the system of Soviet control over the East European countries has been the economic situation in the Soviet Union and in Comecon in general. As a rule, it may be stated that growth of Soviet economic strength has been accompanied by a limitation of the role and freedom of action of the other Warsaw Pact states, while Soviet economic weakness has yielded more freedom of action for these countries and has helped to increase their role in Soviet defence and foreign policy. To be more specific, while the economic integration of the Comecon states is, of course, superficial, the 'transmission' of economic trends (negative rather than the positive ones) is multifarious. This phenomenon is a result less of the policies of the national governments than of the very similar socio-economic systems and of the extremely costly war-economy programmes of the Warsaw Pact.

The USSR bears the political and economic responsibility for these developments. At times of success, it was reasonable to emphasize this responsibility. In an era of continuing economic and political troubles, it is easier for the Soviet leaders to divide the tasks and difficulties among its closest friends. For precisely that reason, their role will increase in the coming years, particularly in the economic area but also in the affairs of Comecon and the Warsaw Pact.

This conclusion is challenged by J. V. Oudenaren, an American analyst who argues that:

> ... with the domination of Eastern Europe of declining utility and perhaps rising cost to the Soviet Union, an evolution in Soviet attitude over time cannot be ruled out ... turning away from reliance on non-military achievements to project global influence, Eastern Europe could become increasingly marginal to world politics.[38]

In fact, as I have shown, the Soviet Union is trying to intensify the role of NSWP states in every respect, especially in the area of defence-related industry.

During the post-war years, Eastern Europe became an important supplier and customer of the Soviet military-industrial complex.[39] To illustrate this point, I would cite only the most recent developments in this area. As we can see from *Table 2*, between 1984-86 the NSWP members increased their share in Warsaw Pact production of tanks, armoured vehicles and other ground forces armaments from 12-24 per cent to 18-33 per cent. They are also producing 100 per cent of the towed AA artillery.

Comecon members are also playing an increasing role in developing defence-related technologies. Recent Comecon decisions suggest that *perestroika* will, in certain crucial sectors, be dependent on the activity and role of the NSWP

TABLE 2
Production of Ground Forces Armament: USSR and NSWP
(1984-1986)

	1984			1985			1986		
	USSR	NSWP	*NSWP Total*	USSR	NSWP	*NSWP Total*	USSR	NSWP	*NSWP Total*
Tanks	3200	450	12.3%	3000	700	18.9%	3000	700	18.9%
Other Armoured Fighting Vehicles	3800	1200	24.0%	3500	1200	25.5%	3000	1200	28.6%
Towed Field Artillery	1900	250	11.6%	2000	200	9.0%	1300	150	10.3%
Self-Propelled Field Artillery	1000	300	23.1%	1000	350	25.9%	1000	500	33.3%
Multiple Rocket Launchers	900	100	10.0%	700	100	12.5%	500	75	13.0%
Self-Propelled AA Artillery	50	0	0.0%	100	10	9.0%	100	50	33.0%
Towed AA Artillery	0	225	100.0%	0	225	100.0%	0	200	100.0%

Calculated from: *Soviet Military Power 1987*, US Department of Defence, Washington DC, March 1987, p. 122.

states. The USSR will try to alleviate this dependence by using Soviet institutions and maintaining a special strategy, a development which can be illustrated by two examples.

According to Comecon plans, ninety-three major new technologies are to be developed in the next 10-15 years.[40] The Soviet Union has reserved the right to co-ordinate and supervise all these projects irrespective of its own share in the expected results. As noted above, the USSR is now pressing its East European allies to open themselves up economically to the West. But 'this openness has to be conducted on the basis of a harmonized strategy', argues Yu. S. Shiryaev, director of the International Institute of Economic Problems of the World Socialist System. Indeed, he demands full co-ordination of the foreign trade policies of Comecon members:

> One of the most important goals of the practical realization of the scientific-technical concepts is to overcome the technological barrier on the world market. It is, therefore, important not only to establish priorities clearly from the point of view of meeting our own needs of up-to-date goods and services but also to conduct *a selective policy, choosing the most likely points for a breakthrough on the markets for high-technology goods.* This is in fact the external orientation of Comecon's Complex Plan for Scientific and Technological Progress. At the same time, the co-ordination of import policies requires very serious attention.

In the absence of sufficient co-ordination of the operations of Comecon states on markets of third countries, separate and disparate contacts with them have objectively become an element in the inhibition of the development of the international socialist division of labour. The large debts accumulated by a number of the fraternal countries have prompted giving preference to those foreign economic operations that make it possible to earn the freely convertible currency needed to service debts. As a result, many kinds of goods vitally needed by community partners have been withdrawn from the Comecon international market.

To this must be added *the adverse effect of uncoordinated purchases of equipment and licences from different Western firms.* This has resulted in a secondary (imported) parallelism linked with puchases of licences and equipment to meet identical social needs. Apart from dissipating resources, this has given birth to a more important problem. Some branches and industries in the fraternal countries that are using foreign equipment have diverged from one another in technological concepts. This, in turn, has created additional obstacles to the organization of mutually profitable co-operation and specialization of production.[41] (*Emphasis added.*)

This is a strategy not necessarily oriented towards long-term peaceful co-operation with the West. It emphasizes the needs of an economy directed towards traditional war-planning.[42] Such a strategy may well meet with stiff resistance from the East European partners in the years ahead. In the next decade, the Soviet leadership will be confronted with the problem of how to punish allies who are trying to improve their own economies by exploiting every opportunity to open up trade relations with the West. It will find the task even more difficult if two or three such allies co-ordinate their activities without Soviet approval and outside Comecon control. If the USSR closes its eyes to such developments, it may lose control over many aspects of East European defence. Should this prognosis be correct, the Soviet leaders may be faced in the years to come with many unpredicted problems in their relations with their Warsaw Pact partners that will run counter to the defence and economic planning that has been the central focus of Soviet policy for forty years.

Notes

1. Pawel Bozyk, *Zagrozone bezpieczenstwo ekonomiczne* (Endangered Economic Security), *Polityka*, No. 49, 5 December 1987, pp. 17-18.
2. Mikhail Gorbachev, *Perestroika, New Thinking for our Country and the World* (Harper and Row, New York, 1987); In fact, Gorbachev is expressing in a more propagandistic way the approach emphasized in the recently approved Programme of the CPSU. See: *Partiinaya zhizhn'*, 1986, No. 6-7, pp. 133-134.
3. Gorbachev, *op. cit.*, pp. 49, 164-165.
4. *Soviet Military Power, 1987*, US Department of Defence, Washington, DC, 1987.
5. Army General V. Varennikov, '*Na strazhe mira i bezopasnosti narodov*' (Safeguarding Peace and Security of Nations), *Partiinaya zhizn'*, 1987, No. 5, p. 12.
6. Army General V. Shabanov, *Shchit Rodiny* (The Shield of the Fatherland), *Ekonomicheskaya Gazete*, No. 8, February 1988, p. 18.
7. Vladimir V. Kusin, Gorbachev and Eastern Europe, *Problems of Communism*, January-February 1986, Vol. XXXV, pp. 41-42.

8. We should mention not only the well-known conflicts between Romania and Hungary on the issue of the Hungarian minority living in Romania, but also the subtle disapproval about western Poland's postwar borders recently expressed by GDR and picked up immediately by the West German newspapers. *Cf.* Werner Kahl, *In Usedom zeigt sich die Grenze Polens, Die Welt*, No. 147, 29 June 1987, p. 4.

9. *Cf.* Programme of the CPSU, *Partiinaya zhizhn*, No. 6-7, 1986, p. 134.

10. *Vneshnyaya torgovlya*, 1987, No. 11, p. 23.

11. *Ekonomicheskoe sotrudnichestvo stran-chlenov SEV*, 1987, No. 11, p. 107.

12. *Dengi i kredit*, 1984, No. 11, p. 5.

13. *Planovoe khozyaistvo*, 1988, No. 1, p. 98.

14. *Zycie Gospodarcze*, No. 51-52, 20-27 December 1987, p. 2; *Voprosy ekonomiki*, 1985, No. 7, p. 140.

15. *Die Welt*, 15 February 1988, p. 9; also *cf.* G. Rybalko, *'Konvertabelnost' rublya v povestke dyna'* (The Convertibility of the Rouble on the Day Schedule), *Ekonomicheskaya gazeta*, No. 9, February 1988, p. 20.

16. *Cf.* the book review in: *Voprosy ekonomiki*, 1987, No. 8, pp. 131-132 by A. Shurkalin and Yu. Sychev of the Czechoslovak book of J. Sereghova, *Intenzifikace prumyslove soucinnosti v podminkach socialisticke integrace a vedeckotechnickeho rozvoje*, Nakladelstvi Ceskoslovenske akademie ved. Prague, 1985.

17. *Ekonomicheskoe sotrudnichestvo stran-chlenov SEV*, 1988, No. 1.

18. *Ekonomicheskaya gazeta*, No. 6, February 1988, p. 21.

19. *Handel Zagraniczny*, No. 9-10, 1987, pp. 3-21.

20. Jacek Morag, *'Wymienialnosc waluty w gospodarce socjalistycznej'* (The Convertibility of the Currencies in a Socialist Economy), *Handel Zagraniczny* No. 8, 1987, p. 12.

21. In May 1987 a special session was organized by the Soviet Main Statistical Administration to prepare a methodological basis to make possible a comparison of statistical data published by the Comecon members, with 373 experts, representatives of 44 ministries and main state committees and 175 research institutes participating. The discussants agreed that the main obstacle to making economic indicators comparable is the lack of any sensible price system in each of the Comecon states. *Vestnik Statistiki*, 1987, No. 9, pp. 76-79.

22. In this context we should mention particularly the discussion related to the estimates of the Soviet subsidization of the East European trade made by Michael Marrese & Jan Vanous, *Soviet Subsidization of Trade with Eastern Europe. A Soviet Perspective*, IIS, University of California, Berkeley, 1983. It is worth noting that *after* Marrese-Vanous's study was published also Soviet analysts discovered that their Comecon partners were in the past subsidized by the USSR, but only by about $50 billion, still less by about $30 billion than calculated by the American experts. *Cf.* A. Burov, *Ekonomicheskoe sotrudnichestvo SSSR so stranami sotsialisma* (Economic Co-operation of the USSR with the Socialist Countries), *Mezhdunarodnye otnosheniya*, Moscow, 1987, p. 72; *Cf.* also L. G. Abramov, *SEV. Kapitalyne vlozheniya-perspektivnaya sfera sotrudnichestva* (CMEA. Capital Investments—A Perspective Area of Co-operation), Nauka, Moscow, 1988, pp. 108-112.

23. Professor V. Dashichev, (Department Director of IEMSS-Economic Institute of the World Socialist System), *'Prioritet razuma'* (The Priority of Reason), *Moskovskaya Pravda*, 16 July 1987, pp. 2-3. It is worth noting that parts of this article were translated into Polish and published under the headline 'The Soviet Economy Cannot Separate Itself from the World', *Polityka*, No. 32, 8 August 1987, p. 12.

24. Jerzy Baczynski, *'Porazka optymistyczna'* (An Optimistic Failure), *Polityka*, Eksport-Import, No. 4 (231), February 1988, p. 17.

25. Morag, *op. cit.*

26. Michael Checinski, *A Comparison of the Polish and Soviet Armaments Decision-making Systems*, Rand, R-2662-AF, Santa Monica, CA, January 1981. In the last two years many Soviet military industrialists have moved to positions in the top economic leadership of the country. The career of Yurii Maslyukov, who became recently Chairman of the USSR Gosplan and a Politburo Candidate Member, is particularly noteworthy. Many believe that such personnel changes are made to capitalize on the experience of the defence industrialists for improving management in non-military branches of the economy. Yet, it may also be

96 MICHAEL CHECINSKI

an indicator that the Soviet leaders want to improve the co-ordination between the war-economy and overall economic planning in general. *Cf.* Viktor Yasmann, 'The New Gosplan Chairman and the Military Industrial Complex'. *Radio Liberty Research*, RL 97/88, 8 March 1988.

27. *Soviet Military Encyclopedia*, Vol. 8 Moscow 1980, pp. 567-569.

28. Shabanov, *op. cit.*

29. First Rank Cpt. A. Plekhov, *'Politika KPSS v oblasti oborony'* (The Defence Policies of the CPSU), *Kommunist Vooruzhonnykh Sil*, 1986, No. 20, p. 18. *Cf.* also: A. I. Sorokin (ed.), *Sovetskie Vooruzhennye Sily v usloviyakh razvitogo sotsialisma* (The Soviet Armed Forces under Conditions of Developed Socialism), Nauka, Moscow, 1985, p. 50.

30. Col. V. N. Maltsev, *'Voennaya deyatelnost' Soveta Truda i Oborony vo glave s V. I. Leninom'* (The Military Activity of the STO Under the Leadership of V. I. Lenin). *Voenno-istoricheskiy zhurnal*, 1980, No. 2, p. 18.

31. Michael Checinski, 'The Economics of Defence in the USSR', *Survey*, Spring 1985, Vol. 29, No. 1 (124), pp. 29-59.

32. Shabanov, *op. cit.*

33. Sorokin, *op. cit.*, p. 225.

34. Gorbachev, *op. cit.* We should also mention the very pertinent remarks of W. E. Odom, about the reasons for reducing in the mid-1920s the Red Army to about half a million soldiers. '... A foreign observer might have concluded that the Soviet regime was quietly disarming itself. ... In reality the Bolsheviks were taking a short-term risk in order to have a large, modern military force in the future...' William E. Odom, 'Soviet Force Posture: Dilemmas and Directions', *Problems of Communism*, July-August 1985, Vol. XXXIV, p. 3.

35. V. Zagladin, *'Kommunistecheskoe dvizhenie v sovremennom mire'* (The Communist Movement in the Modern World), *Kommunist Vooruzhonnykh Sil*, 1987, No. 1.

36. Michael Checinski, *'Moskau informelt die Einflussung und Kontrolle in Ost Europa'*, *Osteuropa*, 1988, No. 7.

37. *Cf.*, for example, the information about the meeting of CC Party secretaries for economic affairs of the Comecon countries. *Vneshnaia Torgovlia*, 1987, No. 11, pp. 1-2, and the meeting of the CC Party secretaries for ideological affairs, held in mid-March 1988 in Ulan Bator, Mongolia.

38. John Van Oudenaren, *The Soviet Union and Eastern Europe. Options for the 1980s and Beyond*, Rand, Santa Monica, Ca, R-3136-AF, March 1984, pp. 83-90.

39. Michael Checinski, 'The Comecon/WTO and the Polish and Czechoslovak Military-Industrial Complex', *Osteuropa-Wirtschaft*, 1988, No. 1.

40. Professor Yu. A. Konstantinov, *'Finansirovanie Kompleksnoi programmy nauchnotekhnicheskogo progressa stran-chlenov SEV* (Financing of the Integrated Program for Scientific-Technological Progress of the CMEA Members), *Dengi i kredit*, 1987, No. 5, p. 26.

41. Yu. Shiryaev, *'Strany SEV: konstruktivnyi podkhod k problemam razvitia mirokhoziaistvennykh sviaze'* (The CMEA Countries: A Constructive Approach to the Problems of the Development of World Economic Ties), *Mirovaya ekonomika i miezhdunarodyne otnosheniya*, 1987, No. 11, pp. 33-34.

42. This is only one aspect of a more complex war-economic programme outlined by Moscow for the Comecon countries. The importance of this programme for Soviet defence planning is explained by Marshal Ogarkov. He argues that the Soviet '... military doctrine fully takes into account the socio-political, economic and military capabilities of the countries of the socialist community...' Marshal N. V. Ogarkov, *Istoriya uchit bditelnosti* (History Teaches Vigilance), Voenizdat, Moscow 1985, p. 76.

SECTION 4
The New Technologies as
Solutions to the Problems
of the 1990s

IN spite of enjoying more than twice the national product of the members of the Warsaw Pact, the Atlantic Alliance possesses a collection of forces that are quantitively inferior, qualitatively uneven and have only a limited ability to rearm, reinforce, support or even communicate with one another. One of the methods by which this situation could be redressed and savings made might be to introduce new technologies.

The economics of the modern battlefield are all important. Pyrrhus pointed to the principle after the battle of Asculum: 'One more victory and we are lost'. Pyrrhic defence is not winning directly but indirectly, exacting a disproportionately high price for any concession, forcing an adversary to pay more for countering a system than its deployment costs. It avails a country nothing to destroy an inexpensive unmanned vehicle for the expenditure of several mobile surface to air missiles, a fact that remains true even in that rare condition called 'air supremacy'. If the cost of deploying the new systems can be contained, they might become the most significant expression of a Pyrrhic defence.

Unfortunately, as is argued in the essay that follows, the cost of such a defence is likely to be expensive both in terms of resources and political credibility. If, as James Sherr argues, their deployment would seriously deny the Warsaw Pact its present advantage in manpower and standardization of weapons, the introduction of the new technologies would be well worth considering. It would not, of course, make asymmetrical conventional arms cuts acceptable to the Soviet Union. Choices are the stuff of politics, but politicians are always reluctant to make them. If I may misquote Leo Labedz 'it is a melancholy thought that whether the omelette is national or international. . . the broken eggs will necessarily loom large'.

CHAPTER 6

The Quest for Technological Submission: Discriminate Deterrence as a Case Study of NATO's Response

CHRISTOPHER COKER

It was Raymond Aron who observed in *The Century of Total War* that conflicts in the twentieth century differed from those in the past because of 'the element of technical surprise'. Ever since 1949 technology has offered an elusive formula for successful deterrence, a formula that has special appeal for an alliance which, by choice rather than necessity, has made minimum use of its greater manpower and maximum use of nuclear arms.

For thirty years NATO has responded to a perceived conventional imbalance (whether real or hypothetical, strategically significant or not), by modifying or updating its nuclear armoury. The introduction of battlefield nuclear weapons helped to make up for deficiencies in conventional force strengths when it became clear that NATO could not, or would not, meet the original force goals agreed in 1952. The deployment of theatre nuclear forces in 1957 made possible the policy of flexible response, which made nuclear deterrence more credible at a time of reduced defence spending by the NATO allies.

Today we are witnessing a renewed interest in the new conventional technologies, an interest made more pressing by the agreement in December 1987 to eliminate all intermediate nuclear weapons within the next five years. This treaty has served to concentrate the minds of NATO's leaders on conventional defence for the first time since the early 1960s when RAND strategists such as William Kaufmann and Alain Enthoven argued for drawing a line (or firebreak) between nuclear and conventional forces, with the emphasis on increased conventional spending.[1]

In 1988, the findings of a fifteen-month commission co-chaired by Fred Iklé, the former Under-secretary of Defence for Policy Affairs, gave a stark warning of the perils which lay ahead if the Alliance failed to spend enough to deter a conventional Soviet attack. Perhaps, the most significant part of the report (entitled *Discriminate Deterrence: report of the Commission on Integrated Long-Term Strategy*) was the conclusion that the US army depended heavily

on its ability to counterattack; to thrust deep into Eastern Europe in response
to an invasion, a policy described as 'discriminate deterrence'.

The extended range and accuracy of the new smart weapons, especially
stealth aircraft or drones, Iklé argued, could capitalize on the Soviet army's
major vulnerability in Eastern Europe: the central role assigned to radar-
based air defences. Stealth aircraft assigned to destroy targets behind enemy
lines could 'take out' four times the number of units vulnerable in an invading
force. Deep-strike attacks in the West could be countered by tactical ballistic
missile defences, endo-atmospheric interceptors and airborne optical sensors.
It was a persuasive, even seductive, vision of the twenty-first century battlefield in which technology would count more than men, technique more
than tactics.

The furore to which the report gave rise in Europe centred largely not on
the conventional force argument, but the fact that the same tactics and
thinking were considered vital for the use of nuclear weapons as well. 'The
Alliance should threaten to use nuclear weapons not as a link to a wider and
more devastating war—although the risk of further escalation should still be
there—but mainly as an instrument for denying success to the invading
Soviet forces'.[2]

In a widely-read rejoinder, Michael Howard, Karl Kaiser and François
de Rose argued that such advice could easily be misunderstood, undermining
in the process the most important basis of the Alliance: the community of
risk. Unless there was a perception that nuclear weapons would not be used
selectively but indiscriminately, as a weapon of last resort not first, Europe
could become a zone of limited nuclear war.[3] It was on this understanding
that, at the Werkünde conference in Munich, West German delegates asked
the US Secretary of Defence, Frank Carlucci, to dissociate the US government
from the report and its findings. For the Germans, as for most other European
observers, the report provided what one French official described as 'further
evidence of the unreliability of American thinking on European defence'.[4]

Even in their reply to their numerous critics, Iklé and his colleagues tended
to address themselves to the nuclear issue: to the fear that deterrence based
on nuclear war in Europe alone would not only bring about a European
apocalypse but also erode European confidence in NATO's capacity to
prevent war from breaking out in the first place. An article written by Albert
Wohlstetter, to which Henry Kissinger, Fred Iklé and Zbigniew Brzezinski
added their names, argued that, far from undermining European confidence,
discriminate deterrence should reassure them. The report, after all, not only
advocated maintaining the US guarantee against a nuclear attack on any
European ally (in contrast to those who advocated 'no first use') but also
against overwhelming conventional attacks. Towards this end, they asked for
modernized nuclear forces to be based in Europe (including American intercontinental nuclear forces).[5]

In truth Wohlstetter and his colleagues were rather naïve in thinking that the Europeans would ever be reassured by an agreement 'for the discriminate, effective use of intercontinental as well as theatre-based forces against military targets in the Soviet Union as well as Eastern Europe'. One of the reasons why Europe rejected President Carter's offer of holding part of the US ICBM force in reserve as an 'intermediate' force, an alternative to deploying cruise and Pershing 2 was its belief that the proposal would decouple the US and Western Europe. It was also signally reluctant to accept sixty B-52 bombers armed with air-launched cruise missiles as part of post-INF modernization. The Europeans could never accept Wohlstetter's conclusion that the main reason they had attacked the report was because of deeply-ingrained habits of thought, in particular the habit of equating the use of 'strategic forces' with assured mutual destruction. Their real concern was that in a Europe without intermediate or modernized short-range systems, US intercontinental forces would never be used.

Asking too many questions about the US guarantee merely unnerves the questioner. What is of real concern to Europe is the use of conventional forces recommended in the report, a use which long predates the publication of *Discriminate Deterrence*, and with it the publicity which followed. With its habitual dislike of living with non-war fighting doctrines, a 'defeatist' belief in an escalation process, a bluff which might one day be called, the United States began as early as the late 1970s to look with interest on new advances in the micro-miniaturization of sensor and guidance systems which appeared to afford an unprecedented opportunity to eliminate hard, dispersed targets at long distances behind enemy lines. By the mid-1980s precision-guided missiles offered NATO a chance to use conventional weapons for many of the missions once assigned to nuclear systems.

The debate about discriminate deterrence is important, therefore, not because of the doctrine itself (which was rapidly dismissed by the Pentagon) but because it was a phase, albeit the most recent, in a debate about conventional deterrence which began after 1980 when Bernard Rogers, then SACEUR, hoped that the new technologies might make the modernization of theatre nuclear forces more acceptable to European public opinion. He was supported in his case by the former US Defence Secretary, Caspar Weinberger, whose main interest in office was to encourage original thinking about defence, and whose residual instinct was to see technology as the answer to most of NATO's problems.

Most Europeans have remained highly sceptical—and many highly concerned—about where the debate is leading. Michael Howard and his co-authors chose to take issue with *Discriminate Deterrence* not only for its emphasis on the possibility of fighting a nuclear war but even more for its proposition that 'the Alliance could defeat the Soviet army, or at least fight to a standstill, without having to reach for nuclear weapons, a proposition they found to be not only impossible (in terms of resource allocation) but also unacceptable (in terms of European public opinion).

For its critics *Discriminate Deterrence* was far more dangerous for its recommendations on Europe's conventional defence than its advice on the use of nuclear weapons. Europe finds the use of new technologies for conventional defence undesirable for six reasons which deserve discussion:

(1) as a pretext for the United States to avoid confronting the cost of direct (as opposed to indirect) defence;

(2) as yet another example of America's elusive quest for technological supremacy;

(3) as a threat to the conventional arms talks on which Europe now relies to 'offset' the perceived damage of the INF Treaty;

(4) as a way of encouraging the Europeans to spend more on their own defence (and thereby to feel more confident about the inevitable reduction of the American commitment to Europe);

(5) as a stage on the road to conventional deterrence;

(6) last, but not least, as a provocation to a peace movement which, though dormant, is not yet dead, a movement which is unlikely to sit out the next decade in a mood of subdued passivity.

1. Discriminate Deterrence as a Pretext;

A pretext for not paying the real price of conventional defence. The primary interest of those—particularly in the United States—who advocate introducing the new technologies seems to be the attrition of Soviet forces not yet capable of reaching the front. The assumption is that more effective conventional forces might replace battlefield nuclear weapons while at the same time offsetting some of the deficiencies in conventional firepower which have been apparent for years. Unfortunately, such thinking gratuitously ignores the reality of the present problem: that NATO has neither the political will nor the resources to redress its front line deficiencies while simultaneously addressing the need to build up its conventional reserves. If NATO cannot hold the first echelon attack, any 'follow on' strategy would cease to have much meaning. As Britain's former Minister for Procurement, Geoffrey Pattie, remarked in 1984 'there is little merit in annihilating the Soviet second echelon at the risk of bringing NATO's early defeat by the first'.[6]

Fearful of being checked in an initial attack, the Soviet military seems to have significantly downgraded the strategic importance of its reserves, focusing instead on Operational Manoeuvre Groups (OMGs), some twenty or thirty in number, powerful enough to punch a hole through NATO's front line. Unlike the West the Soviet Union does not seem to have been deterred by the formula that an attacking side needs a numerical superiority of 3:1, any more than the Germans were in the early years of the Second World War. *Blitzkrieg*, after all, was designed to address a distinct *inferiority* of forces; wars were meant to be won off the battlefield, as well as on it; to represent short, sharp engagements, not prolonged confrontations in which superior manpower would eventually tell. According to some Soviet sources it will only be necessary to prevail in the opening days of a conflict to paralyse NATO altogther, or render it incapable of a concerted response.

It is worth pointing out that the Alliance's conventional front line weaknesses have not been corrected. Fifty per cent of NATO brigades are out of their Corps area, or stationed more than 100km from the front line. The British Army of the Rhine has only 60 per cent of the ammunition it needs. Belgium's decision not to purchase the Patriot anti-aircraft system has highlighted a disastrous short-fall in the Central Region.

I will not dwell on the failure to keep stockpiles at adequate levels—a failure which prompted the US Congress to set a ceiling on the size of the 7th Army in 1984. Spare-part shortages are critical in the 7th Army as well. The 1989 round of cuts forced on the Pentagon by the need to reduce America's budget deficit has fallen largely on ammunition stocks, equipment and maintenance—all low profile items with little political cost. The US military is now on the brink of four years of blood-letting that will inevitably lead to a fundamental re-structuring of its armed forces.

The M60 tank has insufficient spare parts for its fire control system. Replacement parts for the AH 64 helicopter are still not stocked at the direct maintenance level, which means that it could become in wartime not a combat craft at all, but a highly expensive observation platform. Many combat units are still critically short of officers and NCOs. Despite a huge (and unsustainable) military build-up, the 7th Army has fewer units ready for combat than it had in 1979. The same is also true of the USAF. The number of airforce units considered fully or substantially combat-ready has actually declined by 15 per cent.

In short, the Alliance needs to ask itself whether a high priority should be given to discriminate deterrence, or whether the introduction of the new technology is worth the expense. It would surely be wiser to strengthen NATO's direct defences so that it can hold out against a reinforced attack rather than strengthen its indirect defences to prevent the second echelon from ever reaching the front. In the best of all possible worlds it would be desirable, of course, to follow the Panglossian principle of doing both. It would be highly desirable not only to destroy tanks on the battlefield but also before they reached it. As always, the economics of defence will probably force the Alliance to make a choice.

It is all very well relying on 'smart weapons' but technology is no substitute for smart thinking. As the Centre for Security and International Studies' (CSIS) advice to the next President concluded, 'your basic theme in approaching our strategic thinking is to think smart not richer'.[7]

2. Discriminate Deterrence as Revisitation

Revisiting the past, rather than looking to the future, keeping alive what one of NATO's most persistent critics has called its eternal quest for 'technological submission'[8]—the perpetual hope of using gold-plated, essentially 'baroque' technology to reduce increasing manpower requirements. It needs to be asked whether many of the new technologies would actually work. What we do know is that many of the dreams represent a dangerous form of escapism.

Superficially, of course, one can see why discriminate deterrence is attractive. At the moment, alas, the practical application of the concept is many years from being realized. A Congressional study five years ago discovered grave faults in the communications equipment of the 7th Army, on which its field commanders would have to rely to identify putative breakthrough points. It also found grave faults in its wartime intelligence units (CEWI) on which they would rely to determine movements by the second echelon forces.[9]

Even with an indirect defence system such as Assault Breaker—which is designed to support a non-dynamic defence against a first echelon attack— it is highly questionable whether the technological advantages the West enjoys would prevail on the day. Assault Breaker, it must be remembered, is designed to destroy Soviet tanks 300km behind enemy lines. Not only would its operators have to calibrate the target (in the face of sophisticated electronic counter-measures) but all targeting information would have to be passed to a delivery system which would release its submunitions once it had been launched, submunitions which would have to independently search and destroy individual tank units.

It is perhaps worth recalling that by the end of 1983, five failures in the first sixteen Pershing 2 flights were identified as faults in design.[10] The electronic components of the Patriot ground-to-air missile were so failure-prone that at one point the US army decided to stop testing it. In August 1984 the Department of Defence announced that because of 'systemic deficiencies' in design it intended suspending payments to the Hughes Aircraft Company for three of the military's foremost missile systems, namely the Maverick air-to-ground, TOW anti-tank and Phoenix air-to-air missiles. As a result of a micro-chip scare the following month, a third of the US Sparrow air-to-air missiles were found to be defective.

The quest for technological submission, therefore, is likely to remain as unrewarding as the quest for the Holy Grail. To a jaundiced European eye, the US is once again engaged in the wrong debate. It was Jorge Luis Borges who wrote that 'the greatest magician would be he who could cast such a spell upon himself as to believe the reality of his own creations'. It is a sobering thought which should prompt NATO to think very clearly before putting its trust entirely in the new technologies.

3. Discriminate Deterrence as a Threat to the Conventional Arms Talks

One of the most serious of Europe's concerns. However much the Alliance were to spend between now and the late 1990s on conventional forces, it would run up against the paradox that an effective denial strategy might actually lower the nuclear threshold for the Soviet Union and force it not only to reconsider its own policy of no first use, but also the desirability of asymmetrical conventional defence cuts.

While there seems little doubt that the Soviet Union would prefer to prevail without resorting to nuclear weapons, prevail it must. Until recently it could be reasonably confident that at most 10 per cent and probably less than 5 per cent of its tanks would be destroyed by air attack, a strikingly small number.[11] Now some Western analysts believe that the Alliance has it within its grasp to reduce the tank to its traditional role as an infantry support vehicle; to offset the Soviet Union's advantage in terms of numbers; to arrest a *blitzkrieg* attack, if not reverse it. The report of the ESECS study group in April 1983 concluded that NATO could eliminate 60 per cent of a Soviet armoured division (the Soviet military's own criterion of 'annihilation') by conventional means alone, using submunitions. At the moment it could only achieve such a strike rate by launching 2,200 air sorties, or twenty-five missions (using aircraft with 10kt nuclear free fall bombs). Faced with such a threat, the Russians might well feel constrained to carry out a pre-emptive nuclear (or chemical) strike merely to restore the conditions that would allow a classic conventional conflict to be played to a successful conclusion. As a Soviet defence journal recently complained, the US was trying to fight 'a conventional war which was no longer conventional'. The potential lethality of the new conventional missiles 'approached the destructive power of low yield weapons', and thus effectively threatened to erode the threshold between nuclear and conventional battlefield systems.[12]

Analysts of Soviet military thinking have discovered a deep dislike of the integrated battlefield dreamed of by Iklé and his colleagues, the ultimate computerized war. As Colonel Volobyev recently commented, computers do not solve problems; they create them because they deny generals time to think. Most worrying of all for those who take Soviet military writings as reflecting genuine concerns, not manufactured ones, is the growing insistence that the Soviet armed forces must prepare for a surprise attack, for fighting the kind of defensive war which the USSR was ill-equipped to fight in 1941-43.

Whether the generals are likely to get their message across in the Kremlin is an open question. Even if they fail, the adoption of a doctrine similar in its essentials to discriminate deterrence might render it impossible for the Soviet Union to fall back on what some analysts have identified as a major shift in Soviet military doctrine from a reliance on 'absolute security' towards a doctrine of 'military sufficiency'. Even if the doctrine has yet to

be confirmed, verified and tested, the attempt to achieve technological submission would certainly threaten the conventional 'superiority' which, in a
moment of rare frankness, a recent Warsaw Pact communiqué acknowledged
to be the only valid reason for keeping defence spending within limits.[13] At
a time when NATO is about to embark on conventional force reduction talks
in earnest, most Europeans would hardly consider the time is right for
reformulating conventional strategies as radically as Iklé's study suggests.
Whether one takes an upbeat or more sanguine view of the Soviet Union
under Gorbachev, the view is one that argues against a conventional arms race.

4. Discriminate Deterrence as a Way of Rediscovering a Purely European Commitment

Or revising the present 'trans-Atlantic bargain'. *Discriminate Deterrence*
merely confirmed many Europeans in their suspicion that America would
like to reduce its defence commitment to Europe by what Howard and Kaiser
called its failure to factor in 'Europe in the long term considerations of the
report'. They were equally disturbed that Europe appeared only as an 'object
and not an actor in politics—that it was not even considered worth mentioning
as a force which would influence the strategic environment twenty years hence'.

That of course was not always a fear. In 1977 Geoffrey Pattie confidently
predicted that the new technologies would provide 'a new role for the
medium power'; that new electronic devices and precision-guided missiles
might present a European 'challenge' to both Superpowers. 'Translated into
military and diplomatic terms' he argued, '... we are entering a phase where
inadequately-prepared powers of Britain's size can recover some of the diplomatic leverage that massive nuclear deterrence destroyed in the 1960s.'[14] It
was an alluring vision which seemed to offer entry into the wider (non-
European) world.

Perhaps, it is symbolic that, having relinquished his post as Minister of
Procurement, Pattie went on to throw in his hand with the former US Navy
Secretary, John Lehmann, to create yet another defence consultancy in
Washington committed not to European autonomy, but to the two-way
street, the two-way traffic in arms.

For Europe's technical shortcomings are becoming all too apparent now
that for the first time in modern history it has incurred a net technology
deficit with the United States and Japan, especially in some of the 200
systems including stand-off weapons and technologies for targeting and
surveillance which the Independent European Programme Group (IEPG)
decided to develop at a meeting in April 1984. The fact that it is five years
behind Japan in introducing certain integrated chips such as the 256K, and
is falling behind in the race to develop 'intelligent' sensors, would suggest
that even the creation of a European Procurement Agency might now be
too late.

Worse, if the new technologies were to be deployed too quickly they would only throw into stark relief Europe's declining manpower. 'It is difficult to image' wrote Jean-Francois Poncet 'a Europeanization of the defence of the continent without an increase in the resources, both human and economic, allocated by European nations to security.'[15] Unfortunately, the 'demographic winter' through which West Germany is projected to pass in the 1990s will reduce German manpower alone by 200,000 men.

Unless national service is reintroduced in Britain, it will also be increasingly difficult to afford (not find) sufficient resources to maintain four armoured divisions on the Rhine. Manpower is still essential. As Alan Lee Williams wrote in an extended *critique* of Pattie's book, it took NATO years to wake up to the fact that it had wasted its past endeavours by trading men for technology, by placing too much faith in quality rather than quantity, and by squandering its advantage in manpower for a technical lead which had yet to be tested in battle.[16] In September 1976 the young Senator Nunn felt constrained to warn the Alliance that success on the battlefield might depend as much on its ability to absorb losses (a function of mass) as on its capacity to inflict them (a function of performance):

Unfortunately, the price of the West's traditional technological supremacy has been a disinvestment in conventional forces. This is not to deny the importance of technological superiority. It is to say, however, that at some point numbers do count. At some point technology fails to offset numbers. At some point Kipling's thin red line of heroes must give way.[17]

The problem with the new technology ten years on is that in relying on technological superiority more than ever, NATO will inevitably have to find more manpower. It is all very well buying high technology homing shells at $50,000 a time, each capable of destroying a $2 m. tank, but the manpower required to fire the shells is likely to prove more expensive than the tanks.

In Britain manpower cuts in the 1970s led to a 13 per cent increase in the ratio of weapons to troops and a shortage of men which was felt most acutely by the Royal Artillery. The army's Rapier missile units which required seven men per system had to make do with only five. In the Falklands, the shortage of gun crews proved so serious that every available soldier, regardless of his training, had to be pressed into service to keep the guns firing—the price of the endless manpower reviews of the past twenty-five years. In November 1986 additional manpower cuts in the Rhine army prompted the General Staff to predict that Britain would find itself deploying 'a smaller, less well-equipped and less well-trained army'.[18] It is not at all sure whether the BAOR could deploy new technologies without a substantial increase in manpower, the ultimate test perhaps, of its commitment to Europe: a test one too many?

5. Discriminate Deterrence as the Key to Conventional Deterrence

As the poet Philip Larkin once warned 'always too eager for the future, we pick up bad habits of expectancy'. The same might be said of conventional deterrence. Any coincidence of interest which might arise from America's wish to move towards a form of non-nuclear defence and the aspiration of many European opposition parties to implement a policy of conventional deterrence may well founder on their mutually exclusive understanding of the respective terms. If the Left is drifting towards conventional deterrence, it is drifting towards non-provocative defence as well. In Britain the Labour party has already condemned Airland Battle as a *blitzkrieg* strategy which has no role in NATO, and the development of many of the new weapons as a threat to the military balance.[19] Its attitude towards discriminate deterrence echoed the same fears. Even without its nuclear element it appeared to be an offensive, not a defensive strategy.

Of course, it has to be said that the very concept of non-provocative defence is highly specious. The distinction between defensive and offensive weapons is at the best of times difficult to make. A country may decide to forgo the use of certain weapons in war for fear of the consequences; it may even deny itself the same capabilities in peace for the same reason. That is a matter of political judgment. But the argument has gone well beyond a debate about ethics or prudence. In the inter-war years almost the same debate raged between the proponents of offensive and defensive warfare with results that were scathingly portrayed by Churchill in his *History of the Second World War*. The machine-gun, he wrote, which had enabled the German army to hold on to thirteen provinces of France, had been considered virtuous because it had been used for defence; the tank which helped the Allies dislodge the Germans in 1918 was 'placed under the censure and obloquy of all just and righteous men'.[20] Non-provocative deterrence these days does not rule out the introduction of new technologies but it does require that they should be modified for a short-range static defence, an idea which is probably not ahead of but behind the times, an idea whose day may already have passed. Regrettably, it is not the number of Soviet tanks that is of such concern to the Alliance but the increasing number of airborne assault brigades deployed by the Soviet Union. As its confidence in armoured warfare begins to wane, the Soviet military may start to place much greater emphasis on highly mobile units which would spare the Soviet army the very war of attrition on which the advocates of discriminate deterrence have set their sights.

At a time when NATO has so little mobility, it is somewhat disconcerting to find Soviet writers rating the combat effectiveness of an airborne brigade (sixty assault helicopters and 1,900 men) as equivalent or even superior to that of a tank division (10,000 men and 500 combat vehicles). The 'rotary wing revolution', as Richard Simpkin called it, seems to have passed the

European Left by, just as the onset of tank warfare did in the 1930s.[21] It is ironic to find that politicians, like the generals they command, seem happier preparing for the last war than the next. If, as D. C. Watt once noted, war is far too serious a business for politicians, there are a good many politicians in Europe who believe that any move towards conventional deterrence would be tactically disastrous and politically naïve, the kind of move, wrote the British political columnist, Peter Jenkins 'which brings nuclear deterrence into disrepute and peace movements onto the streets'.[22]

6. Discriminate Deterrence as a Form of Disarmament

Rather than an answer to the problem of 'structural disarmament' from which the Alliance has been suffering significantly for the past fifteen years, this may yet prove the most potent objection of all.

The notion of a grand conventional conflict to defeat Soviet forces, Howard argued, would meet with little support in Europe because it would produce the very annihilation the public fears from nuclear escalation. Even in the early 1980s several observers had begun to predict that once the cruise debate had faded in the public memory, attention might be turned instead to conventional weapons.[23]

At the height of the INF debate, the Chairman of the European Nuclear Disarmament Group, the ubiquitous E. P. Thompson, claimed that it was no longer enough to clamour for nuclear disarmament. If the countries of Europe ever again went to war, the distinction between nuclear and conventional weapons would soon be lost. 'We must work to disallow any kind of recourse to war'.[24] It was a remark which was curiously echoed by Sir Geoffrey Howe, who predicted in a speech in March 1987 (before the INF treaty had been signed) that a conventional war in Europe would be almost as devastating as a nuclear one: 'A dozen Tornados armed with precision bombs', he observed, 'could do the same job as 600 Lancasters in a raid in the Second World War.'[25] It is, perhaps, significant that Marshal Ogarkov, the former Soviet chief of staff, also voiced a similar fear.[26] The propaganda value of opposing the new technologies is unlikely to be ignored.

The Peace Movement is unlikely to disappear with the INF Treaty. It has become part of the European psyche, the populist version of a profound crisis of confidence in traditional tactical doctrines and received strategic wisdoms. On the one hand, the United States and its European allies are seeking to build a more stable relationship with the Soviet Union by improving the conventional balance; on the other, the Peace Movement is looking for a 'security partnership' with the East based on a non-provocative defence posture.

In reality both crises of confidence are really the same: conventional deterrence haunts an Alliance that suffers from an inate fear that it will not be able to sell nuclear deterrence to the public indefinitely; for the Peace Movement it represents an opportunity rather than a threat, an opportunity to escape the fate of living in a permanent state of armed peace. The movement's enthusiasm for conventional deterrence clearly represents a passive rejection of the past, rather than an affirmative belief in the future. It could hardly be otherwise. Convinced of the need for change, it is not in a position to bring it about.

Conclusion

In the aftermath of the INF Treaty the Western Alliance is bound to maintain the military balance in central Europe by favouring land-based missiles and artillery with increasing range, and stand-off missiles capable of being fired by aircraft hundreds of miles from their targets, in the vain hope, perhaps, of reducing manpower needs, and thus defence expenditure.

If I have taken a depressingly negative view of the new doctrines which come with the technologies, it is because I believe it unlikely that NATO will ever work out a strategy in which the new weapons can be used. Unfortunately, the institutions for debate are silted up. If a strategy should emerge it is likely to be reactive, a response to Gorbachev's latest initiative, to the perceived threat of the United States decoupling from Western Europe, to serious differences over the concept of conventional deterrence. Fractured and beset by doubts about the INF treaty, NATO, alas, is not the best vehicle for promoting an allied consensus, only allied cohesion and with it the corrosion that cohesion in the past has tended to bring.

Perhaps, it is better that NATO should fail in this respect than that new technologies be deployed on an *ad hoc* basis. As Napoleon once remarked, 'It is a principle of war that where it is possible to make use of thunderbolts they should be preferred to cannon'. That does not mean that their use is necessarily desirable, or should be pursued. When the Alliance comes to formulate a new doctrine in the future it should remember that the premature introduction of the tank in the First World War, like the V2 missile in the Second, illustrated how the eternal quest for 'technological submission' can provide almost unlimited scope for ineffectiveness.

Notes

1. William Kaufmann, 'The crisis in military affairs', *World Politics*, July 1958, pp. 579-603.
2. Fred C. Iklé, Albert Wohlstetter (eds), *Discriminate Deterrence: Report of the Commission on Integrated Long-Term Strategy* (January 1988), p. 30.
3. Michael Howard, Karl Kaiser and Francois de Rose, 'Deterrence Policy: a European response', *International Herald Tribune*, 4 February 1988.
4. *The Independent*, 12 February 1988.
5. Zbigniew Brzezinski, Henry A. Kissinger, Fred Iklé and Albert Wohlstetter, 'Discriminate Deterrence won't leave Europe dangling', *International Herald Tribune*, 24 February 1988.
6. Cited 'ET: where to now?', *International Defence Review*, March 1984, p. 718.

7. Denis M. Hertel, Thomas T. Ridge, William Taylor (eds), *National Security Choices for the Next President* (CSIS: Washington DC, 1988), p. 9.

8. Dan Smith, *The Defence of the Realm in the 1980s* (London: Croom Helm, 1980), p. 78.

9. *Department of Defence Appropriations for 1983,* Hearings before the Sub-committee of the Committee on Appropriations, House of Representatives, 98th Congress, 2nd Session (Washington DC, 1984), p. 694.

10. *International Herald Tribune,* 10 August 1983.

11. D. E. King, 'Survival of tanks in battle', *RUSI Journal,* March 1978, pp. 26-31.

12. See Colonel Volobyev, 'The Airland (Battle) Operation', *Foreign Military Review (ZVO),* July 1984; Colonel Viktororov 'NATO's new concept; the Rogers plan', *ZVO,* February 1985; and Colonel V. Kirsanov, 'The exploitation of second generation cruise missile technology in the US', *ZVO,* March 1985. For one of the best discussions of Soviet reactions to emerging technologies see James Sherr, 'NATO's emerging technology initiative and new operational concepts: the assessment of the Soviet military press', *Soviet Studies Research Review* (Sandhurst), AA15 (1987).

13. Warsaw Pact Communiqué, Berlin, 29 May 1987.

14. James Bellini and Geoffrey Pattie, *A new world role of the medium power* (London: RUSI, 1978), p. 2.

15. Jean-Francois Poncet, 'The European Pillar', *Atlantic Focus* I (Paris: Atlantic Institute, October 1987).

16. Alan Lee Williams, 'A new world role for the medium power—Review Article', *RUSI Journal,* September 1978, p. 61.

17. *Ibid.*

18. *The Sunday Telegraph,* 2 November 1986.

19. *The Times,* 17 November 1987.

20. Cited Albert Wohlstetter, 'Swords without shields', *National Interest,* Summer 1987, p. 32.

21. Richard Simpkin, *Race to the swift: thoughts on twenty-five century warfare* (London: Brasseys, 1985), pp. 118-31.

22. Peter Jenkins, 'An illwind blowing across the Atlantic', *The Independent,* 11 February 1988.

23. 'The anti-nuclear movement wonders how to stay airborne', *The Economist,* 4 February 1984; Avie van der Vries, 'Airland Battle in NATO: a European view', *Parameters,* Summer 1984, pp. 11-12.

24. E. P. Thompson, 'The image and reality of war', *New Society,* 23 August 1984.

25. *The Times,* 12 March 1987.

26. Stan Sloan, Paul Gallis, *et al., Conventional arms control and military strategy in Europe* (Washington, DC: Congressional Research Service, 16 October 1987).

CHAPTER 7

Strategy, Economics and the New Technologies—The Soviet Response

JAMES SHERR

To a degree which is both unmatched and unappreciated elsewhere, the USSR bases its military strategy on a 'scientific' understanding of the likely adversary. To achieve this understanding, Soviet specialists do not simply analyse the military and economic capabilities associated with the bourgeois notion of 'balance of power'. In their eyes, equal effort (and equal rigour) must be devoted to discerning the mentality of opponents, the social ('class') cohesion of their societies, the will and capacity of governing élites, and the ability of an opposing coalition to act as one. It is the contest between all these factors—tangible and intangible, political and psychological, material and organizational—which determines the 'correlation of forces' between the USSR and its opponents; and it is the correlation of forces that Soviet policy seeks to alter, in peace and in war.

For all this, as seasoned Marxists, the Soviet Union understands that power cannot exist, let alone be sustained, without an economic and technological base to support it. To Soviet military scientists, 'military doctrine'—the official set of views about war and how to conduct it—is something which develops dialectically as the state's goals are reconciled with changing techno-logical possibilities. At times in Soviet history this doctrine has taken a revolutionary leap forward in response to technological innovation. Just as frequently, capabilities (and possibilities) have lagged far behind the agenda which 'doctrine' has specified. No matter how 'morally' deficient an advanced rival, if he has grasped the potential of new technologies and, worse still, begun to match them with new forms of 'military art', he poses a challenge that must be taken seriously.

For those immersed in this way of thinking, the report of the Commission on Integrated Long-Term Strategy (*Discriminate Deterrence*) was but the latest indication that Western security élites had grasped the significance of the 'revolutionary turn in military affairs' identified by Marshal Ogarkov in 1982.[1] There have been other indications which have caused—and will continue to cause—even greater concern: 'AirLand Battle' (the doctrine of the US army, adopted in 1982) and 'Follow-on-Forces Attack' (FOFA), SHAPE's 'deep-strike' concept, adopted by NATO in 1984. The new revolution, founded on micro-electronics, sensor technologies and directed energy systems, threatens to supersede a far earlier revolution founded on nuclear weapons and guided missiles. The devil the Soviet Union knows—and which, thanks to the 1965-80 build-up, it largely mastered—is one with which it must now part; or so, at least, it fears. It is a fear this report will reinforce, despite the controversy it has aroused in the West.

This Chapter addresses four questions. What does the Soviet Union believe the latest 'emerging technology' (ET) initiatives and concepts say about NATO's strategic intentions? How does it believe these initiatives will affect NATO's military capabilities? How adequate will the operational and tactical principles of the Soviet armed forces prove in response? To what degree will Soviet policies and priorities need to be changed?

The most plausible (unclassified) root to their answers lies in a critical assessment of the Soviet military press. 'Critical' it must be because of the nature of 'open' writings in a system which regards deception as a prime objective of policy. Such an assessment is, nonetheless, possible. Military writings which, day in and day out, yielded a diet of imaginary problems and ignored real ones would serve no useful purpose. Set in the context of other indicators of Soviet thinking—exercises, force structures and the classic texts of military science—the press can be an important source of insight.

Soviet assessment of NATO strategy is, at the end of the day, an assessment about the challenges for Warsaw Pact strategy. That strategy must, therefore, be our point of departure.

Background to Warsaw Pact Strategy

Warsaw Pact strategy is Soviet strategy. The Pact remains essentially what it was when first established in 1955: a diplomatic counterweight to NATO and a mechanism for imposing Soviet military doctrine upon national armed forces. In peacetime, NATO tries to reconcile national concepts to the common purpose, but its *authority* to do so is non-existent. It is in wartime that NATO comes into its own. In wartime, the Warsaw Pact disappears. Non-Soviet formations (restricted to divisional size) will be slotted into higher formations (Armies and Fronts) under Soviet commanders who answer not to a Pact equivalent of SACEUR or CINCENT, but to the High Command (GK) of the theatre (TVD) and, through that organ, to the Supreme High Command (VGK) of the Soviet Armed Forces.

Soviet 'military doctrine' (*voyennaya doktrina*) is the official (Party) view of the goals and nature of future war and of those measures required to prepare the armed forces and the country for it. This intellectual framework, supported by a centralized institutional structure, imposes coherence on all aspects of military policy. In the USSR doctrine and strategy determine the roles of services and the procurement of weapons, not the other way round.[2]

Even in 'this nuclear age', the task assigned to doctrine and strategy is waging and winning war, not 'deterrence' as many Westerners think of it. The Soviet Union does indeed believe in deploying capabilities for 'holding back' the adversary (*sderzhivaniye*)—and the missiles of the Strategic Rocket Forces are a good case in point. But the notion that armed forces as a whole should be designed for something less than winning—to 'discourage' adversaries and, in turn, 'reassure' allies—is, in Soviet eyes, a suspect notion: naïve as well as over-sophisticated, and profoundly unhistorical. Indeed, the Soviet Union never seems to be sure whether such 'deterrence' really is a Western notion or simply a Western ploy.

Nonetheless, as Clausewitz stated (and as Lenin tirelessly reiterated), war is an instrument of policy. If it is to remain so, it had best be short, particularly if NATO is the opponent envisaged.[3] This belief finds firm support in Marx and Engels, who argued that the economically stronger contestant would prevail in drawn out conflict, and who documented the 'revolutionary effects' of war on victor and vanquished alike.[4] Today the social infirmities of Warsaw Pact allies and the perils of nuclear escalation give these arguments powerful reinforcement. The Soviet Communist Party (CPSU) is unlikely to consider any prize to be worth the break-up of the 'socialist camp', the destruction of the Soviet system, or the initiation of a global holocaust. Having said this, the Soviet military establishment plans for long as well as short wars,[5] and needs no reminding that the war one likes may be very different from the war one gets. But if at a point of crisis it is clear that war will be protracted, the Soviets will not be the ones to launch it.

Nor will they launch it if they cannot achieve strategic surprise. By definition, strategic surprise must be a joint military and political enterprise and, of necessity, a product of integrated, detailed and long-term planning. Even in an age of intrusive intelligence-gathering and advanced technology, surprise is possible, and it has been achieved. Technically, it may not be possible to achieve *total* surprise but militarily, total surprise has rarely been necessary. The weak links of intelligence and warning—political, institutional and intellectual—have been surprisingly resistant to technical 'improvement', and may continue to be so in future.[6]

The Soviet Union believes that surprise, if achieved, could have telling results against NATO. When it compares its own position with that of its opponent, it notes five key deficiencies. Three of these—insufficient reserves, poor terrain preparation and the limited operational depth of the Central Region—require no discussion. But a fourth, the maldeployment of NATO forces in peacetime, is a clear reminder of Moltke's warning that 'he who is wrongly deployed at the start of hostilities never recovers'. But it is the final weakness—doctrinal disunity—that Soviet writers consider crucial. In NATO there are sixteen different ways of training, equipping and commanding forces. In the Warsaw Pact there is one. Not even individual NATO members can boast a 'military doctrine' in the sense of a binding and inclusive set of assumptions tying together national policy, military strategy, deployment of forces, procurement of weapons and training of troops.

Finally, it bears noting that NATO is *vulnerable* to surprise, because a coalition of democratic and genuinely sovereign states is unlikely to take decisive action until challenges are direct and unmistakable. The dependency of Flexible Response on a period of strategic warning—on warning which is promptly *utilized* by NATO's political authorities—is no secret to Soviet leaders. To them, crisis management is synonymous with crisis manipulation, and the manipulation of perceptions is a continuous peacetime activity. Should war be decided upon, *maskirovka* (military deception) would not only encompass the well known (and ever more sophisticated) arts of concealment, simulation, camouflage and disinformation, but a co-ordinated effort by all arms of the state at cloaking intentions and ensuring that NATO is in disarray on the day that robustness is needed.[7]

If surprise is achieved, Soviet strategists believe they can impose their style of war upon NATO. Whereas most NATO armies set store by tactical flexibility, the Soviet military prizes flexibility at the *operational* level: Army and Front (roughly equivalent to an Army Group). It is mastery of this level of warfare and this alone that enables armies to achieve strategic results. The oft-cited 'operational rigidity' of the Soviet armed forces is a misnomer for its *tactical* rigidity (*ie* at the level of division and below): the corollary to a structure affording the higher commander the ability to manoeuvre forces at theatre-wide scales and concentrate force at the decisive time and place.[8] Doctrinal fragmentation deprives NATO's commanders of similar flexibility and leaves their formations vulnerable to operational outmanoeuvering. In the Great Patriotic War of 1941-45 operational flexibility played a crucial role in defeating a tactically more proficient opponent. It should be noted that the German army of 1941-45 had greater operational capability than NATO has today. The Soviet Union believes that NATO's commanders may find themselves highly constrained in the sort of war the Warsaw Pact would fight.[9]

For these reasons, it believes that NATO will be forced to resort to nuclear weapons to defeat its offensive. It is of overriding importance, therefore, for the Pact's forces to achieve their end before these weapons can be employed effectively. It follows that this end must be carefully defined. If the political objective is NATO's destruction—and an attack in the Central Region would be an act of madness if the objective were anything less—then the military objective must, at the minimum, include what Clausewitz termed the Alliance's 'centre of gravity': in brief, the Federal Republic of Germany. With the likely additions of Denmark and the Low Countries, this could well be the *maximum* zone of operations envisaged.

Clearly, the greatest obstacle to this strategy will be nuclear weapons based with deployed formations in the theatre of war itself. Even if they can be substantially disabled, the Soviet forces must waste no time in encircling and then destroying the enemy's most active combat formations. Otherwise, the short war will lengthen and, as it does, the risk of a nuclear strike from forces outside the theatre of operations will increase.[10]

Four tasks are therefore vital: (1) achieving air superiority; (2) inserting forces into the strategic depths; (3) disabling nuclear systems in the theatre of operations; and (4) encircling major force groupings. The first task, air superiority, is essential if enemy defences are to be shattered, momentum maintained and formations prevented from breaking out of encirclement.[11] The Warsaw Pact's 'air operation', a combined arms undertaking (aircraft, missile strikes, and airborne *desants*) would target air bases as well as nuclear assets and command-and-control centres. It would be launched concurrently with, or even before, the Pact's strike groupings crossed the Inner German Border.

The second task (and much of the third and fourth) would fall to Operational Manoeuvre Groups (OMGs). These highly mobile armoured and heliborne forces would be inserted as early as the first day of operations, once strike groupings had succeeded in punching a hole in the enemy's forward defences. They would conduct reconnaissance in depth and destroy command-and-control, nuclear weapons and other systems which could slow the attacker down (*eg*, multiple rocket launchers). The aim of OMGs would be to blind, deafen and gag, not deprive the enemy of life and limb. Creating purposeful havoc, they would speed the passage of the main body of forces which, along with the OMGs, would aim to deprive the enemy of the force separation he needs for safe nuclear targeting.[12]

The real muscle behind encirclement operations would be provided by strike groupings (motor rifle and tank formations, supported by aircraft, missiles and artillery) penetrating NATO's forward defences at their weakest points and with overwhelming force. To achieve these penetrations, a flexible force structure is called for, because the terrain and the opposition confronting the attacker will vary. Moreover, to achieve the breach by conventional means, striking power must be well forward. For both these reasons, the deep and rigid structure of echeloning required on the nuclear battlefield loses its purpose.[13]

The superiorities the Soviet military believes it needs for breakthrough operations are considerable (4:1 being preferable). However, NATO should find this no cause for celebration. By constructing immense strike groupings on narrow breakthrough sectors (sometimes only six per cent of the zone of advance), the Red Army achieved its dramatic encirclements of 1943-45 (*eg*, Stalingrad), despite force ratios in the *overall* zone of advance inferior to those which exist today. In support of the main effort, some sectors in the theatre would confine their offensive to the tactical depths and others (Armies or even an entire Front) would adopt a defensive posture. A Soviet strategic offensive operation would unfold, therefore, as a mixture of offensive and defensive operations. It would not require superiority throughout the theatre, but it would require massive superiority at the critical place and moment. This in turn requires winning the battle for time: forcing an enemy to react to you before you are forced to react to him. To date, thanks to NATO's vulnerability to surprise and its weaknesses at the operational level, Soviet commanders could have some confidence that NATO would lose the battle for time and, with it, the battle itself.[14]

The aim of Soviet strategy is to achieve a conclusive victory before any nuclear response can take place. With Soviet armies deep inside NATO territory and NATO's main force concentrations encircled, a nuclear response at that stage is more than likely to be militarily pointless: an act of retaliation rather than defence, against an enemy far better equipped to dominate the escalation process than at the moment the threshold of war was crossed. Soviet commanders hope that, so constrained, the opponents who remained would accept the facts on the ground and refrain from rolling the nuclear dice.

Soviet strategy is as ambitious as it is ingenious. The attention still given to nuclear warfighting and, increasingly, to a second, longer phase of operations testifies to reasoned Soviet scepticism about the effectiveness of their capabilities in practice and the 'realism' of their adversaries in the heat of war. Whilst the Soviet Union would never confuse technological proficiency with military proficiency, it does recognize that its ability to implement its strategy is sensitive to the technological level of its combatants. With this thought in mind, we can turn to NATO's initiatives and the Soviet reaction to them.

'Emerging Technology' Initiatives in NATO

For all the affinity between them, the 'emerging technology' (ET) initiatives in NATO are diverse and even divergent. So far, none have moved far from the realm of paper into the nuts and bolts of trained and equipped forces. Even if they do, they will not amount to a unified military doctrine, as the Soviet Union would recognize it. Of the principal concepts at issue, the most ambitious, AirLand Battle, is strictly a national concept: since 1982 the official doctrine of the US Army (FM 100-5 (1982)) and endorsed by the US Air Force the same year. A product of combined arms specialists from several US army establishments, it departs markedly in substance—and even more strikingly in spirit—from the doctrine it supersedes, 'Active Defense' (FM 100-5 (1976)). Its *motifs* are mobility, manoeuvre and the fluid battlefield; combined arms and the 'integrated battlefield'; 'deep strike' and the 'extended battlefield'; surprise, disorientation of the enemy and the imposition of one's own style of war upon him. Its most significant feature is its recognition of the importance of the operational level of war. But by far its most controversial feature is its recognition that a defender loses if he simply defends. As a doctrine for war of manoeuvre at an operational scale, AirLand

Battle goes so far as to envisage counterthrusts by US ground forces into Warsaw Pact territory itself.

'Follow-on-Forces-Attack' (FOFA), launched at the instigation of General Bernard Rogers, is a SHAPE concept, approved by NATO's Defence Planning Committee in 1984, and hence officially part of NATO strategy. Wresting the maximum potential—and the maximum optimism—from new technologies of target acquisition, communications and firepower, it aims to deprive an attacking force of support and reinforcement by mounting 'deep strikes' against his rear and flanks. It seeks to achieve by advanced conventional means what can only be achieved at present by nuclear weapons. It is at the same time more grandiose than AirLand Battle and more modest.

Whereas AirLand Battle is a national corps-level doctrine, FOFA is a strategic concept, theatre-wide in scope. But in contrast to AirLand Battle, FOFA consists of a set of goals and planning guidelines, rather than detailed operational and tactical principles for conducting campaigns and battles. Whereas AirLand Battle aims to integrate firepower into a doctrine of manoeuvre, FOFA concerns itself solely with the centralized employment of air, missile and artillery assets. Its notion of 'deep strike' does not extend to counterattacks by NATO ground forces into Warsaw Pact territory, and both General Rogers and his successor, General Galvin, have affirmed that such counterattacks are contrary to NATO policy.[15]

Although commissioned by the US President, the report of the Commission on Integrated Long-Term Strategy, *Discriminate Deterrence* has no official status in NATO or in the United States. Its subject is US grand strategy. It offers a framework not only for war in the Central Region, but for numerous military contingencies—and also for peacetime budgeting and programming. But on this wider canvas, it exhibits details of the same picture which has emerged elsewhere: the insistence on initiative, a refusal to accord sanctuaries to opponents, and a preoccupation with developing and exploiting technology in a disciplined and comprehensive way.[16]

Finally, the US Strategic Defence Initiative (SDI) warrants mention, even though it is neither self-evidently (nor ostensibly) addressed to a Warsaw Pact conventional offensive in Europe. As we will note, the Soviet Union claims to believe otherwise—and may even have reason to do so.

Soviet Press Commentary on NATO Initiatives

The Soviet press exaggerates the momentum of NATO's efforts and their coherence. Innocently or otherwise, it presents a view of NATO thinking which mirrors long-standing Soviet thinking about how war should be fought. It also maintains that these initiatives are indicative of a profound and menacing change of attitude in the Alliance.

One of the more curious features of the Soviet press reaction is its tardiness. Although FOFA got under way in 1979-80 and AirLand Battle became official US army doctrine in 1982, open Soviet sources devoted little attention to either initiative before 1984. This delay is not surprising. A potentially momentous subject such as doctrinal change in NATO will not be exposed to public scrutiny until it has first been scrutinized by the leadership. But the delay is a clue which signifies interest, and it appears to signify that Moscow takes NATO's change of direction seriously. In July 1984 the journal *Zarubyezhnoye Voyennoye Obozreniye* (*'Foreign Military Review'*) published a 5,000-word summary of AirLand Battle by two authors, Colonel V. Volobyev and Lieutenant Colonel N. Nikolayev. Apart from two ritualistic references to 'America's aggressive plans', it records the essentials of FM 100-5 (1982) without flamboyance. But three points in the summary are worth noting.

First, the authors characterize AirLand Battle as a concept for 'the total destruction of enemy forces at all depths of his operational force formation by nuclear, chemical and highly accurate conventional means'. This characterization has all the limitations of a literal truth. AirLand Battle doctrine stipulates that if nuclear operations commence, they must be integrated into the scheme of ground and air battle. In short, nuclear weapons must be used as weapons of war, *if they are used*. The Volobyev-Nikolayev summary leaves one in no doubt that they will be.

Secondly, the authors assert that US strategists have relied on 'a comprehensive study, analysis and evaluation of the tactics and operational art of the potential enemy' in devising the doctrine. Without going so far as to accuse them of purloining their concepts from the Soviet armed forces, the reader is left with this impression (and with some degree of justice!).

Thirdly, the larger part of the article is devoted to Deep Strike. Whilst AirLand Battle is said to aim at 'the isolation of the region of combat operations by delaying or destroying the Pact's second echelon', the authors are at pains to note that AirLand Battle is a doctrine of *manoeuvre* and that NATO fire assets would assist manoeuvre forces in targeting the flanks of first echelon formations. The reader is therefore warned that AirLand Battle is not simply a Deep Strike concept designed around a dated concept of Soviet operations (*ie*, deep and rigid echelonment).[17]

Subsequent articles about NATO initiatives take up most of the themes raised by Volobyev and Nikolayev and draw noteworthy lessons from them:

1. The Integrated Battlefield.

Many Soviet writers express anxiety lest ET weapons *strengthen* the capabilities of NATO's nuclear forces. Their interpretation of the relationship between these forces differs starkly from NATO's own. Few in NATO would deny that the attractiveness of ET lies in its potential to raise the nuclear threshold (or, at least, ensure that it does not fall further), yet it is difficult to find any public Soviet acknowledgement of this aim. In the main, Soviet commentators are keen to establish that such weapons will merely diminish inhibitions about nuclear use. The Soviet reader is persistently told that ET weapons, NATO Intermediate-range Nuclear Forces (INF) and SDI are the three pillars of a co-ordinated enteprise to restore US nuclear superiority and make the integrated nuclear, chemical and conventional battlefield a reality.[18]

The message is double edged, to say the least. On the one hand, Soviet commentators indict NATO with plans to fight a 'conventional war which is no longer conventional'. Air-fuel explosives, precision-guided missiles, the multiple-launch rocket system (MLRS) and homing artillery with sub-munitions are described as weapons which 'approach' (or, more recently, 'equal') the effectiveness of 'low yield weapons of mass destruction', eliminating the threshold between nuclear and conventional war and forcing the nuclear threshold down to 'a threateningly low level'. The Soviet Union plainly wishes to make clear that if this is NATO's game, it will not play it by NATO's rules (a threat of first use?) Yet, for good measure, it also wishes it to be known that NATO's *real* game is to eliminate this threshold and make nuclear warfare acceptable.

2. The Extended Battlefield.

Soviet discussion of Deep Strike capabilities is a highly-charged combination of 'doomsday'-mongering and myth-making in which the distorting mirror image is ever present. There is repeated reference to the 'vast scope' of the war which NATO contemplates, a theatre strategic operation in all but name, waged on Warsaw Pact territory. Until the end of 1986 at least, Soviet articles did not acknowledge General Rogers's downward revision of FOFA's Deep Strike to the operational-tactical depths (120 km), let alone his declaration (May 1983) ruling out deep attacks by ground forces across the NATO-Warsaw Pact frontier. Indeed, even large NATO combined-arms exercises (such as Autumn Forge '84 and '85) are turned into object lessons as to how such exercises 'could very easily grow into operational level offensives'.[19]

It would be very un-Soviet to dwell upon such projects without specifying the political aims they would serve. A major theme has become the Alliance's 'change of attitude': an Alliance now intent on 'seizing foreign territory'. Soviet insistence on this point may provide a flavour of the 'worst case' wisdom in Moscow. Does the Soviet leadership fear that the disintegration of the Warsaw Pact has become NATO's war aim? Or does it simply fear that a war waged by Deep Strike systems would bring about its disintegration whatever NATO's aim? The theme presents obvious difficulties for Soviet commentators, keen to remind the reader of NATO's intrinsic aggressiveness, yet also keen to impress upon him that a menacing 'change of attitude' has taken place. If NATO is now intent on seizing foreign territory, what was its aim before.[20]

3. The 'Rogers Plan'.

A third theme in Soviet writings—but altogether absent from Volobyev's and Nikolayev's account—is the coherence of NATO's efforts. Whereas Western specialists tend to dwell upon divergences between NATO's initiatives, Soviet commentators boldly fuse them together. The 'Rogers Plan' of Soviet description is an amalgam of AirLand Battle, pre-1983 vintage FOFA and fiction. As a literary device, it serves a convenient purpose. It enables the Soviet Union to stress American dominance of NATO and at the same time raise the spectre of an Alliance-wide threat pooling R&D resources as well as national armed forces.[21]

Soviet articles devoted to NATO and its intentions are a good reminder of the perils of assuming a correspondence between Soviet statements and Soviet views. The peril may be all the greater in articles about the Soviet armed forces, precisely because it is less obvious. Serious, detailed and technical in nature, these articles can be richly informative. Whether this makes them wholly trustworthy is open to question.

The press has long contained pertinent criticism of Soviet military performance, but within the past three years there has been sign of a deeper dissatisfaction and restlessness. First, warnings about the inadequacy of traditional ways of thinking are becoming commonplace. Citing Lenin's warning that war is rarely fought as expected, military writers draw attention to the enemy's more complex tactics and equipment and also to the challenges which the latest *Soviet* equipment poses to traditional ways of operating. Colonel Volobyev (the author of *ZVO*'s article on AirLand Battle) warns that computerizing the battlefield will not in itself solve problems because computers give people less time to think. Like a good many others, he stresses that time is a 'decisive factor for success'. Therefore, not only must decision-making be accelerated, but also the implementation of decisions by subordinates. Indeed, a large number of Soviet commentators now sound a radical note: not only must subordinates act more swiftly; they must also learn to think for themselves.[22]

Secondly, experience in Afghanistan is now marshalled to reinforce insights into 'wars of the future' which occasionally seem to be nothing more than transparently coded warnings about war against NATO. The need to train for 'non-standard combat situations', to develop proficiency in independent small team operations, to accept that security of the rear can no longer be taken for granted are becoming general refrains about war itself, rather than variants for dealing with 'bandits'.

A third departure in thinking concerns defence, traditionally the poor step-child of Soviet military art but, since the early 1980s, a respectable subject of study and a vigorous subject of discussion. In the era dominated by the (nuclear) 'revolution in military affairs', defence was considered counter-productive, if not hazardous. In the emerging era of the (conventional) 'revolutionary turn in military affairs', defence has been deemed, at least, good in parts. True enough, a defender who only defends will lose. But on the fluid battlefield, an attacker who only attacks will dissipate his efforts and be halted or outflanked. Most Soviet discussion, therefore, concerns defence at the tactical and operational levels: defensive battles and operations pursued as components of a strategic offensive. But when an article faults Soviet military art before 1941 as lacking a doctrine for defensive operations above the operational level and practical experience above the tactical it may be inferred that strategic surprise is arousing concern again. Indeed, Mikhail Gorbachev himself has cited 22 June 1941 as an example of what happens to those who become complacent.[23]

Such warnings may reveal alarm at the intentions which underlie NATO's new concepts—or may simply be designed to express it. To date, military-technical discussion does not express alarm, but it does reveal concern—partially about NATO's intentions, but more fundamentally about the pace of change as such. To all appearances, the Soviet armed forces have been engrossed in a debate since the 'revolutionary turn' was first acknowledged. Do the latest concepts in NATO pose a concrete threat or, given the Alliance's built-in 'contradictions', only a notional one? Should the Soviet forces attempt to counter 'emerging technologies' or master them? If emulation is necessary, can structures, skills and habits of mind keep pace with technological innovation (Soviet as well as Western)? Can tactical initiative be fostered without jeopardizing cohesion at the operational level? Can the old imperative of centralized control and the new imperative of decentralized decision-making be reconciled? In sum, will new technologies and concepts be needed to preserve the effectiveness of the armed forces, or will they undermine distinctive Soviet strengths?

Assessing the Soviet Assessment

The Soviet Union has made out a 'worst case' for NATO's new initiatives, if not a false one, and it has clearly done so for a purpose, if not several. To what extent are Soviet anxieties genuine and to what extent contrived? Given the exacting demands of a short-warning short-war strategy, the Soviet Union does have reason to fear NATO's new technologies and concepts if efforts are targeted at the right areas.

1. Intelligence and warning.

A force structure on today's conventional pattern, concentrating the bulk of armour and *matériel* forward, would present a rich target set to a warned and prepared defender. Given Soviet refusal to attack unless surprise is assured, it follows that improvements in intelligence and warning could curtail the Warsaw Pact's freedom to resort to war.

2. Deep Strike.

Responsive and accurate deep strike systems would make surprise more difficult to exploit. Whatever their utility against a (now diminished) second operational echelon, they would menace the flanks of the first operational echelon and complicate lateral movement; and they would pose a clear threat to targets in the operational-tactical zone (*eg* army level HQs and air bases). By allowing NATO to launch strikes from further back in its own rear, Deep Strike systems would afford the defender more time to recover from attack, and they would be more dificult for the attacker to destroy.

3. Battlefield Mobility and Firepower.

The overriding battle in a short war is the battle for time. If a strategy of lightning conventional war is to succeed, the Pact must remain inside the enemy's decision-making cycle once the initial advantage of surprise is secured. In other words, battlefield threats must develop more quickly than an adversary's ability to respond to them. Surprise, in short, must be exploited—and friendly and enemy forces themselves must be sufficiently intermingled to frustrate any hope of a battlefield nuclear strike. The significance of NATO's projected target acquisition, fire systems and mobile strike forces is that, in combination, they could turn time into the attacker's enemy. If the defender can assess and respond in time, he will slow down the battlefield and gain the respite he needs to restore a defensive line. NATO seeks these capabilities in order to defer or prevent nuclear use. The Soviet Union sees them as the *prelude* to nuclear use because they will arrest the mobility of Soviet forces and turn them into feasible targets. For these reasons it now attaches as much importance to destroying 'reconnaissance strike complexes' and multiple rocket launchers as it does to nuclear weapons.

Even if NATO does target its resources with discrimination, it is unlikely that the Soviet military will be acutely worried about the viability of its strategy between now and the end of the century. Within this time scale, it is likely to be confident of its ability to hold the ring, thanks to:

1. Counters.

Soviet generals are past masters at countering strengths they cannot match. For every exotic weapon deployed by NATO, a straightforward counter or spoof will be sought. Having long regarded the best as the enemy of the good, they will be encouraged by the over-sophistication of many ET weapons, their vulnerability to *maskirovka* (*eg* chaff, simple emitters and deflectors) and to enhancements of current hardware (*eg* longer range SAM's, look-down-shoot-down radar, and composite and reactive armour). While at least in an order of magnitude more lethal in accuracy, range and power than today's generation of weapons, many 'smart' weapons are easily fooled, and many are also in an order of magnitude more vulnerable than the weapons they replace.

2. Resourcefulness.

Whilst lagging behind NATO in the latest technology, the Soviet armed forces have often led the way in *applications* of technology (*eg* interfacing SAMs with air defence guns). They have also been resourceful in converting NATO's 'defensive' innovations to offensive use (*eg* mounting ATGMs onto tanks, integrating SAMs into manoeuvre formations). They are astute improvisers who stretch old technology to its limits and deploy new technology where it will do the most good.

3. Quantity.

No matter how revolutionary the weapon, Soviet generals will disparage its impact if it is not deployed in quantity. For the past twenty years the USSR has consistently overtaken NATO in re-equipping its armed forces with weapons that NATO had first introduced (*eg* SAM, anti-tank guided missiles). This has given them a qualitative as well as a quantitative edge over their opponent. The present political climate makes deployments in quantity most unlikely. The new 'smart' artillery shell costs twenty times as much as the one it replaces. This sort of trade-off will not endear itself to cost-conscious publics in North America and Europe, particularly at a time when many perceive arms control to be the chief task of defence policy.

4. Doctrine.

To date only one NATO member, the United States, has coupled advanced weapons with major doctrinal innovation. But as a corps level concept, AirLand Battle can only make itself felt at the lower end of the 'operational' scale, and it is therefore vulnerable to outmanoeuvring. It is not the Soviet style to challenge an opponent's strong suit, rather to bear down upon his weakest link. In Soviet eyes, strategy is the art of manoeuvring the opponent into a contest where his weaknesses are telling and his strengths irrelevant. Until the Commanders of NORTHAG and CENTAG acquire the resources and prerogatives of their Warsaw Pact counterparts (*ie* Front commanders), and until NATO takes serious steps towards doctrinal unity, it may have little ability to shape this contest, and may find this style of warfare difficult to withstand.

As strategists, Soviet commanders deal in realities rather than potentials. But as planners, they are guided by the long term and the 'worst case'.[24] The radicalism of the Gorbachev leadership is a sign of pessimism over the longer term, and there are ample grounds for it.

1. Technological.

Countering advanced technologies with resourceful applications of earlier ones is a short-term solution, not a long-term one. The Soviet Union regards technology as a cornerstone of the socio-economic base determining national power. Unsurprisingly, each major shift in Soviet military doctrine has been associated with a corresponding technological revolution. The Soviet Union can prevail with a technological base inferior to its rival's, but not with one on a qualitatively different level. Unsophisticated tanks can prevail against sophisticated tanks; cavalry cannot. Gorbachev, for one, believes that unless the latest technological revolution is mastered, the USSR will find it difficult to remain a Superpower in the next century.

While on the strength of past experience the Soviet Union believes this revolution will be mastered, it also recalls that past struggles against advanced opponents have succeeded thanks to the militarization of Soviet society and the unwillingness of these opponents to impose similar rigours upon themselves. The Soviet military build-up of the 1960s and 1970s was a taxing undertaking, despite the Americans' lack of appetite for serious competition. The Soviets fear some of the latest initiatives— SDI in particular—just because they are initiatives: because the strengths of the opponent may be mobilized rather than left to develop piecemeal. Given the relevance of SDI-related technologies to the conventional battlefield, Soviet hostility to the programme is sincere, if not for the reasons usually cited.

2. Strategic.

The USSR's strategic worry is that extended deterrence can be revitalized and a semblance of superiority restored to NATO. In Soviet eyes NATO's effectiveness hinges on its ability to maintain countervailing nuclear trumps against Soviet conventional strengths. Far from believing that advanced technology could soon replace such trumps, they fear the contribution that more robust conventional forces might make to the overall strategy of Flexible Response—and to the viability of NATO's nuclear forces. As devotees of the principle of combined arms, Soviet strategists have assessed the combined impact of advanced technology, INF, European nuclear force modernization and SDI and assume that the West has made a similar assessment. To be sure, the INF Treaty markedly improves the Soviet assessment, and the present climate in NATO makes it unlikely that 'compensatory measures' would be welcome to those who would have to consent to them. Soviet leaders will do their best to make this climate irreversible, particularly by 'doing business' with right-of-centre governments. But (*qv* the post-Nixon reverses of the 1970s), there is no guarantee that they will succeed. Today's triumphs provide a decent interval, not an end to Soviet problems. The USSR will not remain a Superpower merely by guile and stratagem.

3. Political.

Since 1980, the USSR's political worry has been that NATO's intentions might change. As people who conceive of politics as struggle, the Russians view NATO's defensive intentions as the product of Soviet might rather than NATO's goodwill. As Brezhnev stated at the 25th Party Congress, 'the advent of *détente* was largely connected with the emergence of a new correlation of world forces'. He and his successors have used this correlation of forces to consolidate a dynamic *status quo* favouring 'socialism'. Behind Brezhnev's warnings about the 'impossibility' of 'turning the clock back', was a fear of those in the West who might create such a possibility and exploit it. Behind the press vituperation about plans to 'seize foreign territory' is the fear that a restoration of NATO superiority would restore the psychological initiative to NATO in Europe and stimulate the 'export of counter-revolution' in the Third World. SDI, AirLand Battle and *Discriminate Deterrence* show that such forces exist and that they have the ability to make themselves felt.[25]

Conclusions

In its consideration of NATO initiatives the Soviet Press has given vent to real fears, albeit in a disingenuous way. The most effective way to mobilize people against a long-term danger is to speak as though the wolf were already at the door. The Soviet press campaign is largely a propaganda campaign. It distorts what is taking place in NATO, yet it expresses an honest fear of what might take place if the USSR is complacent. To be sure, it is also a weapon of political struggle by a leadership determined to extend *perestroyka* to the armed forces. There can be no doubt, however, that Gorbachev believes that *perestroyka* is in the USSR's interest and not simply his own. Threats are being exaggerated for a national purpose, not simply because of 'manoeuvrings at the top'. To judge by the military press at least, his concerns are shared by a large part of the military establishment.

For the four questions set out at the beginning of this Chapter, answers can now be formulated:

1. NATO's Political Intentions.

The Soviet Union believes that NATO's new initiatives have stemmed from a new spirit in the Alliance and not just from new technologies. These initiatives are seen as but one part of a co-ordinated (military, economic and moral) offensive against socialism by 'well-known circles' who would 'reverse the course of history' and roll back all of 'socialism's' gains since Khrushchev's fall. To be sure, those circles have been isolated and marginalized of late because of Gorbachev's astonishing impact, not least upon the political Right itself; but they have not disappeared. The Soviet leadership respects the rebound of the anti-*détente* cause in the West, despite its many setbacks.

2. NATO's Capabilities.

The Soviet Union doubts whether NATO's current initiatives will remedy its fundamental weaknesses. But it fears the longer-term potential of advanced conventional technologies, both in space and on earth, and worries lest the doctrinal innovation accompanying it gathers momentum. Whereas NATO looks on its present initiatives as goals rather than realities, the Soviet Union sees them as forerunners rather than final products. Its greatest fear is a sustained development of new technologies coupled with systemic doctrinal change. If NATO convinces the USSR that advanced technology is an *alternative* to systemic change, Soviet fears will recede.

These fears will recede still further if NATO convinces it that advanced technologies are an alternative to nuclear weapons. The Soviet Union fears NATO's nuclear capabilities more than it fears the new technologies, and is likely to do so for a considerable period of time. Added to them, these technologies can revitalize Flexible Response and deny the Warsaw Pact the quick victory mandated by Soviet military doctrine. But in the absence of nuclear weapons, the pressure to win quickly will diminish, and war itself will become easier to plan and wage.

3. Soviet Operational Concepts.

Far from invalidating basic operational principles (surprise, flexibility, mobility and tempo, combined arms and operations in depth) improvements in NATO's capabilities will place even greater reliance upon them. But there is a difference between the principles and their realization. Although simple counters can be found to the relatively crude 'ET' weapons under development today, it may not be so easy to fool the genuinely smart generation of weapons which will follow. New technologies and skills will be required in the Soviet armed forces, as well as proficiency in operational concepts given little emphasis today (*eg* defence and small team operations).

4. Soviet Priorities.

Soviet commanders find that they must once again 'catch up and overtake' a more advanced opponent. The first means of doing so is the *perestroyka* (reconstruction) of the economy and society. *Perestroyka* is possible (in foreign policy terms at least) because the capabilities of the armed forces provide the margin of safety needed to pursue it. But it is also necessary because this margin of safety will disappear in the next century unless a comprehensive refurbishment of the economy is undertaken. Crash efforts in priority areas will not suffice, and there is no certainty that the economy or society could withstand them.

The second means of 'catching up and overtaking' is international *détente* because, without a *peredyshka* (breathing space), gaps with competitors may persist or even widen. In practical terms, buying time for modernization means finding ways to retard Western investment in the capabilities sought and, simultaneously, to effect a relaxation of Western vigilance about technology transfer. Like Lenin's strategic retreat of the 1920s, Gorbachev's retreat is also an offensive. In the vocabulary of Soviet military scientists, the 'new thinking' is an operational-level, combined arms offensive designed to ensure that the *strategic* defensive operation succeeds.[26] Behind the *leitmotif* of the 'new thinking'—an 'interrelated, interdependent and integral world'—is a policy of new linkages for old: a policy designed to render associations unfavourable to Soviet interests (*eg* NATO) ineffectual and irrelevant.[27] Like Lenin's *peredyshka*, Gorbachev's is active and creative. It will be successful if, at its completion, the world as well as the USSR ends up 'reconstructed'.

Ever conscious of historical precedent, Gorbachev, like Stalin (though not in the manner of Stalin), seeks to haul Soviet industry fifty years forward in one decade. Also, like Stalin, he wisely opts against rearmament today for investment in the industrial base which will support rearmament tomorrow. Like Lenin, he asks for a breathing space from his rivals in order to become a fitter rival himself. NATO's advanced technology initiatives prompt fears that his rivals may not give him one. These fears run deep. The danger, however, is that, as on earlier occasions, the Soviet Union may discover its fears are excessive and, on the strength of its own efforts, return to the offensive.

130 JAMES SHERR

Notes

The author gratefully acknowledges the assistance provided by the staff of the Soviet Studies Research Centre, RMA Sandhurst and, in particular, Christopher Donnelly, Charles Dick and the late Joe Chachulski for their comments on an earlier draft of this paper.

1. N. V. Ogarkov, *Vsegda v gotovnosti k zashchite otechestva* (Always in readiness to defend the fatherland) (Moscow: Voyenizdat, 1982), p. 31, in Notra Trulock III, *Soviet Perspectives on Limited Nuclear Warfare* (Camberley: Soviet Studies Research Centre, RMA Sandhurst—hereafter, SSRC, 1987), p. 30.

2. *Ibid.*, p. 53. Also Major-General S. N. Kozlov, ed., *The Officer's Handbook*, Moscow, 1971 (US edition, trans. by US Air Force), pp. 61-66. 'Doktrina Voyennaya' (Military Doctrine), *Voyennyy Entsiklopedicheskiy Slovar'* (Military Encyclopedic Dictionary) (Moscow: Voyenizdat, 1983), p. 240.

3. General S. P. Ivanov, *Nachal'nyi Period Voiny* (The Initial Period of War) (Voyenizdat, 1974), from P. H. Vigor, *Soviet Blitzkrieg Theory* (London: Macmillan, 1983). Vigor's book provides the most comprehensive treatment of the subject in English.

4. For a concise summary of these writings, see P. H. Vigor, *The Soviet View of War, Peace and Neutrality* (London: Routledge & Kegan Paul), pp. 16-23. James Sherr, *Soviet Power: The Continuing Challenge* (London: Macmillan/RUSI, 1987), pp. 95-107.

5. Michael MccGwire, *Military Objectives in Soviet Foreign Policy* (Washington, DC: Brookings, 1987), pp. 18-19 and *passim*.

6. C. J. Dick, *Soviet Views on Strategic and Operational Surprise and Deception* (Camberley: Soviet Studies Research Centre, RMA Sandhurst—hereafter, SSRC, October 1986), Paper C57; P. H. Vigor, *Soviet Blitzkrieg Theory*, pp. 1-9, 144-167. A recent and important Soviet source on surprise is M. M. Kir'yan, ed., *Vnezapnost' v Nastupatel'nykh Operatsiyakh Velikoy Otechestvennoy Voiny* (Surprise in Offensive Operations of the Great Patriotic War) (Moscow: Voyenizdat, 1986).

7. Roger Beaumont, *Maskirovka; Soviet Camouflage, Concealment and Deception*, Stratech Studies SS82-1 (College Station, Texas: Center for Strategic Technology), 1982. Also chapters by John J. Dziak, Richard J. Heurer, Jr., William R. Harris and Notra Turlock III in Brian D. Dailey and Patrick J. Parker, *Soviet Strategic Deception* (Lexington, Massachusetts: Lexington Books and Hoover Institution Press, 1987).

8. The belief in the relevance of operations in the Great Patriotic War to future conventional war with NATO is occasionally made explicit; *eg*, Major General S. Shtrik, 'The Encirclement and Destruction of the Enemy during Combat Operations not Involving the Use of Nuclear Weapons', *Voyennaya Mysl'* (Military Thought), no. 1, January 1968, FPD0093/68, 22 May 1968, in *Selected Readings from Soviet Military Thought*, (US Government Printing Office: Washington, DC), 1982, p. 188. Army General P. Lashchenko, 'Sovershenstvovaniye Sposobov okruzheniya i unichtozheniya krupnykh gruppirovok protivnika po opytu velikoy otechestvennoy voiny' (Perfection of Methods of Encirclement and Destruction of Large Enemy Groupings based on the Experience of the Great Patriotic War), *Voyenno-istoricheskiy Zhurnal* (Military Historical Journal), January 1985, cited in John G. Hines, 'Encirclement' (Camberley: SSRC, April 1985), paper A74.

9. To quote the American authority, John G. Hines: 'The NATO army group commander co-ordinates the activities of four or five subordinate national corps which, in the Soviet view, are mostly "higher tactical units", and he depends on the Allied Air Forces, Central Europe (AAFCE) for "air support" of his operations. The Soviet Front commander *commands* two to six combined-arms or tank armies, each of which the Soviets consider to be a large operational formation, and, perhaps most important, he *commands* his own air army.' John Hines, *op. cit.*, p. 1.

10. Because these weapons will be under attack, pressure would be all the greater to release them in a timely fashion. The Soviets could not exclude the possibility that the US President and SACEUR (in his capacity as Commander-in-Chief of US Forces in Europe) would bypass NATO's release procedures *in extremis*. Since GLCM and Pershing II can strike the USSR, they are strategic weapons from the Soviet point of view. It requires no imagination to grasp how much simpler Warsaw Pact operations in West Germany would become once these systems were withdrawn.

11. R. Pawloski, *Changes in Soviet Air Combat Doctrine and Force Structure* (Camberley: SSRC, January 1986), paper B25.
12. C. N. Donnelly, 'The Soviet Operational Manoeuvre Group: A New Challenge for NATO', *Military Review*, (9/1983).
13. Army General A. I. Radziyevskiy, *Tankoviy Udar* (Tank Strike) (Moscow: Voyenizdat, 1976), cited in C. N. Donnelly, *Echeloning* (Camberley: SSRC, December 1984), Paper A64.
14. Lt. General V. G. Reznichenko, ed., *Taktika* (Tactics) (Moscow: Voyenizdat, 1984); John Hines, *op. cit.*, pp. 15-21; Stephen R. Covington, *The Role of the Defence in Soviet Military Thinking* (Camberley: SSRC, September 1987), Paper C64.
15. For a good summary of AirLand Battle and FOFA, see Boyd D. Sutton *et al.*, 'Deep Attack Concepts and the Defence of Central Europe', *Survival*, vol. xxvi, no. 2 (March/April 1984).
16. *Discriminate Deterrence: Report of the Commission on Integrated Long-Term Strategy* (Washington, DC: US Government Printing Office, 1988).
17. Col. V. Volobyev and Lt. Col. N. Nikolayev, 'The AirLand Operation (Battle)', *Zarubezhnoye Voyennoye Obozreniye* (Foreign Military Review)—hereafter *ZVO*, (July 1984).
18. Lt. Col. V. Kulikov and Lt. Col. V. Stroginov, 'S Becpetsedentnym Razmakhom' (On an Unprecedented Scale), *Krasnaya Zvezda* (Red Star), 16 January, 1985. General-Lieutenant M. Proskurin, 'Shto Kroyetcya za "Planom Rodzhersa"?' (What Lies Behind the Rogers Plan?), *Krasnaya Zvezda*, 3 December 1985.
19. Lt. Col. U. Andreyev, 'Bundesver: Udarnaya Sila NATO' (The Bundeswehr: NATO's Striking Force'), *ZVO*, (September 1984).
20. Lt. Col. V. Viktorov, 'Novaya Kontseptsiya NATO "Rodzhers Plan"' (NATO's New Concept: The "Rogers Plan"), *ZVO*, (February 1985).
21. *Ibid.* General-Lieutenant M. Proskurin, *op. cit.*
22. General-Major I. N. Vorobyev, 'Novoye Oruzhiye i printsipy taktiki' (Tactical Principles for the New Weapons), *Sovetskoye Voyennoye Obozreniye* (Soviet Military Review), No. 1-2 (January and February 1987).
23. Stephen R. Covington, *op. cit.* See also Kerry L. Hines, *Emerging Soviet Concerns and Countermeasures to the Advanced Conventional Munitions Threat* (Arlington, Virginia: Pacific-Sierra Reserach Corporation, August 1987), PSR Note 796.
24. General Ye. Ivanovskiy (C-in-C of Soviet Ground Forces) stated that 'in the new training year (1986) it is necessary to pay particular attention to mastering effective examples and methods of fighting against an enemy who employs precision weapons'. Army General Ye. Ivanovskiy, 'Glavnoye v deyatel'nosti voysk-boevaya ucheba', *Voyennyy Vestnik* (Military Herald), No. 1 (January 1986), p. 4. In Kerry Hines, *op. cit.*, p. 22.
25. While 'disarmament' is no doubt the most publicized element of the 'New Thinking', it also embraces reconciliation with estranged states (China and Israel), regional diplomatic initiatives, both conspicuous (Middle East) and not (Southern Africa), economic overtures (*eg*, ASEAN) and—perhaps most far-reaching in its implications—the healing of wounds within the (long-fragmented) international Communist movement. For a similar assessment, see *Gorbachev and the Struggle for the Future* (Fort Leavenworth, Kansas: Soviet Army Studies Office, December 1987).
26. Mikhail Gorbachev, *October and Perestroika: The Revolution Continues* ('Jubilee speech' to the CPSU Central Committee, 2 November 1987), (Moscow: Novosti Press Agency Publishing House, 1987), p. 59.

SECTION 5
Alliances in Transition

IN a famous passage, J. H. Elliot, the historian of seventeenth-century Spain, explained the country's decline as a failure of readjustment. It was Spain's misfortune that in its hour of need its ruling class

> ... lacked the breadth of vision and the strength of character to break with a past that could no longer serve as a reliable guide to the future. ... At a time when the face of Europe was altering more rapidly than ever before, the country that had once been its leading power proved to be lacking the essential ingredient of survival—the willingness to change.

Ten years later Alistair Buchan in End of the Post War Era echoed almost exactly the same thoughts about the Atlantic Alliance—an institution whose 'ossification' he attributed in large measure to a failure of political leadership.

In recommending the revitalization of the Western European Union (WEU) David Harvey and Dexter Jerome Smith believe that it is the Europeans who must set an example, an example which might inspire the United States—the Alliance's 'leading power' and a country which might also be said to be in a state of 'decline'—to come to grips with the problems outlined in this volume of essays. Their essay is an unadapted version of a paper produced in 1987 by a British Conservative party lobby which was particularly well received by the West German government, as well as the WEU itself.

In Eastern Europe Jonathan Eyal suggests that the lead will be set not by the Europeans but the Soviet Union, and not in the Warsaw Pact, but COMECON. Through greater economic integration lies the road to translating the Warsaw Pact itself into a true alliance, not a coalition of powers whose interests and those of the USSR are not always immediately apparent to the outside observer. One thing is clear; the time for empty gestures is long since past. If both alliances are to survive the economic challenges of the 1990s they will have to change—an argument, alas, which is not unfamiliar to those academic writers who have been arguing the point since 1974.

CHAPTER 8

In Defence of Europe— The Western European Union Reinvigorated

DAVID HARVEY and DEXTER JEROME SMITH

Introduction

The need for a strong and balanced NATO continues. The former NATO Secretary-General Lord Carrington concluded that the problem is 'not that America is too strong but that Europe is too weak'. A concerted effort by the seven member nations of the Western European Union (WEU)— Britain, France, West Germany, Italy, the Netherlands, Belgium and Luxembourg—could help redress the balance.

There have been numerous efforts to strengthen the European pillar of NATO since the 1950s. This essay asserts that a stronger European partner in the Alliance is in the interest of both the United States and the peoples of Europe. The economic and political need for a successful initiative has never been greater. The European Community has, so far, consistently rejected embracing a security dimension. In these circumstances the initiative to revive the Western European Union (WEU) provides the best hope for progress.

The process of European construction is lengthy and difficult. The recommendations made here are all attainable but in some cases represent more long-term goals. The important thing is to establish landmarks to work towards. The approach outlined in this essay is an incremental one and includes many proposals of a more near-term nature to help the process along.

A More Purposeful Union

Attempts to reinvigorate the WEU do not imply dissatisfaction with the NATO Alliance. There is nothing inconsistent about a strong WEU within a strong NATO. The one should lead to the other. Advocating the restructuring and revitalization of the WEU recognizes both that the organization needs an overhaul to work better, and that when working well the WEU has the potential to do things that NATO as a whole cannot.

135

In its early years, in the mid-1950s, the WEU provided the treaty framework for a war-torn and defeated Germany to enter the new interdependent community of nations being established by the Western powers. This led to German membership of NATO and the European Community. The WEU also helped resolve the Franco-German sovereignty dispute over the Saar territory. It became the only institution through which France could work out the detail of its contribution to the common security of Western Europe after the French withdrawal from NATO's integrated Military Command in 1966. It provided the only European forum for Britain to meet regularly with the original six members of the European Community prior to Britain's EC membership in 1973.

Today, the WEU provides the only European forum where member Defence and Foreign Ministers can sit around the same table and discuss defence matters. This does not happen in the European Community because that institution still has no security dimension, and it does not happen in NATO's EuroGroup either, essentially because French membership of NATO is confined to the political level: France being a member of the Atlantic Council but not of the Integrated Military Command.

The Treaty of Brussels, one of the foundation stones upon which the WEU rests, contains a binding commitment to afford fellow members 'all the military and other aid and assistance in their power' should one come under armed attack. Like NATO, the WEU operates on the premise that an attack on one is an attack on all. But, unlike NATO, there is no scope for fellow members to interpret, ignore and delay in their response to an encroachment on Allied territory. Moreover, whereas WEU treaty obligations allow for member countries to engage in military operations 'out of area' in concert wearing their WEU colours, NATO treaty obligations do not give similar latitude for out-of-area operations.

In the field of armaments co-operation too, the WEU is empowered to go further than NATO. NATO is making some encouraging progress here through, for example, bodies like the Independent European Programme Group (IEPG). However, the WEU actually has an agency in being for the development of armaments collaboration with a remit to pursue not just collaborative armaments production (which the IEPG does), but to go beyond that to establish common programmes for procurement, sustainability, support and logistical reinforcement.

It is because the members of the WEU coincidentally represent the hard core of the European defence community, as well as the greater latitude offered within the WEU format, that the WEU has such tremendous potential. Moreover, the need has never been so great for the WEU to take up the challenge it was created for, namely to be an embryonic European Defence Community. With a US-Soviet agreement on intermediate-range nuclear forces now signed, it should be apparent that future progress on disarmament in Europe will require Europeans making European initiatives in the field of arms control, and it is the WEU countries that would necessarily be the key players, because they are the most directly affected.

With regard to defence procurement, all the WEU members are well aware now that their domestic markets are too small for economic acquisitions for the larger, more expensive and highly sophisticated items of military equipment that need to be bought. WEU countries could collaborate better in purchasing defence items, not least because they all have similar requirements and similar technological and industrial capabilities.

Also, the need for out-of-area international peacekeeping operations seems to be growing daily. Often the 'hot-spot' countries have historical and sometimes colonial ties with the member nations of the WEU. These WEU nations may retain considerable influence that might be appropriately harnessed to bring peace to countries in turmoil, but at the same time few WEU countries have much in the way of means when it comes to projecting military power to far flung places all by themselves. Too often the United States is left to police trouble-spots too far away for effective action by a single European power, and the risks of a regional crisis becoming a point of conflict between the superpowers is ever present as a result.

Even those Americans most understanding of the European situation are still inclined to warn Europe of the dangers of not bearing its fair share of the burden of maintaining the security of the Western world. America's concern for Europe and understanding of its position is likely to diminish in the years to come if for no other reason than that American interests, concerns and sympathies will be drawn to other corners of the globe. Already, America trades more across the Pacific than across the Atlantic; and by the year 2000 more than one quarter of America's population will be of Latin American and Asian origin. Strong forces are pulling America's attention away from Europe; Europe had, thus, better be able to stand on its own two feet to keep NATO/US relationships strong and healthy.

Making WEU Work

Given the suitability of the WEU to take up the slack between NATO and the European Community and be the catalyst for creating a true European defence identity—a forum for exploring European security issues—why has it not risen to the challenge?

There are two answers to this question. First, the gap WEU could fill is so ill-defined that a gradual evolutionary process must be adopted. Secondly, although the engines of change are working, the interests of the parties concerned have not necessarily been focused enough to produce much in the way of an end result. The creation of the common defence identity, lacking in Europe today, necessitates the growth of a public perception of European common interests. WEU Secretary-General Alfred Cahen states that the 'reactivated Western European Union must justify its existence by actions and by deeds'. After four years of revival it is time that we saw both.

Reactivation Progress

Progress has been slow. To quote St. Augustine, the WEU powers appear to want 'Chastity, but not just yet'. To be fair, the WEU's founders also wanted the organization to function as a pillar of NATO and European construction but they found the same problems of contradictory interests and half-heartedness. Their failure left WEU descending into an inactivity that has taken some considerable time and effort to amend.

The founders of WEU quite clearly intended to establish a close association between Europe's unity and security. The 1948 Brussels Treaty and the 1954 Paris Agreements, which established WEU in the form that it has held for most of its life, followed directly from the failure of the French Pleven plan to create a European Defence Community with its own army. With the passing of time both NATO and the emerging European Community appeared to be more appropriate forums to consider European security issues. The question of a European defence dimension raised only intermittent interest. WEU became a centre for the performance of secondary tasks, such as monitoring the arms build-up and providing a link between the Community and the United Kingdom before 1973. WEU became a twilight organization.

Member governments could hardly dissolve a symbol of their unity. There were other, more subtle, means of marginalizing this body. One senior UK parliamentarian remarked that the officials he had met as a junior member of the Assembly in the 1950s were still there upon his return to a senior WEU post, twenty years later; the only difference was that they were slightly more hard of hearing. The organization was allowed to atrophy. During a great part of the 1970s and early 1980s the Ministerial Council did not meet. The Permanent Council, comprising Ambassadors to the Court of St. James's and charged with day to day supervision, met only a handful of times a year. Only the Assembly's vociferous attempts to assert itself suggested that the WEU might still be alive.

When the WEU came to be revived by the 1984 Rome Declaration most commentators were unwilling to take the organization's 'rebirth certificate' seriously. This was an honest reflection upon the WEU as it stood. The first task had been to wake the organization from its slumber and give it strength and purpose. This has been a gradual process so as to avoid having a semi-comatose WEU crashing into the path of either the European Community or NATO. A steady and discreet approach overcame much of the legacy of twenty years of inactivity and helps explain the slow progress and the frequent fogginess of the awakening sleeper.

The Rome and Venice Declarations

The 1984 Rome and the 1986 Venice Declarations established a channel for the harmonization of security policy. Since 1984 the Ministerial and Permanent Councils have established common principles in a number of areas of concern. The Strategic Defence Initiative, terrorism and the current Gulf crisis provide three examples. Progress has been made either by direct action or, more in keeping with the nature of the beast, by discussion, debate and then leverage upon other institutions.

The re-establishment of the meetings of the Ministerial and Permanent Councils as regular features in the diplomatic calendar have given WEU the credibility that it so obviously lacked before. The Ministerial meetings have achieved a consistently high media profile. Behind the activities of both Councils, the Secretariat was largely restaffed and the existing structure, if under-resourced, was made reasonably effective. In anticipation of the increasingly important role that the WEU will take in European defence policy development and research three experimental agencies were established:
— an agency for the study of arms control and disarmament questions;
— an agency for the examination of security and defence questions;
— an agency for the development of co-operation in the field of armaments.
These bodies have largely superceded older structures and are beginning to serve both the Councils and the Secretariat as intended. The arms control agency was involved in briefing European governments on Soviet negotiating tactics. The arms co-operation agency has begun to exercise its liaison function between the more technical bodies directly involved in project work, such as the Independent European Programme Group (IEPG) within NATO.

The Western European Union has started to provide a means for the dialogue necessary for the emergence of a European defence identity. Thus it has begun to achieve what the signatories of the Rome Declaration were asking for. Yet the achievements today have been, on the whole, administrative, rather than concrete, and very much on the lower end of the scale of difficulty. Major question marks remain over the public's perception of the WEU, the suitability of its present structure for achieving objectives as well as the real extent of the commitment of member nations.

Europeans find it hard to accept that they have common security interests, requiring a closer unity. The issue is not one that merits a serious place on most political agendas. It is not hard to point to particular areas of vulnerability. The German SPD and Green Parties and the British Labour Party are potentially suspect friends to the North Atlantic Alliance. They represent a swath of vague anti-American sentiment that goes wider than the bounds of their own parties. None of these groups has any concept of a European defence identity. A realization of common interest would serve to strengthen, rather than weaken, the appreciation of the American presence in Europe.

Both NATO and the Western European Union need to be underpinned by popular understanding and support. The WEU policy document *WEU and Public Awareness* came to this conclusion in 1985 and its recommendations were accepted by both Councils. Yet in April 1987 the Assembly noted, 'The absence of effective and adequate information given to the public on the (Ministerial) Council's activities'. Such a situation left 'considerable doubt about its intention to set up a European pillar of the Atlantic Alliance'. The strategy had not been implemented. The issue might be placed in context if it is noted that the limitations placed upon resources means that, at the time of writing, the Secretariat is only just able to consider circulating the speeches of the Secretary-General to an audience beyond the walls of his headquarters.

WEU ORGANIZATION

The following criticisms can be made:

1. A Permanent Council manned by Ambassadors accredited to the nation hosting the Secretariat is not an appropriate executive body to lead the revitalized WEU. Although the major features of policy will continue to be decided by the Council of Ministers, a permanent day-to-day management committee is needed with the time to keep a firm hold on the reins. The present team of Ambassadors have a full range of diplomatic duties and do not have that time.

2. The present organization of WEU lacks the independence necessary to allow it to put pressure on those member nations lagging behind.

3. No business would locate interdependent departments of its head office in two different capital cities. Most of WEU's policy and research functions are in Paris, while the executive is located in London.

4. The WEU Assembly is composed of European parliamentarians. The same MPs meet at WEU, the North Atlantic Assembly and a number of similar bodies. They are also expected to shoulder a full range of parliamentary duties in their home countries. A revived WEU will make increased demands upon its Assembly. It is doubtful if many MPs would be able to meet these demands effectively. Furthermore, European construction is a matter for interests and expertise beyond the purely political. It could be said that the Assembly requires a wider skills base, including industrialists, civil servants, diplomats and members of the academic community to provide a wider talent pool to prepare the intellectual and policy framework necessary for the creation of a European defence identity.

5. The Assembly has noted that the functions allocated to the new agencies for research and policy are 'inadequate and vague'. The role of these agencies is defined only in the most general terms, certainly without the detail necessary to allow the development of policy frameworks. The structure of the Permanent Council is such as to leave it unable to

provide regular direction that might substitute for clear mandates. The Council meetings are too infrequent.

6. The Secretariat is largely the revived structure found in place in 1984. Most of the support services that the Secretariat can provide are diverted toward the Assembly. There are inadequate resources available for full servicing of the two Councils or for external functions, whether educative, promotional or diplomatic.

7. The WEU member governments have made a general agreement to restrict the availability of new resources. If revival is to become revitalization then fresh funds will have to be made forthcoming to see that the job is done properly.

8. The debate over the admission of new members to WEU is a source of embarrassment. Portugal has already applied to join and Spain would like to do so. The Assembly recognizes the need to proceed with the Portugese application because of the importance of maintaining good relations with NATO's non-WEU members. These non-WEU countries can hardly be impressed by the insult done to one of NATO's firmer adherents by the length of the delay in the processing of its application. The Councils, on the other hand, adhere to the general principle that the admission of new members must be preceded by the drafting of a set of entry qualifications. This is the best way to preserve the WEU as the defence hard core of Europe while still allowing for the entry by new members. In any event the issue must be faced quickly.

9. All of the WEU institutions recognize their contributory role to the Atlantic Alliance. During the initial stages of revival, informal links with NATO were all that were needed, but these should now be formalized. The members of NATO not in the WEU need an open channel for consultation. Good lines of communication with the European Community are essential. The WEU is merely a substitute forum until such a time as the European Community can bring itself to develop an effective security dimension. If the Community were ever to bring itself to grasp the nettle, the WEU would be redundant.

One recent Assembly report suggests that structural and policy deficiencies are symptomatic of a lack of commitment from some if not all the WEU powers. 'Implementation of the principles agreed on in Rome seem to have run up against various obstacles which are difficult to define since the governments have done the utmost to conceal them. In any event ... one has to record a succession of uncertainties and evasions in the Council's work, which has fallen far short of the intentions expressed in Rome'.

Each of the ailments diagnosed here could be cured. Effective growth toward the achievement of the longer term aims implied by the Rome Declaration will only be achieved if member states are willing to put at least some of their doubts behind them, face up to the WEU's problems and take their medicine.

Policies for Progress

If previous agreements hold, the butterfly will emerge from the chrysalis, even if, as is only to be expected, it looks a little fragile to begin with. The decisions made at the WEU Ministerial Council meeting on 26-27 October 1987, particularly the Platform on European Security Interests, define the way in which the WEU will develop and determine the degree of success that it is likely to encounter. The WEU Secretary-General has written: 'The question we must now ask is whether the Western European Union is able to discharge the responsibilities which have been given to it . . . the proof of the pudding is in the eating'.

The changes that the Ministerial Council ought to impose should attend to the structural problems of the WEU and to its position in the world as a whole. Some of our suggestions are trial balloons but only because they try to see the problems of a more distant European future. This is always a most difficult task but it is one that has to be and, eventually, is the function that WEU must perform if it is to prove its continuing worth.

THE WEU SECURITY COMMUNIQUÉ

The Platform on European Security Interests adopted at the WEU Ministerial Meeting of October 1987 should be taken as a statement of credo. In particular, it should be regarded as:

—A reassertion of the commitment of the WEU powers to the North Atlantic Alliance and of the need for the European members within it to play a more purposeful and united role.

—A statement of support for the NATO strategy of Flexible Response, including nuclear deterrence, identifying it as the most effective defence posture for Europe and stating the need for unified European action to make Europe's contribution to that defence both more effective and fairer in terms of burden-sharing.

—A statement of the need for the WEU powers to speak in unison both within the Alliance and in world affairs as a whole. The present babble of sixteen different voices in NATO expressing sometimes sixteen different views on just about every issue has been one of the major reasons for the success of Soviet diplomacy. The existence of two strong pillars in NATO would still allow for a diversity of opinions but would also allow quicker and more effective decision-making.

—Recognition that WEU members expect their organization to take part in foreign affairs outside of NATO's EuroGroup structure, and sometimes outside the NATO area of responsibility. Better burden-sharing means that the Europeans must also assist in part of the policing activity that the United States presently conducts around the world.

—Recognition of the need for at least a semi-official umbrella organization to guide European arms procurement. The long-term aim should be the establishment of a European free market in defence products that will allow European companies to compete on the same footing as their American counterparts.

—Recognition that signing the communiqué acts as a threshold to be crossed by new WEU members to ensure that WEU continues to represent 'the hard core' of the European defence community.

However, even a Platform statement with all these elements will accomplish nothing unless it is supported by other material actions; in which case it will at last symbolize a new European unity to the world. Ultimately, as with the 12-nation European Community, there must be recognition that the WEU should be able to act upon a majority vote of its members, which would allow that majority the right to embark upon a course of action as they felt appropriate without always having to achieve unanimity.

ACADEMY OF DEFENCE SCIENCES

The creation of an academic centre of excellence for the defence community in Europe should be a realizable long-term objective. WEU has been seeking to bring together numbers of the great and the good for regular brain-storming sessions and this is the first stage. Potentially, bringing together such a brains trust could help member states to work together in this field and create a mindset conducive to greater co-operation. But, as with other areas of WEU activity, without a focused near-term objective progress is likely to be a long time in coming.

Under an independent initiative, an agreement has been reached on forming a consortium between three NATO colleges aimed at establishing a common core curriculum for the study of international arms collaboration programmes. The Defence Systems Management College in the US, the Royal Military College of Science at Shrivenham in Britain and the Federal Academy at Mannheim in West Germany are to participate as partners in establishing centres of educational excellence in the field of armaments co-operation.

The US Defence Department has advanced $100,000 to facilitate two conferences for these participating NATO colleges, the first in May 1988, the second in May 1989, both at the Defence Systems Management College at Fort Belvoir, Virginia. After the second of these it is envisaged that the consortium will launch into a study to produce the desired common curriculum, but to support this latter activity a budget of $7 m. has to be raised in voluntary contributions from governments and industry. A contribution from the WEU, perhaps in exchange for some involvement in the curriculum study, would be a very positive development likely to produce good results. It would also be a good first step on the road toward establishing a WEU Academy of Defence Sciences.

As well as offering courses on international armaments co-operation programmes, including project management, the WEU Academy should aim to offer studies and research opportunities advancing understanding and practices related to arms control matters, strategic affairs, and military doctrine and operational tactics, all topics which a more purposeful European defence community might perhaps increasingly have to approach from a distinctively European perspective.

A project management school at the WEU Academy could offer training to all those involved in administering defence procurements—civil servants, military personnel and contractors—teaching the necessary skills for effective management. Too many major European procurement programmes have nose-dived into disaster. Some programmes, such as the Nimrod airborne early warning system and the SP70 howitzer, both recently cancelled, and the still struggling Franco-German Common Anti-tank Helicopter (CATH) and the eight-nation NATO NFR-90 frigate, show little attention to sound project management principles. This shortage of management skills needs to be rectified; unchecked it just speeds up the process of structural disarmament, eroding Western defence capabilities.

In addition, a WEU Academy of Defence Studies would provide the focus for a series of shorter-term programmes to bring together a wide range of talented people who might otherwise not get the opportunity to meet and learn from each other.

WEU AND THE PUBLIC

The Assembly's criticism that the Secretariat has failed to publicize the institution's work needs to be answered with action. The Secretariat should have a full Press and information department to ensure the widest possible circulation of information. The work of the various agencies of the WEU should also be more widely publicized.

The essential part of this public affairs function should be exercised through the establishment of WEU offices in each member state. Each office would:

—Provide a regular circulation of information to the defence community.

—Organize courses and seminars in host nations, perhaps in future in conjuction with the proposed Academy of Defence Sciences.

—Establish links between the procurement agencies of the WEU and the business community.

—Provide the central institutions of the WEU with feedback from member nations.

—Provide a flow of information to the general public.

Institutional Reform

THE PERMANENT COUNCIL

The Permanent Council should be composed of Ambassadors specifically accredited to the WEU, who would hold the post for a fixed term to give them some degree of independence, and it would continue to be chaired by the Secretary-General.

REFORM OF THE ASSEMBLY

The Assembly should be a pool from which the Councils and Secretariat of the WEU can draw specialist skills and knowledge to assist in the conduct of studies and the business of policy formulation as and when necessary. The applications of the European defence identity are ill-defined. The Assembly can field the expertise to fill in the picture.

To help the Assembly in continuing to uphold its brief, monitoring the work of both of the WEU Councils, while also reflecting the expanded role of the organization, the structure of the Assembly should be changed. Member states should formulate a list of Parliamentarians, industrialists, civil servants, diplomats and experienced commentators or academics, and draw from that list as required. A second group of delegates would be sent to the Assembly from the European Parliament where national groups from WEU member states would despatch a small expert party in accordance with the party political composition of their representation. This European parliamentary element would be essential to confirm the WEU's political legitimacy as a representative body.

Each delegation would be led by its own accredited Ambassador. The role of delegation members would depend in part upon their status and specialism. All would be able to take a part in committee work but some, such as the civil servants, would play a less active part in the meetings of the Assembly. The Assembly meetings would continue to monitor the work of the Councils and the Secretariat. But a primary function of the new Assembly would be to provide committee personnel for working groups. The presence of an Ambassador on WEU national delegations in the Assembly would allow delegates a second channel through which to monitor and question the work of the WEU's Executive.

THE SECRETARIAT

The Secretariat needs to be better resourced to allow it to establish a full-scale public affairs department both to back up the work of the new committees of the Assembly and handle external relations with other European and Alliance bodies. In the longer term, thought should be given to appointing a political figurehead to lead WEU as an executive President, chairing the meetings of the Assembly and the Ministerial Council; the Secretary-General continuing to chair the Permanent Council and be administrative head of the Secretariat.

A Rapid Deployment Force

In NATO, the forces of the sixteen member nations are organized so as to be able to fight side-by-side in the event of war. There are no truly international units in the sense of, for example, soldiers from different countries being in the same battalion or brigade in the field; (though in Command headquarters it has proved possible to achieve such an international mix).

The dream of creating an internationalised European Army has existed in the minds of European federalists since the creation of that movement. It was pursued by the countries of the WEU and might have become a reality in 1954 had an agreed proposal not been voted down by the French Assembly of Deputies. In 1987, the idea sprung to life again; France and the Federal Republic of Germany have agreed to form a Franco-German infantry unit commanded, at least initially, by a French officer. At a Press conference after the conclusion of a Franco-German military exercise (Cheaky Sparrow) in south Germany in September 1987, President Mitterand of France and Chancellor Kohl of West Germany made it known that they would be willing to see other European countries sending forces to join and further internationalize the Franco-German Unit.

Though there are no plans for this at present, this offer might be something that WEU countries could, and certainly should, seriously consider, representing, as they do, the hard core of the European defence community. An enlarged Franco-German Unit could grow into a WEU force *de facto*. It could grow to Corps-size, and this 'European Corps' might ideally include amphibious and air elements giving it a combined arms operational capability. Such a force would, of course, not be under NATO command because of France being outside NATO's Integrated Military Command Structure. But there would be some advantages in that. A European Corps involving all WEU members would necessarily be operating within the context of supporting the North Atlantic Treaty Organization without requiring a change in the French position on NATO membership.

This force could do a very useful job, for example, in the rear of the area of NATO's forward defences in a logistical and support role or chasing down a deep penetration by a Soviet Operational Manoeuvre Group (OMG). Or it could support neutral friendly countries like Sweden, Finland or Austria, which could not take help from NATO. It might even be able to serve a broader out-of-area role, engaged in international peacekeeping duties around the world, thereby taking some of the burden off the shoulders of the United States, which has been forced into the role of a sort of global policeman.

There may be some areas where the European Corps would be a very welcome substitute, either because European influence is actually greater, or else because there exists a high risk of superpower confrontation.

If all this seems somewhat remote it should be noted that in 1988 five out of the seven WEU members (France, Italy, Belgium, the Netherlands and the UK) sent naval vessels to the Gulf; of the other two, Luxembourg did not have a navy, and West Germany's naval force did not have a 'blue water' capability because of the way in which German's Constitution limits the country's military potential. Nevertheless, West German naval vessels for the first time were sent into the Mediterranean to cover for absentee ships. It can be noted that the WEU did not need a joint command structure in place to achieve this, and some have argued that the absence of such a command structure in this case is politically advantageous. This is not to say, however, that the creation of a WEU joint military command would be a bad thing, and it certainly would not exclude the possibility of WEU members working separately but together.

Perhaps the creation of a WEU European Corps is a long way off, though maybe some immediate benefit could be gained by WEU members' armed forces simply exercising together. The point is that the Franco-German Unit could represent such a force in embryo; an offer is on the table from the French and the Germans for others to join, and if other WEU members do join that will *de facto* bring us closer to the creation of a WEU European Corps.

A WEU Procurement Agency

If a WEU military force were to be created it would logically have to have standardized equipment and supplies, and it would make sense for that equipment and supplies requirement to be met collectively rather than individually. Apart from this, however, it is clear that if countries can agree to buy items together, they can get better value for money, exploiting economies of scale from long production runs, and they will also exercise more power in the market place being able to dictate improved terms of sale.

The recent Anglo-French purchase of the E-3 airborne warning and control system (AWACS) aircraft has demonstrated that one does not necessarily need a joint procurement agency to achieve these advantages. At the same time, however, if this approach confers advantages with a single purchase, how much greater would the advantages be if such an approach were to be systematized through the creation of an international agency?

The criterion for any collaborative purchase has to be that it makes economic sense in the first place. If it is not economically efficient to collaborate, such collaboration should be avoided. A WEU procurement agency makes sense because the member nations of the WEU have a great deal in common both in terms of the technological requirements of their military forces and the production capabilities of their respective industrial sectors.

A NATO-wide procurement agency might be even more desirable but not necessarily as realistically achievable, given that NATO includes countries with little in the way of a defence industrial capacity. If a WEU procurement agency were to be created there would be nothing to stop it from being absorbed at a later stage into a NATO procurement agency if that proved appropriate. Certainly, if an individual procurement would be more economically efficient in the context of a body larger than the WEU, such as NATO or the European Space Agency (ESA), then that is where it should be.

Like a WEU European Corps, a WEU procurement agency may be a long way off. Perhaps the role and policies of such a hypothetical organization ought to be one of the first research tasks that the proposed WEU Academy of Defence Sciences should address.

Conclusion

Regardless of whether any of the proposals contained in this essay are taken up, the process of reactivating the Western European Union has begun, and not before time. The proposals considered here are meant to be helpful both to the future development of NATO and to the future development of the WEU. Such developments will necessarily be incremental, and so the objectives outlined range from the near-term to the far-distant. What should be emphasized most is the belief that a strong Europe means a strong NATO. The members of the WEU, representing the hard core of the European defence community, have both an obligation and an opportunity to give a lead, and in so doing to respond positively to the challenges now besetting the Atlantic Alliance.

This Chapter is published with the kind permission of the Bow Group, a policy research organization serving the British Conservative Party. It was first published as a Bow Paper in October 1987 immediately prior to the WEU Ministerial Meeting in The Hague at which the Platform on European Security Interests was signed.

CHAPTER 9

Gorbachev, Comecon and Eastern Europe: Attempting to Forge a True Alliance

JONATHAN EYAL

All Soviet leaders since Stalin have attempted to derive the maximum strategic benefits from their possession of Eastern Europe, while minimizing their financial commitment. Eastern Europe, a belt of buffer states which could be used both for the protection of the Soviet hinterland and also as a platform for the launch of any military offensive against Western Europe, remains strategically important. Furthermore, its military contribution is not insignificant: more than one third of all mobilized forces in Europe came from the region. Possession of these European states served as obvious evidence of the Soviet Union's Superpower status and confirmed the supposed accuracy of Marx's interpretation of the historical dialectic, under which a victory of the working class in a particular country remained irreversible.

These were the major advantages of the continued Soviet presence in Eastern Europe. During Stalin's rule and immediately after the establishment of Communist governments in all the states of the region, the balance of benefits accruing to the USSR from its possession was overwhelmingly favourable. Czechoslovakia was an industrial country with a disciplined workforce; the German Democratic Republic (GDR) boasted an educated population which could be made to work; Poland and Romania were rich in raw materials and sources of energy. Stalin was content to establish joint companies which only disguised a policy of plunder on behalf of the Soviet Union.

Soon after his death, however, it became clear that the economies of the countries which Stalin had incorporated in his socialist 'commonwealth' were rapidly sinking. The Soviet Union, as the manager of the empire, tried to find a solution. Every Soviet leader since the early 1950s has attempted to implement his own ideas and every one of them has failed. This was essentially because Moscow attempted to square a circle. It wanted to encourage self-sustaining economies, but desired them to be independent of any Western economic support. It sought to obtain economic advantages from the East

Europeans and thus minimize the costs of maintaining its empire. At the same time, it imposed on the region its own political, social and economic priorities. As the guardian of the true faith, which combined scientific analysis of history, international relations and economics, every reform implemented in the Soviet Union was, by definition, considered applicable to East European situations. A mishandling of East European events, insensitivity to the region's history, downright Soviet ignorance and arrogance and the systemic failures inherent in all command economies combined to prevent the adoption of any long-lasting solution to Eastern Europe's malaise.

From the Soviet viewpoint, the worst combination of events actually happened. Local Communist governments were not more secure, but less. Standards of living did not rise to keep up with the West, the commonwealth refused to become a showcase of social engineering; and military force still had to be used to restore order. Once this solution became increasingly difficult in the era of *détente* in the 1970s, Soviet financial help was increasingly required to prevent fresh social revolts. The empire did not become cheaper to maintain, but more expensive. It was not more homogenous, but more diverse.

This was the situation which Gorbachev found in 1985. In his handling of the East European problem, the new Soviet leader has shown that he has learned the lessons of past mistakes, identified the major problems and boldly set out to solve them. The nexus of the Gorbachev solution is a closer integration in which the Warsaw Pact and Comecon would become essential pillars. He has sought to strengthen these institutions with real powers which would bind his allies into a genuine association, based on mutual self-interest. Ever the realist, he has accepted that only self-interest could serve as a durable element in East European relations. Gorbachev's desire to fill the blank spots in Polish-Soviet relations, his almost explicit repudiation of the Brezhnev Doctrine, his emphasis on each Party being entitled to map out its own development strategy are all part of the same package.

The nexus of the integration package is economic and social reform. This may appear to be no different from Gorbachev's internal priorities at home but a careful reading of Soviet behaviour in Eastern Europe would suggest that the new leadership in the Kremlin is aware that the USSR's experience cannot be transferred immediately to the entire region. While he remains personally convinced that no socialist society can sustain its vitality unless economic reforms are combined with political change, the Soviet General Secretary is prepared to compromise on political change in Eastern Europe, at the price of achieving genuine economic co-operation. Gorbachev remains a *Soviet* leader, who looks at the Comecon states from his own national interest. His policies may still provoke a social explosion in Eastern Europe and may still fail. Nevertheless, should they succeed, if only partially, the East Europeans may still remember with fondness Brezhnev's 'period of stagnation' when all was unwell and yet manageable.

East European Economies until 1985

As long as the East European states were not incorporated directly into the Soviet 'family of nations', the independence of their régimes and their legitimacy both inside and outside their countries was important. Both Moscow and the East European governments opted for a policy of legitimization by tolerance; a slow but inexorable rise in the standard of living, coupled with the régimes' predictability and a reduction in the use of terror as means of social control, reinforced by impermeable frontiers would, it was argued, drive home the point that the régimes were there to stay.

As the examples of Hungary, Poland and the GDR show, the way the mixture of policies was applied did not concern Moscow greatly, as long as it was sure that basic rules were not broken: that the control of the Party over all walks of life and adherence to the alliance with the Soviet Union were beyond question. One country which perceived the pecking order of Soviet priorities and used it to its advantage was, of course, Romania. It is also Romania which currently presents the best example of the ultimate failure of Soviet policy to manage its alliance through a mixture of *diktat* and national independence, without laying solid foundations based on joint economic and security interests. It was a half-way house which produced little integration, perpetuated inherently unstable régimes and still portrayed the Soviet Union to the world as an imperial power.

During the 1970s, in particular, Brezhnev was convinced that the formula had worked. He genuinely believed that long-term economic growth could be achieved, resulting in turn in political cohesion, without undertaking unacceptable political reforms. This strategy, which grew directly out of the invasion of Czechoslovakia in 1968, entailed pursuing *détente*, which brought the region financial and technological assistance from the West and allowed their economies to expand, coupled with half-hearted attempts at integration within Comecon. Some of the region's economies did, indeed, register spectacular industrial growth rates which promised full employment and a seemingly unstoppable rise in local standards of living. Hungary is the most cited example of a country which benefited from the ability to shape its own economic policies while not straying outside the bounds of permissible behaviour. The GDR was equally successful in the 1970s. In fact, the Brezhnev solution unravelled very soon.

Poland was the prime example of this failure. The Polish government accepted massive credits from Western banks but handed them over to the bureaucracy. This bloated body of Party and state activists proved incapable of absorbing new technology or directing resources to the industries of the future—an essential step, for most East European states aimed to repay their debts through increased exports. White elephants sprung up everywhere, industrial production still proved unable to compete on open markets, hard currency could not be obtained and debts mounted. The party was over by the end of the 1970s and resulted in an explosion in Poland; Hungary and Romania, however, were also on the brink of economic collapse.

The Soviet Union had two options. The first was to allow the East European economies to cope as best they could with the situation, partly by restricting local consumption and imports in order to repay their debts and partly by diverting more products to exports. This could risk further social crises. Moscow's alternative was to step in and redeem the East European's debts. That would prove difficult for the Soviet economy, which was itself under severe strain. The solution adopted by Brezhnev was typical of him: a compromise between these two options. Assistance, mainly in the form of raw materials supplies, was provided on a selective basis. At the same time, the East Europeans were expected to undertake their own belt-tightening policies.

The Soviet Union gave no indication, however, of having perceived the irony of the situation: yet another of its policies was falling apart. Governments could not assure prosperity and at the same time fulfil their societies' political aspirations. Eastern Europe remained an economic liability for Moscow. At the end of Brezhnev's rule Comecon's members owed almost $54 bn. in hard currency.[1] In 1973, Eastern Europe ran a surplus of $600 m. in its trade with the USSR. By 1980, the deficit stood at $1.6 m. and was growing rapidly. Moreover, Soviet subsidies to the region reached a staggering $18 bn. by 1982. Clearly, this situation could not be allowed to go on for much longer, yet, as a sick leader succeeded a dying one in the Kremlin, little was done until 1985.

Gorbachev's Succession

Gorbachev's rule was marked, in its first year, by a period of caution. Disarmament negotiations, relations with the United States, economic and social reforms at home all required far more immediate attention. Yet it was inevitable that, sooner or later, his interest would be directed at the situation of his allies in Europe. The reasons for this were more than just economic. First, the Soviet leader seems to have grasped the lessons of history—as he is fond of calling them—fairly well. As with most colonial adventures, there is little to be gained from handling social and economic crises in Eastern Europe and everything to be lost. Every reform in the Soviet Union can have an impact in Eastern Europe and usually not in the direction Moscow expects. Stability was, therefore, the first prerequisite for future change and Gorbachev's first eighteen months in power were devoted to that. He personally attended the 11th Congress of the GDR's Communist Party and congratulated Erich Honecker on his country's achievements at a time when Berlin felt particularly insecure about his attitude to inner-German relations. Similarly, in June 1986, the Soviet leader attended the Warsaw Pact summit meeting in Budapest and assured the Hungarians of his support for their own economic mechanism. Indeed, Gorbachev's increased emphasis on more frequent consultations within the Pact pleased everybody, even though the GDR, Czechoslovakia and Romania, in particular, suspected that the price of greater consultation might be greater integration and waited for Moscow to name the price.

FROM TEACHERS TO PUPILS

To their surprise, Soviet economic demands were slow in coming, while the East Europeans enjoyed greater freedom in their foreign affairs. The tactic worked well in presenting yet another facet of the new leader's apparently benign appearance while still achieving strategic objectives. The ban imposed on Communist relations with China was lifted as part of Gorbachev's aim of normalizing relations with his Far Eastern neighbour and the East Europeans were encouraged to lead the way. Honecker travelled to Beijing, relishing this apparent Soviet acknowledgement of his country's relative primacy in Eastern Europe.[2] The East Germans were also congratulated for signing an agreement with the Federal Republic's Socialists on the creation of a 'nuclear-free corridor' in Central Europe.[3]

The GDR and Hungary felt genuinely flattered at persistent hints that the Soviet Union was actively studying the possibility of implementing their own methods of economic reforms. Their joy and pride were certainly premature: hints that the Kremlin looked with interest upon the GDR's and Hungary's economic mechanisms dated back to Andropov's rule[4] and were revived in 1986 by Abel Aganbegyan, one of Gorbachev's closest economic advisers. It is unlikely, however, that the possibility of copying East European economic reforms was ever seen as a viable proposition.

While it remains undeniable that the Soviet Union's new leaders did devote some attention to the GDR's and Hungary's economic experiments during 1985 and 1986, this was probably due more to intuition than a serious economic analysis. The fact was that the GDR forged ahead to the top of the East Europeans' economic performance during the 1970s and Hungary's reforms succeeded in creating greater prosperity and assuring the population a reasonably decent standard of living and increased personal consumption. Both results were, therefore, enticing. What probably attracted some leaders in the Kremlin even more was the fact that the GDR's economic performance was not accompanied by a dilution of the Party's rigid control over society or by a relaxation in central planning. In fact, the GDR proceeded to liquidate the last relics of private enterprise just before launching its economic reforms in the early 1970s. In Hungary, some private enterprise was allowed but, again, this did not appear to result in great dislocation or the diminution in the Party's role. Surely, some members of the Politburo felt, the GDR and Hungary were living examples of the possibilities still available to central planners. Unfortunately, they were not. First, the reforms introduced in the GDR and in Hungary could not be translated or applied in the Soviet Union. Secondly, even these reforms were slowly grinding to a halt and threatened greater dislocation in the future.

The GDR's success owed its existence to the *Kombinat* model, which united producer, supplier and seller. This accorded priority to certain branches of the economy and was applied to a society which was historically and linguistically homogenous and which was used to discipline and the ethos of hard work.[5] In short, success in the GDR relied on all the basic factors which the Soviet Union did not possess. In any case, the Soviet Union did not enjoy the fruits of this success. In 1973, it exported 2 bn. roubles-worth of goods to East Germany, of which a quarter was heavy machinery and 10 per cent oil. Ten years later, Soviet exports to the GDR did, indeed, grow almost four-fold, but no less than 60 per cent of the total was in the form of gas and oil.[6] Increasingly, the Soviet Union was relegated to the status of a supplier of raw materials. This was not all. The GDR in return sold to the USSR only the goods which could not be sold in the West for hard currency.

From Gorbachev's more radical viewpoint, it did not matter that the GDR's example made command economies and the socialist system more respectable and even workable; what mattered very much was the fact that as the years went by, the Comecon economies did not become compatible but competitive. All competed with each other in the production of some items but especially in the penetration of hard-currency markets. Only success in these markets assured them a steady opportunity to buy necessary raw materials and technology which the Soviet Union was unable to supply. The Soviet Union found itself at the bottom of the export priorities for all of them, both in quality and quantity. With the possible exception of Bulgaria, which prudently—and in retrospect in the late 1980s also successfully—continued to rely on the Soviet market for most of its finished goods, all other East European states delivered their lowest quality goods to the Soviet Union.

There are fairly clear indications that, despite these facts, Gorbachev genuinely studied the applicability of Hungarian-style reforms. Their attraction to him was obvious. Given his personal background, he found Hungary's ability to increase agricultural production and assure a sizeable export surplus of food particularly enticing. It is reported, however, that members of the CPSU Central Committee were strongly against applying them,[7] although the debate lasted a long time.[8] The conclusion, therefore, was that Eastern Europe could not teach the Soviet Union any useful lessons and Gorbachev's attention turned to the economic difficulties in the region the moment it became clear that even these two 'model' East European economies were beginning to falter. Hungary was jolted by the general drop in credit from the West in the wake of the Polish debt crisis; its inefficient industries were nearing breaking point and fairly radical reforms were still needed. The GDR's economy was also contracting. The alarm bells came soon enough—even

if Berlin still refused to recognize them—in the shape of sharply lower growth
rates for such key industries as coal, energy and heavy machinery.

While during 1981-86 the coal and energy sectors grew by an annual
average of 8 per cent, this dropped to no more than 2.1 per cent by 1987 and
the heavy machinery sector's growth rate halved over the same period. This
was coupled with stagnant exports and increased competition from West
German producers who themselves encountered difficulties in exporting
to the Third World and increasingly regarded their own country as their
only hope for growth. Given these factors, the East German economy was
comfortably following the Czechoslovak path; an industrial country which
became an economic disaster. With Romania on the point of starvation and
Poland a basket-case economy crippled by foreign debts and an undisciplined
labour force, the time for learning had passed; it was now Gorbachev's turn
to do the teaching. The honeymoon with Eastern Europe came to an end.

The problems which Gorbachev intends to tackle are very great. His
general and ultimate goal is to assure stability and prosperity; to transform
the region into a genuine alliance. This requires social and economic reforms
which will encounter great opposition. His middle-term goal is to achieve all
these with the political and financial commitment to his own country. His
short-term solution is to begin integration in specific areas between different
East European states. The problems which he has to face are related both to
the presentation of these new priorities and their application, for Comecon
has been and continues to be riddled with difficulties which hinder genuine
co-operation.

In command economies, prices for all products are usually decided not by
supply and demand, or costs of production but by administrative fiat. There
are usually two broad price bands: one for the producer, the so-called
wholesale price, and one for the consumer, the retail price. The structures
of these two prices are usually unconnected because of the different levels of
subsidization and taxation. Thus, the essential basis for trade co-operation is
not available. Furthermore, there is the question of currencies. Within
Comecon's transactions, the so-called 'transferable rouble' was introduced in
1964. At that time, it was equivalent to a Soviet domestic currency unit, but
the rate has remained unchanged ever since. In practice, the transferable
rouble is not a currency at all but a book-keeping device. It is issued only
in response to imbalances in bilateral trade within Comecon and has no
circulation in other countries. As a consequence, most of the trade between
Comecon states is conducted at the level of barter. It is a barter system which
does not benefit the Soviet Union. Most of the USSR's exports consist of
energy products and other raw materials. In return, Eastern Europe, heavily
dependent on sometimes cheap and always available supplies of oil in particular, pays with products of the lowest possible quality after having satisfied
all possible orders in hard-currency markets. Hard currency promises access
to advanced Western technology and, by being freely convertible, also allows

local governments the flexibility to choose their own future economic priorities. Thus, Gorbachev lacks the means to establish better economic collaboration quickly. Comecon lacks proper prices, proper currencies to conduct trade and the political will to do this.

Gorbachev nevertheless has considerable advantages. First, the sharp downturn in trade with the West and the performance of East European economies has made them more dependent on Soviet supplies of raw materials since they lack the ability to purchase these on the open market. Secondly, because of the five-year moving scale which Comecon operated in fixing the price of oil, Soviet oil has become cheaper. The Soviet leader can thus appear to be magnanimous by appearing more responsive to his allies' needs while at the same time pressing home his political advantage.

THE FIRST SHOCK

At the beginning of November 1986, the 42nd Comecon session was held in Bucharest. From the first day, it was clear that the Soviet position had changed radically. The Poles and East Germans treated the delegates to long expositions of their 'achievements'; Moscow's representative curtly replied that more co-ordination of these 'achievements' was needed, in the form of 'stable economic, scientific and technical ties between states and the effective utilization of the possibilities of social and economic integration'.[9] The plans which were unveiled went further than anything the East Europeans expected, mainly because they underestimated Gorbachev as a leader. From subsequent pronouncements, it is clear that Gorbachev had learned the lessons of Khruschev's integration failures thoroughly.

Khruschev had sought to establish a division of labour in the socialist community. Particular countries, with strong industrial traditions and good infrastructures were allocated the tasks of industrial production; others, such as Romania, were given the job of supplying the socialist community with raw materials and food. The idea was misconceived, for it attempted to impose a unified plan on the entire socialist community. Secondly, it was offensive to the East Europeans' national pride and to their own economic aspirations. Most of the region's leaders, graduates of the Stalinist school of economics, still believed that more steel smelters, more heavy industry and more furnaces was what Communist rule was all about. In the context of Eastern Europe, industry represented progress; the larger the industry, the better it was; to be condemned as an agricultural country would entail remaining in the backyard of Europe. Romania's dissention within the Warsaw Pact could be partly traced to Khruschev's hare-brained scheme. Thirdly, the plans of the 1950s and their further refinement under Brezhnev did not allow for the fact that the East European allies were themselves operating command economies in which export priorities were not dictated by market prices but by administrative fiat. Thus, from Gorbachev's viewpoint, it was not enough to agree with the governments concerned on a new programme of co-operation, since this was likely to remain a dead letter as long as the East Europeans still controlled the manpower, the allocation of resources and the production facilities, and decided upon export markets. For genuine co-operation, which would be beneficial to the Soviet Union, it was necessary to break this monopoly of individual governments over their key industries.

That in itself is a larger task than Gorbachev can handle and involves a whole host of social and political problems, among which the role of the party as a guiding force in society is the most obvious. A middle way had to be found between hurting the East Europeans' sense of pride in their own achievements and attachment to nationalism, the continued operation of a command economy throughout the bloc and the desirability of greater economic co-operation and specialization. This may have appeared elusive but Gorbachev succeeded by looking at the East European economies as a mirror of his own. The East European leaders could be compared to the bureaucratic elements in the Kremlin; their economic troubles were similar to those of the Soviet Union. The solution, in the short run, could not be found in dismantling the command economy, but rather in improving on its most glaring failures. The Soviet leader decided to insist on co-operation between his country and his allies at the enterprise rather than state level. Once contracts were signed, once targets were set, it would be more difficult for any government to frustrate them. It was precisely this insistence which aroused the greatest apprehensions in Eastern Europe.

From the East European point of view, this technique implied integration not with a stronger economy, but with a weaker one. Secondly, the East Europeans suspected that such co-operation would be dictated by Moscow's economic priorities and would not address their own needs. In this respect, the fact that the Kremlin insisted on collaboration in electronics and machine-building industries was particularly worrying, since the USSR required help in precisely these fields.[10] Finally, co-operation at the enterprise level is inherently more difficult to control nationally, which is precisely why Gorbachev preferred it. In the absence of real prices, convertible currencies or any other accurate economic indicators, the performance of such joint enterprises would always be open to manipulation. For all these reasons, the East Europeans put up stiff resistance at the Bucharest Comecon meeting. Indications, however, that Gorbachev was serious in his intention came soon enough. Within days of the Bucharest meeting, all the leaders of the Warsaw Pact were summoned to Moscow[11] for what was officially termed as 'frank' discussions.[12]

We still do not know what was decided at that meeting, but the 1987 Soviet State Plan did flatly declare that there would be a 'considerable development' in co-operation within Comecon, especially in the field of 'direct production links'.[13] The opposition of the East Europeans, nevertheless, continued, for the GDR's 1987 plan spoke pointedly of co-operation on the 'mutual advantage' principle between state economies.[14] Gorbachev expected opposition and was well prepared for it. In late November 1986, therefore, the Soviet Union shifted from a general emphasis on co-operation to attention on specific branches of industry in particular East European states. The GDR came in for most of the attention as became clear during the regular meeting of the USSR-GDR economics commission in December.[15] Honecker was nevertheless confident that he could withstand the pressure. He was wrong; Gorbachev played his second card with consummate skill.

THE SECOND SHOCK

In January 1987 the Soviet leader introduced another element into the argument: that of political reform. His speech to the Central Committee Plenum on 27 January 1987 was indeed remarkable. He admitted the failure of previous Soviet economic policies; he berated the bureaucracy and blamed high Party officials for the situation; he attacked aspects of central planning for stifling initiative and called for greater investment in consumer industries. Ultimately, he blamed nepotism and promotions within the Party on account of personal relations, rather than merit. The speech sent a seismic shock through Eastern Europe. Gorbachev could afford to criticize Brezhnev's inheritance for it was not of his own making; the East Europeans represented the system which the new Soviet leader was now attacking.

Hungary and Poland, which had already embarked on efforts to mobilize forces outside the Party to the task of economic reconstruction enthusiastically embraced the speech. Romania's Stalinist leader, Nicolae Ceausescu, reacted violently to Gorbachev's criticisms and vowed that they would never be applied in Romania. The GDR and Czechoslovakia were stunned by the criticism of policies which they had faithfully applied for years. The argument between Moscow and the East European capitals was no longer one about economic reforms and co-operation but about the survival of the régimes themselves. In Czechoslovakia, Gustav Husak's *raison d'etre* was the application of Brezhnev-style government and that was now rejected by the mentors themselves. Gorbachev may yet regret the implications of his reforms in Eastern Europe for there is little doubt that they have tended to destabilize the local régimes.

At the same time, the immediate effect, from the Soviet Union's viewpoint was quite beneficial. The spectre of united opposition from Eastern Europe evaporated within weeks. If the real question was one of the leaders' actual survival, economic co-operation was the lowest common denominator on which they could agree, provided Moscow could be persuaded not to insist on the application of social and political reforms in the region. The breakdown was amply illustrated by the debates which followed. Ceausescu desperately tried to resurrect a united front with the support of Czechoslovakia and East Germany; unfortunately for him, his country was already in such an economic mess that no one was particularly interested in what he had to say. As both East Berlin and Prague realized, supporting wayward Romania could be politically unwise and the benefits which could be derived from such support would be derisory. The debate in East Germany and Czechoslovakia, however, changed from economic to political reforms. Czechoslovakia's tame trade unions were encouraged to continue with 'democratic centralism', a euphemism for total political control over all walks of life.[16] Honecker told his people that he had 'not the slightest reason to conceal the course' which his country had followed in the past.[17] Brave words indeed, but not the sort of pronouncements which would push the Soviet leader off his course. Within weeks of these events, Soviet Foreign Minister Shevardnadze visited both East Berlin and Prague and pointedly told the Press that he came on 'the orders of Comrade Mikhail Gorbachev' to discuss economic matters. The Hungarians sat on the sidelines, shedding crocodile tears about the fact that Eastern Europe had not 'evaluated the changes in the USSR in an identical way'. That, for the moment, suited the Soviet Union well enough.

In April and May 1987 Gorbachev paid visits to his difficult allies: East Germany, Czechoslovakia and Romania. In all three countries, he was careful to emphasize that each Communist state would be allowed to implement its own policies; in each one, however, he insisted that his country would no longer accept shoddy goods in return for energy exports and repeated his view that only co-operation at the enterprise level would succeed. The main aim, for the moment, remained economic co-operation, as Soviet officials were quite happy to point out. Professor Albakin, the Director of the USSR Academy's Institute of Economics and one of the main architects of the Soviet reform programme, repeatedly followed Gorbachev's travels with assurances that the economic mechanism which the Soviet leader was attempting to replace had outlived its usefulness but nevertheless had been essential in its time. The implication was that the past need not be denigrated as long as the present economic mechanism was reformed.

The fact that economic co-operation took priority over political considerations was starkly obvious for all to see. Throughout the post-war period, tiny Bulgaria remained the Soviet Union's most reliable ally. Its leader, Todor Zhivkov, pursued every twist of Soviet policy and applied it immediately in his own country. It must have been particularly galling to him—and interesting for the other Comecon members—that in May 1987 it was Bulgaria which was openly criticized by the Soviet Press for engaging in merely 'superficial' contacts with the USSR and for being 'unadventurous' in the goods it wanted to produce.[18]

Moscow was this time determined to achieve what it wanted from Eastern Europe. Political reforms were not always the most important and certainly not the most immediate priority. When the conflict between hard-liners and reformers within Communist parties became especially acute, as was the case in Czechoslovakia, the Soviet leadership supported compromise rather than a radical political solution: Milos Jakes was appointed to succeed Husak in Czechoslovakia. With hindsight, it is clear that this was part of Gorbachev's greater strategy: economic reforms would bind the region together ever-closer. Once co-operation was a reality there would be time enough for the political reforms which the Soviet leader still believes are essential. However, as long as the political situation was fluid, it would be better to sustain the leaders already in power, provided that they are prepared to co-operate as required. Deliver they will, for they understand that Moscow is now aiming at higher stakes and that their survival depends on accepting Soviet demands. Within two years, Gorbachev has managed to achieve what no other Soviet leader has done: to impress on the East Europeans that the USSR would not support bankrupt economies for ever. He has limited their room for manoeuvre while at the same time appearing to the world as a more enlightened, liberal and lively personality. The East Europeans have been told that they are free to run, but back into the camp rather than outside it. They have been assured that their independence will henceforth be respected, but that closer economic co-operation is a necessity. Ultimately, they have all fallen into line.

Development of Co-operation

The decree of the Soviet Council of Ministers on 19 August 1986, paved the way for twenty-one government ministries and departments and seventy-six of the largest enterprises to have direct access to foreign markets. The Kremlin claimed that in 1987, such firms accounted for 20 per cent of the Soviet foreign trade turnover, and more than 65 per cent of the country's engineering exports in particular.[19] These companies were given very broad powers to trade with their East European counterparts. With Bulgaria, it appears that the co-operation was concentrated on the production of transport and manufacturing machinery, such as motor-trucks and electric hoists which comprise almost 25 per cent of all Bulgarian machinery exports to the Soviet Union. A joint venture, *Avtoelektronika*, works on electrical motor equipment and combines Soviet production with the factories at Plovdiv. With the GDR, the majority of co-operative ventures centres around robotics and chemical-processing plants. East German planners have admitted that their country's exports of microelectronics to the USSR are set to reach a record DM4 bn. by 1990 alone, conducted through 120 joint production agreements.[20]

From Hungary, the main area of expansion is in the manufacturing of motor cars, of which the Raba plant in Gyor supplies rear axles for Soviet buses, while the Soviet Union delivers power units, front axles and pumps. In addition, 6,600 buses were bought in 1988.[21] A joint Soviet-Hungarian venture, *Micromed*, develops and sells medical equipment in the city of Esztergom.[22] With Czechoslovakia, the main areas of co-operation are in specialized steels, chemical industries and pig-iron and, again, trade is planned to rise rapidly.[23] With Poland, co-operative ventures account for 25 per cent of all joint trade and agricultural tools, ships and navigation equipment and manufacturing tools are also scheduled for special attention.[24]

With Romania, a different technique was applied which nevertheless still underlines Gorbachev's ability to draw his allies together through economic co-operation while refusing to be drawn into long political arguments. Ceausescu's attraction to the West was based on his claim to be independent from Moscow. He mediated in the Middle East and between the two Superpowers; he acted as a diplomatic channel between the USSR and China. With the appearance of Gorbachev, all this disappeared. The Soviet Union has conducted summit meetings with the United States, opened a dialogue with Israel with a view to setting up an international conference in the Middle East and negotiated with China. Ceausescu was simply marginalized and exposed for what he always was: a ruthless dictator, ruling a marginally useful country. With his charm gone, his economy in tatters and his population on the brink of starvation, Ceausescu came back into the Soviet fold. Gorbachev stipulated his conditions, which entailed greater co-operation in oil extraction in Siberia as well as Romanian deliveries of what were always hard currency goods, such as food, and clothing.

By being persistent, Gorbachev has solved a problem which had bedevilled all his predecessors. Romania's 'independence' is a thing of the past and the country is kept alive by Soviet support. By refusing to rise to Ceausescu's bait, Gorbachev has exposed the dangers inherent in moving away from the socialist camp. As long as Ceausescu remains in power, he will be the best advertisement for what happens to wayward allies. Romania is kept afloat by the Soviet Union mainly because the Kremlin would not wish to see the régime collapse; at the same time, even in this case, Gorbachev has insisted on exacting a price: goods which do not meet the specified quality controls are returned.

The Soviet Union has claimed that prices for Comecon co-operation are based on the world market. We have little indication whether this is so, but we do know that the main problem does not reside in pricing the finished product, but rather in the price decided for labour, expertise and spare parts utilized in this joint production. On this score, the Soviet Union has admitted that 'the situation is less favourable', since no comparable world prices are easily obtainable.[25] By mid-1987, over 400 Soviet enterprises had direct ties with Eastern Europe. Moscow wants this expanded to 700 'in the near future'. This is particularly the case in the machine-building sectors, in scientific R&D and the design of new manufacturing processes. Most of the co-operation involves items on which the pricing mechanisms are by no means clear. The Soviet leadership had one opportunity on 1 January 1987 to reform the pricing mechanism in Comecon trade but this was not seized upon when new legislation came into force. On the contrary, the

USSR insisted on establishing individual prices for particular items supplied through direct production links although it allowed one concession to the East Europeans by accepting that one price would not be taken as a precedent in the formation of future prices for similar products.[26] In effect, the debate on price formation was postponed, while co-operation is being immediately enforced.

Moreover, in the absence of firm rules on prices, Soviet enterprises were allowed to negotiate their own contract prices. Since much of the co-operation at this stage is politically-motivated, the Soviet enterprises probably have the power to dictate their own prices. There is evidence, however, that haggling continues; Alexei Antonov, the Minister responsible for most of the Comecon negotiations, has indicated that his country insists on taking into account the 'larger scale of production' which the availability of the Soviet market entails.[27] The East Europeans have indicated their concern on this point many times[28] but their options are limited. If anything, Soviet pressure has intensified, especially in the area of production quality. At least in Bulgaria, quality control is assured by the physical presence of Soviet inspectors who make sure that what is shipped to the USSR is of the specified standard.[29] It is quite probable that the additional costs implicit in this stringent inspection may be passsed on to Bulgaria.

RESEARCH AND DEVELOPMENT

The Soviet Union has insisted on co-operating in R&D, claiming that duplication of research within the socialist camp has resulted in 'losing' 5-7 bn. roubles a year.[30] Losing what? Presumably, Soviet economists were referring to money spent on research in the development of similar products in many East European countries.

R&D in most countries is not co-ordinated. However, because of the presence of proper price mechanisms, workable patents protection legislation and flexible applications of technological discoveries in market economies, duplication is reduced and different branches of Western economies can rely on each other. The one area where duplication in R&D exists is in the defence field, precisely where the forces of market economy in the West apply least. In the command economies of Eastern Europe, the duplication is massive, not so much because of nationalist policies as because of a systemic factor. By insisting on direct co-operation, the Soviet Union is attempting, for the moment, to retain command economies while reducing their disadvantage in R&D. The fact that Moscow insists on co-operation in the very area in which it is weak can hardly be reassuring from the East Europeans' point of view.

CONVERTIBLE CURRENCIES

The discussion on convertible currencies has displayed similar trends: the

Soviet Union promised greater flexibility in the future while pushing for greater integration in the present. Despite the fact that the East Europeans regularly demanded the establishment of a convertible currency, or at least concrete steps towards this goal, at the 43rd session of Comecon in October 1987, a decision on the full convertibility of the transferable rouble was again postponed although the member states agreed to a Soviet proposal that national currencies could be made convertible on a bilateral basis with each other, and also accepted the Soviet-inspired need for a 'division of labour' among them in the period of 1991-2005.[31]

A programme aiming at full convertibility of all currencies is to be phased in over a ten-year period beginning in 1991.[32] Although joint ventures will be the first to implement the new system,[33] the rouble is still overvalued by about 400 per cent against the US dollar and thus continues to be a most unreliable unit of accounting between states.[34]

The debate on the convertible currency reveals another important aspect of Gorbachev's policy: his impatience with formal rules of conduct within the alliance. Important decisions of this nature are always taken on a unanimous basis. Nevertheless, despite the fact that the East Germans and Romanians abstained, the decisions were still carried and the plan will certainly be implemented. Czechoslovakia and the USSR agreed on the convertibility of their currencies in February 1988.[35]

This merely means, of course, that co-operating enterprises will be able to conduct their accounting in their own national currencies and does not solve the problem. Commercial credits to these enterprises will still be accorded on the basis of what Prague termed an 'appropriate' exchange rate, without elaborating further;[36] it has subsequently been admitted that much more liberalization of currencies would be required to make the agreement effective.[37] Thus, not only has the debate on currency convertibility been postponed while East European criticism has been deflected, but the ability of one country to block changes has been arbitrarily removed and the rules of the game changed.

Gorbachev has, in fact, made a virtue out of the East Europeans' dissention. Unlike previous Soviet leaders, he has abandoned the chimerical hope of the 'socialist camp' although he persists in paying perfunctory eulogies to the idea. The practice, however, is of a Soviet Union that deals directly with each East European country on the basis of a mutually satisfactory trade. In the words of the Soviet leader:

> The only important thing is that any country's lack of desire or interest to participate in a project should not serve as a restraint on others. Anyone who wants to participate is welcome to do so; if not, one can wait and see how the others are doing. Every country is free to decide if it is prepared for such co-operation and how far it is going to be involved.[38]

He could have added that any country which does not want to join projects dear to the Soviet heart, would have to see for itself how it could manage without Soviet help. Integration, therefore, does take two forms. On the one hand, there is bilateral co-operation in technological and R&D fields; on the other, there is multilateral co-operation in areas such as pricing and marketing raw materials. And finally there is Soviet economic help on a case-by-case basis, such as Romania's.

FORMALIZING THE NEW INTEGRATION

Gorbachev was not content merely to implement his new integration policies; he also attempted to have them recognized as such by the West as well. This was exemplified through Soviet efforts to regulate relations with the European Community (EC) which previously had been denied recognition as a separate entity. Despite the fact that Gorbachev persisted in denying any attempt at transforming Comecon into a supranational organization,[39] he hurried along negotiations with the EC, which he hoped would lead to the recognition of the two bodies at the same time.[40]

Should this agreement be concluded, it is bound to have an effect on the GDR in particular. East Germany already has free access to the European Community through unhindered inter-German trade but, according to the conditions attached to the mutual recognition of the two trade blocs, its status may be changed. The recognition of Comecon as a separate entity would also entail, by implication, the acceptance of the Soviet Union as the leader of its bloc, the acceptance of the division of Europe according to different economic systems and more, rather than less, integration within Comecon itself. Although the Kremlin hopes to improve on its $22.6 bn. exports with the EC through this forthcoming accord,[41] its most significant aspect would be symbolic, in reinforcing Moscow's position above that of its East European allies. Significantly, the Soviet Union always refers to an economic community, which foreign affairs specialists in Moscow are at pains to point out their country would not recognize as a united European political entity, but merely an economic organization comparable to Comecon.[42] It is precisely for this reason that some West European countries are prevaricating, although Chancellor Kohn was reputedly eager to conclude an agreement by the time his country's presidency of the community expired in the summer of 1988.[43]

Conclusions

Comecon has undergone major changes in the last years. This is not, in itself, novel, for most Soviet leaders have attempted to tackle the seemingly intractable problem of Eastern Europe. What makes Gorbachev's efforts stand apart is their persistence and their durability. Should he succeed, he would remove, at a stroke, the ability of many East European states to conduct an independent foreign and economic policy for, with economic integration, closer political co-ordination would follow. The East European governments are at the moment engaging in industrial collaboration in the hope that Gorbachev's insistence on political reform will subside. It will not; the demands for political reforms have been postponed until economic integration succeeds. By appearing receptive to East European complaints— while assuring his allies of his best attention to their needs and by recognizing their diversity and national requirements—Gorbachev may succeed in forging, for the first time since 1945, a true alliance based on, at least, real economic requirements.

The Soviet Union certainly shows no intention of relaxing its demands on co-operation, as Talyzin, the Chairman of the USSR State Planning Committee stated when unveiling the 1988 Soviet Plan.[44] At the same time, Moscow has also been more open about its assistance to the region, especially in the field of oil deliveries. During the signing of the trade protocol with Czechoslovakia in November 1987, which heralded a great increase in bilateral trade, Moscow pointedly announced that Prague would benefit the following year from deliveries of oil which would be '11 per cent to 13 per cent cheaper' than in the previous year.[45] The Soviet Union has also encouraged co-operation between the East Europeans themselves. In 1987, for instance, a full 35 per cent of all Bulgarian-GDR trade was in goods jointly produced; in 1988, this was scheduled to rise to no less than 85 per cent.[46] Co-operation is proceeding apace in nuclear energy programmes and the sharing of electricity.[47] Comecon's own administrative structure has been revamped. Reports speak of a 25 per cent staff reduction at the organization's headquarters in Moscow[48] with responsibilities passed over to certain joint enterprises.

The intention is clear. Soon, the most plausible way for co-operation will be, of necessity, through joint production ventures. To be sure, most of the problems will still remain unsolved. The problems associated with currency convertibility and price formation will remain outstanding. Nevertheless, by not allowing these to prevent the application of his ultimate aims, Gorbachev may forge an alliance which could offer Eastern Europe markets that the West could not. The Soviet Union has already shown that it can offer guaranteed supplies of raw materials, provided the East Europeans participate in their extraction.

Gorbachev's policy is certainly sophisticated and he is playing for high stakes. A social explosion and a major challenge to the Soviet Union's position may still come from the area in the future. If, however, the present integration efforts are implemented, they could make any 'defection' from the socialist camp much more difficult. The Soviet leader has implemented his reforms in Comecon with great skill, but the reforms he has enforced are still dictated by Soviet priorities. These remain unchanged: how to rule an empire, while reducing the liabilities and deriving all the benefits? This is a much wider question, for which the answer must depend on Gorbachev's performance as a leader. For once, a Soviet leader represents progress rather than orthodoxy. The least that could be said about Comecon's reforms is that they have prepared the ground for the political battle between the Soviet Union and Eastern Europe, in forums other than Comecon, in particular the Warsaw Pact, in which the Soviet Union's allies will be expected to play a much greater role than hitherto.

Notes

1. Bond and Klein, 'Impact of changes in the global environment on the Soviet and East European economies', in US Congress, Joint Economic Committee (*East European Economies: Slow Growth in the 1990s*, Washington, DC, USGPO, 1985).
2. *Neues Deutschland*, 26 October 1986.
3. *Pravda*, 25 October 1986.
4. See Y. V. Andropov, *Speeches and Writings* (Oxford, Pergamon Press, 1983), p. 9.
5. For further details, see Bryson and Melzer, *Planning Refinements and Combine Formation in East German Economic 'Intensification'*, Carl Beck Paper No. 508 (University of Pittsburgh, Center for Russian and East European Studies, 1987).
6. *Vneshnaya Torgovlya SSSR*, Moscow, Finansy i Statistika, various years.
7. Z. Medvedev, *Gorbachev* (Oxford, Blackwell, 2nd edition, 1987), p. 204.
8. For its official manifestations, see *Soviet Weekly*, 3 October 1987, p. 5.
9. *Pravda*, 4 November 1986.
10. See, for instance, *Pravda*, 4 November 1986.
11. *The Financial Times*, 30 October 1986.
12. *The Guardian*, 13 November 1986.
13. *Pravda*, 19 November 1986.
14. *Neues Deutschland*, 27 November 1986.
15. *Neues Deutschland*, 17 December 1986.
16. *Rude Pravo*, 10 February 1987.
17. *Neues Deutschland*, 7 February 1987.
18. *Trud*, Moscow, 21 May 1987.
19. N. Baturing and V. Demchuk, 'USSR-CMEA Member-Countries: Further Progress in Production Cooperation', in *Foreign Trade*, October 1987, p. 14.
20. ADN, 13 January 1988; G. Beil, 'The GDR-Largest Trade Partner of the USSR', *Foreign Trade*, November 1987, pp. 22-23; for the Soviet interests in the GDR economy, see the results of bilateral conversations as reported by ADN, 11 January 1988 and *Neues Deutschland*, 14 Jnauary 1988.
21. *MTI*, 16 October 1987.
22. Other joint ventures with Hungary are listed in 'Joint Ventures on Soviet Territory', *Foreign Trade*, January 1988, pp. 45-47.
23. V. Monakhov, 'USSR-Czechoslovakia: Economic and Technical Co-operation', in *Foreign Trade*, January 1988, pp. 2-4.
24. Y. Voinov, 'USSR-Poland: Co-operation Forms are Improving', in *Foreign Trade*, January 1988, pp. 5-7.
25. Baturin and Demchuk, *op. cit.*, p. 15.
26. For previous pointers to the price formation debate, see E. I. Punin, *Scientific and Technical Revolution and World Prices* (Moscow, Mezhdunarodniye Otnosheniya, 1977).
27. A. Antonov, 'New Mechanisms of Co-operation', in *New Times*, No. 47, November 1987, p. 4.
28. See, for example, Hungary's Mihaly Simai, 'There is Much to be Changed by the Third Millennium', in *New Times*, No. 38, 1987, pp. 10-11 and 'CMEA Reform: Complexity and Gradual Progress, in *Figyelo* (Budapest), 10 December 1987.
29. See *Sofia News*, 2 March 1988.
30. *The CMEA Member-Countries in the International Exchange of Technologies* (Moscow, Mezhdunarodniye Otnosheniya, 1986), pp. 107 and ff.

31. *Pravda*, 13 October 1987; Y. Shiryaev, 'CMEA: Restructuring the Co-operation Mechanism', in *International Affairs*, January 1988, pp. 20-32.
32. J. Diehl, 'Soviet Rewriting East Bloc Economic Rules, in *International Herald Tribune*, 14 October 1987.
33. See *International Herald Tribune*, 15 October 1987.
34. G. Merritt, 'Rouble: For a Grand Slam, Free It Up', in *International Herald Tribune*, 22 January 1988; see also V. Loshak, 'The Rouble and Perestroika', in *Moscow News*, 7 February 1988.
35. L. Colitt, 'Moscow, Prague agree currency convertibility', *The Financial Times*, 29 February 1988.
36. *CTK*, 2 March 1988.
37.

38. M. Gorbachev, *Perestroika* (London, Collins, 1987), p. 168.
39. *Ibid.*
40. G. Dadyants, 'CMEA and EEC—Moving Towards Each Other', in *Moscow News*, 6 March 1988.
41. 'Comecon trick', in *The Economist*, 17 October 1987, p. 47.
42. For a clear statement of this fundamental distinction, see Y. Rubinsky, 'European Community: Political Dimensions', in *International Affairs* (Moscow), February 1988, pp. 41-49, and compare with *Kommunist*, No. 15, 1987, especially p. 34.
43. J. M. Markham, 'Comecon Edging Toward Trade Accord with EC', *International Herald Tribune*, 3 December 1987.
44. *Pravda*, 20 October 1987; see also V. Krivosheyev, 'CMEA: Facing Perestroika', in *Moscow News*, 29 October 1987.
45. TASS, 27 November 1987.
46. Bulgarian Radio Home Service, 28 November 1987, 1830 GMT, in BBC, Summary of World Broadcasts, EE/W0004 A/1, 10 December 1987.
47. J. M. Kramer, 'Chernobyl and Eastern Europe', in *Problems of Communism*, November-December 1986, p. 40 and ff; for a list of existing projects, see V. Sobell, 'The CMEA's Post-Chernobyl Nuclear Energy Programme', *Radio Free Europe Research*, Background Report No. 19, 15 February 1988.
48. V. Sobell, 'Reform of the CMEA Makes Cautious Progress', *Radio Free Europe Research*, Background Report No. 37, 8 March 1988, p. 2.

SECTION 6
Pessimism—or Hope?

IN this concluding essay Harry Maier presents an 'upbeat' picture of two alliances which may eventually 'drift together', not apart—a picture it must be confessed which is not shared by all. Perhaps, our only hope is that both sides, like Orwell, will eventually accept that the only 'ism' which has proved itself in the twentieth century is pessimism; but that, unlike Orwell, they will use the premise to construct a more hopeful future.

Even if they were to try, the question must be asked whether the future is in their grasp, or whether history has moved on leaving the Superpowers struggling in its wake.

CHAPTER 10

Drifting Together?
New Challenges Facing
The Two Alliances

HARRY MAIER

The new challenges faced by the Warsaw Pact and NATO arise from the realization that the present cycle of rearmament, far from leading to greater security, involves the risk of military disaster. There is no doubt that the military potential of both alliances has by far exceeded their respective security needs. It has even become apparent that the race to create new and more lethal weapons has not increased the security of the people of East and West but diminished it to a degree unimaginable until recently for two main reasons:

1. In both systems military-industrial complexes have developed which, in becoming independent, have become increasingly difficult to control.
2. Their demands from the taxpayer have reached such a dimension that we are losing the capability to solve the world's major problems from which tensions and conflicts tend to arise.

The new optimistic aspirations of the 1970s to diminish the economic differences between North and South by concerted efforts, to end hunger, the destruction of the environment and the deterioration of the conditions of life have proved to be an illusion. On the contrary, the calamity of the developing countries has become a disaster characterized by growing indebtedness, hunger and increasing overpopulation.

The arms race has prevented the solution of these problems not only by absorbing the resources required for this purpose, but also by creating an international climate which has made it impossible to solve them. Instead of more security, it has led to incalculable risks for both sides.

The realization of this fact has led both sides to the formula: more security with less arms, the basis for a new policy aimed at a perceptible improvement of the East-West relationship. The intrinsic logic of this formula requires a complete change of the military doctrines of the Warsaw pact and NATO and means, above all, giving up any search for military superiority. Changing the military doctrines of the two alliances, therefore, is not just a question of verbal reformulation; it must be the result of a single-minded policy aiming at disarmament guaranteeing the security of both blocs.

171

An important step on the way was undoubtedly the meeting between Ronald Reagan and Mikhail Gorbachev in December 1987. On that occasion, not only a global elimination of an entire class of arms—intermediate-range nuclear missiles—was agreed upon for the first time, but also an agreement in principle was reached to reduce strategic offensive arms by 50 per cent. The Soviet-American statement of 10 December 1987 was historic not only because of its aim—the complete destruction of a whole category of nuclear weapons—but also because of the novelty and the extent of the intended measures of verification.

The common statement also suggested the broad outline of a way to reach a common goal; 'more security with less weapons':

— giving up the search for military superiority;
— accepting that existing differences of opinion must not be an insurmountable obstacle for progress in those fields of common interest to both sides;
— the obligation to adhere to the Anti-Ballistic Missile (ABM) treaty in the version signed in 1972 rather than withdraw from it over an agreed period of time;
— an agreement to further intermediate restrictions for nuclear tests as a phase in their complete cessation;
— adherence to the treaty on the non-proliferation of nuclear weapons;
— working out a comprehensive and effective international convention on the prohibition and destruction of chemical weapons;
— reduction of conventional arms and the elimination of all asymmetries in different arms systems;
— co-operation in solving regional conflicts, from Afghanistan to the Gulf;
— the development of the economic, scientific-technical and cultural co-operation between East and West in an attempt to realize their common obligation to solve global problems, particularly in the field of environmental issues.

Different political observers have claimed that this improvement in East-West relations was the result of political actions in the past. In the West, the politicians, who—despite protests from their own population—were able to deploy US intermediate-range nuclear missiles in Western Europe, claim to have forced the Soviet leadership to enter into disarmament negotiations in earnest. In the Soviet Union, some politicians insist that the breakdown of the Geneva negotiations showed the West that the Soviet bloc was not willing to accept the deployment of cruise and Pershing 2 without a matching response.

In other socialist countries, politicians like Erich Honecker and Janos Kadar opposed in public the intentions of part of the Soviet leadership to end a political dialogue with the West. All these different actions may have had some influence in improving East-West relations. But they were not the *most* important factors. More important were the changes in Soviet politics connected with the takeover by Mikhail Gorbachev in 1985. The real cause of the improvement in East-West relations were the important changes in the Soviet Union since then.

Indeed, in order to identify the new challenges facing the Warsaw Pact and NATO, we must first understand the driving forces of the transformation process in the Soviet Union itself.

Radical Social and Economic Reform in the USSR

At present there are three different groups within the Soviet leadership: the conservatives, the technocrats, and the radical reform group associated with the General Secretary. These groups have very different conceptions about the future of the Soviet Union and its role in the international arena. The conservatives claim that there exists no demand for a radical change in domestic and international activities. Their inability to react to the worldwide technological changes in the 1970s was the main reason for the decline in the innovation potential of Soviet industry. The Brezhnev Group tried to compensate for the growing technology gap with the West with a sharp increase in oil and gas exports. The fall of the oil price in 1986 showed that the Soviet Union had no competitive high-tech products for export, except in the military field. The result was a serious deterioration in its terms of trade and an increase in its foreign debt. In 1986 the terms of trade *vis-à-vis* the OECD countries fell by more than 60 per cent, while the debt burden increased from $15.2 bn. (1985) to $24.0 bn. (1986).

THE CONSERVATIVES' POSITION

For the conservatives, the improvement in East-West relations is only acceptable if it will help change the balance of power in favour of the Soviet Union; to secure, not foreclose, any opportunities for extending its sphere of influence. The political miscalculations of this group were one important factor in ending the process of *détente* in the 1970s. The political strength of the conservative group derives from a coalition between the different power centres of the Soviet leadership: the military-industrial complex, the security apparatus and the central planning bureaucracy.

The military doctrine of this group is to achieve military superiority, not so much to threaten the West militarily, but to push through politically any opportunities for extending the Soviet sphere of influence. For this reason, the conservative group is willing to do anything to strengthen the position of the military-industrial complex.

In the last ten years the military-industrial complex was able to use the deterioration in East-West relations to extend its power and to bring a growing part of the Soviet Union's economic and technological resources under its control.

The conservatives tried to interpret the stagnation of the Soviet economy as the result of an economic war by the Western countries against the USSR and of the need to keep military parity with NATO on a higher level. They have since tried to discredit the reform activities and the 'new thinking' about East-West relations of the radical reform group as changes of wallpaper, which are more symbolic than real.

THE TECHNOCRATIC POSITION

The technocratic reformers accept the need for reforming the socialist economy. But their purpose is not the elimination of the existing over-centralized planning and decision-making process. Through the elimination of inefficient decision-making procedures and the use of new information technology, they hope to make the existing system of directive central planning much more efficient and flexible. From their point of view the main function of international relations is to expand the Soviet economy and the economies of the other socialist countries. Consequently, they are against the integration of socialist economies into the world economy and the interaction of the socialist and Western worlds. They are interested in reducing the burden on the economy and society of the Soviet Union, which resulted from a growing confrontation with the West. The policy of extending the Soviet sphere of influence at any price is, from their point of view, too expensive and too dangerous. The technocrats are the group with the greatest interest in maintaining the *status quo*.

THE POSITION OF MIKHAIL GORBACHEV

The position of the radical reformers has emerged in the past two or three years. This groups's main criticism of the existing planning and decision-making mechanism is its inability to react adequately to the new wave of basic technological innovations which emerged in the 1970s. Existing economic policies could not give the Soviet Union a significant position in any one of the new basic innovation fields, either in micro-electronics, or in the new information- and communications-technology, to say nothing of the field of flexible automation.

The same economic policies which were able, in the 1950s and 1960s, to reduce the technology gap with Western industrial countries were unable to respond to the challenges of the 1970s. The result was growing stagnation both in the Soviet economy and society at large.

In contrast to the conservative and technocratic groups, the radical reformers are convinced that, without radical reconstruction (*perestroika*) of the economy, society and foreign policy, the USSR and the other socialist countries will be unable to compete or keep up with the United States and its allies. At the June session (1987) of the Central Committee, Gorbachev labelled existing economic policies as a brake-mechanism. To smash the powerful coalition between the conservative and the technocratic groups, the radical reformers are using democratization and openness (*glasnost*) as an important weapon. But these are also goals in themselves.

In a relatively short time Gorbachev was able to wrench the initiative from the conservative and technocratic groups. His success was not immediate. During the January session (1987) of the Central Committee his position was so weak that he was forced to postpone the session three times. By the summer his position was much stronger, strong enough, in fact, to persuade the majority of the Central Committee to approve his programme of radical economic reform up to 1990. The key element of this reform programme is full economic independence of all state enterprises, the creation of a market mechanism and the elimination of the central command economy. The success of this radical reform programme depends very much on the development of the balance of power between the three groups within the Soviet leadership.

The foreign policy concepts of the radical reform group are very closely connected with their concept of the future development of the Soviet economy. Without economic and cultural co-operation with the West, it would be impossible to implement any programme of reconstruction. That is why, in the thinking of this group, the end of confrontation with the West, the arms race, and a fundamental improvement in East-West relations must play a key role. The success of reaching an agreement between the US and the Soviet Union on destroying their intermediate nuclear force is not only the result of an intelligent diplomatic bargaining process. Progress in East-West relations is much more the result of the change in the balance of power within the Soviet leadership in favour of radical reform.

In October 1987 Gorbachev's activities met a setback. After a phase of confusion and helplessness, the conservatives succeeded in realigning their forces, taking advantage of the political naïvity of a prominent member of the radical reform wing, Boris Yelzin, to deal a blow to Gorbachev and his supporters. They were supported by some of the technocrats. A political stalemate resulted, which led to a considerable slowdown of the reform process.

In foreign policy, this setback has not yet become fully perceptible. Here Gorbachev can still rely on support from the technocrats. But there can be no doubt that, if the interrelation of forces within the Soviet leadership continues to change to the disadvantage of the radical reformers, and the reform policy comes to a standstill, then the return to the old military doctrine, the struggle for military superiority, will be inevitable. This would lead to a new round of the arms race. In such a case, the Washington agreement would prove to be just a breathing space, no more than one of history's false trails. Recognizing this, Gorbachev has insisted again and again on the reciprocal connection of disarmament and the success of his radical reform policy at home.

That is why the concept of *perestroika* deserves special attention. Within the Soviet leadership there is now a belief that co-operation with the West should help to solve two crucial problems:—

1. to contain the military-industrial complex, which was able to extend its control over the economic, scientific and technological resources of the Soviet Union.
2. to establish a link to the new combination of productive forces, which are the driving engine of the next wave of productivity growth.

The Role of the Soviet Military-Industrial Complex

The military-industrial complex is becoming more and more of an economic burden for the Soviet Union. In the US the share of direct or indirect R&D expenditure for military purposes has increased from 50 per cent to 60 per cent since the beginning of the 1980s. In the USSR this share has increased from 60 per cent to 80 per cent, reaching a level which is unacceptable for any industrial country. But the social costs of the military-industrial complex in the Soviet Union are much higher than in the US. In the former the military-industrial complex is isolated from the civilian economy. There is little technology transfer from the military to the civilian sectors. The military leadership is interested in avoiding any social control of the defence industry. That is the reason for so little exchange of technicians and scholars. In the US, a great part of the research relevant to military and civilian uses takes place in the same laboratories. Companies use military-based expertise for military and civilian purposes. That is one reason for America's competitive edge in important high-tech fields.

Only if the radical reformers are able to eliminate the exclusive status of the military-industrial complex, will they be able to acquire control of the resources necessary for the modernization of the Soviet economy. This will only be possible through a fundamental improvement in East-West relations. By means of economic co-operation with the Western countries, they hope to improve industrial production and close the technological gap with the Western industrial world.

THE CONCEPT OF 'JOINT-HOUSE' EUROPE

An important concept in reaching this purpose is the vision of Europe as a 'joint-house' and of the growing interdependency among the world's regions. The conservative groups in the Soviet leadership have always stressed the existence of two opposing world markets: the socialist and the capitalist worlds, two markets that are completely independent of each other. In contrast to this point of view, the radical reformers are stressing the importance of the economic integration of both European blocs. At the 1987 Summer session of the Central Committee, Gorbachev described the Soviet Union as part of the world economy, without mentioning the existence of the two antagonistic world markets.

This position also reflects the disillusionment of part of the Soviet leadership with the efficiency of economic co-operation between socialist countries. Without a convertible currency, trade among the Comecon countries is very inefficient. That is why the radical reformers are supporting plans to introduce a convertible currency which will help to integrate the socialist countries into the world economy and to create a network of natural interest between them and the West. Were they to succeed they would achieve a significant step towards integrating the Soviet Union and its Comecon partners into the world economy.

They would also strengthen the already discernible tendency of the small and medium-size socialist countries to extend their relations with the West. While the conservative and technocratic groups have observed such efforts with distrust and viewed them as a subversion of the 'Brezhnev doctrine', for the radical reformers such activities mark a step towards closer economic interrelationships of both parts of Europe. That is why they are not opposed to negotiations between Comecon and the European Community.

THE GERMAN-GERMAN RELATIONSHIP

The relationship between the two Germanies is of special importance. For a long time the troubled relationship distorted East-West relations. Since the late 1970s, it has become increasingly evident that the relationship between the two Germanies may instead be a more positive factor in the process of *détente*. Even the end of *détente* and NATO's Long-Term Modernization Programme (LTMP) at the beginning of the 1980s did not set back the improving relationship between the Federal Republic and East Germany. Erich Honecker's visit to West Germany in 1987—which was postponed twice because of the intervention of the conservative wing of the Soviet leadership—indicates the emergence of a new basis for an intensification of economic, technological and cultural co-operation between the two German states. This will undoubtedly contribute to making the division of Germany more acceptable politically, without, of course, removing the demand for greater unity. The reformers around Gorbachev in Moscow assume that the improvement in the relationship between the two Germanies will have positive effects on *détente* and that, while the Germans will occupy different apartments, they will not necessarily occupy different floors in the 'joint-house' that Europe may yet become.

New Thinking about Military Doctrine

Although it created a number of lasting positive results, the process of *détente* in the 1970s came to an abrupt end. Without doubt, one of the reasons was that the conservative group around Brezhnev had no interest in combining disarmament, *détente*, and a reduction of areas of conflict within an internal restructuring of the economy. The reform group around Gorbachev has realized in time that the one is impossible without the other.

The concept of combining these two components is represented by Gorbachev's 'new thinking' which he was able to include in the newly-formulated military doctrine of the Warsaw Pact on 29 May 1987.[1] The 'new thinking' assumes that a war between the two power blocs would not represent a continuation of politics by other means, but the end of mankind. In contrast to the earlier military doctrine, which presumed that, while a military conflict should be prevented, were it to break out it would mean the end of the Western world, it is now emphasized that there will be neither victors nor defeated in a war; that every effort must be made to prevent an intentional or unintentional triggering of a military conflict, to use peaceful means for eliminating enemy images and solving existing political disputes.

In this context it is recognized that the present military parity of NATO and the Warsaw Pact is a major factor in preventing a war. But in contrast to the conservatives, whose policy is to create parity on a higher level, the reform group hopes to secure the military balance of power on a lower level than hitherto.

Gorbachev believes that the realization of his programme for restructuring economic life will make internal and external enemy images superfluous to social stability and the Soviet Union increasingly less useful as an enemy image for others. The competition between the two systems is to be fought by peaceful means. Instead of extending the political sphere of influence of one system at the expense of the other, there should be a joint effort in solving the global problems of mankind, overcoming underdevelopment, the fight against hunger, the protection of man's biosphere, to name but a few of the most important.

Much of this, of course, represents a declaration of intent. It may, however, steer the thinking of the élites of the two Superpowers in new directions and undermine the spirit of confrontation. It would be frivolous, therefore, to dismiss the 'new thinking' in Moscow as pure propaganda. For achieving military parity on as low a level as possible, the Warsaw Pact has formulated a new military doctrine:

- — complete and general prohibition of nuclear tests and the prevention of the arms race in outer space;
- — reduction of armed forces and conventional arms in Europe to a level which would make a surprise attack impossible;
- — strict verification of all disarmament measures;
- — creation of nuclear-free and chemical weapon-free zones in various regions of Europe and other parts of the world;
- — overcoming the division of Europe into military blocs by the simultaneous dissolution of NATO and the Warsaw Pact, beginning with the elimination of their respective integrated military commands.

It would certainly also be of great advantage to the West, if East-West relations were not limited to disarmament negotiations. Broad scientific, technological, economic, ecological and cultural co-operation between East and West might help to reduce areas of conflict and the potential for confrontation. This would also include the development of direct relations between the Warsaw Pact and NATO. The time is finally past when the cohesion of the two military alliances could only be preserved by enemy images and the fear of threat. Neither NATO nor the Warsaw Pact were created as alliances for rearmament, but as alliances for mutual security. Today, security has become indivisible. This will necessitate direct negotiations and consultations. In their new formulation of military doctrine, the Warsaw Pact countries have drawn up a catalogue of issues for such a dialogue, such as the reduction of existing imbalances and asymmetries between the individual arms and armed forces on as low a level as possible.

The success of these negotiations will, of course, depend significantly on the development of the balance of power of the different leadership groups in the Soviet Union. This does not mean that the West ought to remain a passive observer standing in the wings of history. There is too much at stake. By constructive reaction to acceptable bargaining talks, which will also produce more security for everyone, the West might actually strengthen Gorbachev's position at home.

The Washington treaty is an important step in the right direction, but further steps will have to follow very soon. The following points will be of particular importance:—

1. In its negotiations with the Warsaw Pact, NATO will have to formulate its interests very precisely in order to balance the different interests of its members. Above all, it must prevent zones of diminished security from coming into being. It is particularly important to work out a joint conception for a step-by-step reduction of the arms arsenals, with a guarantee of the same security for all member countries. The more precisely the consequent effects of particular disarmament steps are identified, the more stable and permanent will be the solutions striven for. It makes no sense to strive for solutions which set off a chain of demands for offsetting treaties or modernizing existing weapons.

2. The West must also do everything to support the integration of the socialist countries into the world market. The plans of the radical reformers about the introduction of a convertible currency and the co-operation with IMF, GATT and World Bank should be taken seriously and be supported. This also includes the promotion of joint enterprises and projects, an important contribution to an interweaving of interests between East and West.

3. In the creation of scientific-technological co-operation between East and West, interdisciplinary institutes, where possible, should be

established where the intellectual élites of both blocs could meet to discuss the solution of common problems. In this context, the increased promotion of existing institutes, such as the International Institute for Applied Systems Analysis (IIASA) in Laxenburg, near Vienna, are of particular importance. This Institute has deserved well of its considerable contribution in preparing Gorbachev's 'new thinking'. Unfortunately, the US and the United Kingdom have virtually ended their co-operation with this Institute, for reasons which appear to be narrow-minded in view of the enormous task of creating an intellectual basis for greater East-West co-operation.

Note

1. The German version of the new formulation of the military doctrine of the Warsaw Pact is published in *Neues Deutschland*, Berlin (East), 30/31 May 1987, p. 1; see also M. Gorbachev, *Perestroika* (Munich, 1987), pp. 341-342.

Index